Pearson's Canal Companion
WELSH WATERS

Published by Wayzgoose
www.jmpearson.co.uk
enquiries@jmpearson.co.uk

WAY Z GOOSE

Copyright: Michael Pearson
11th edition 2022
ISBN 978 0 9928492 8 3

Lock-wheeling

Over half a century ago, during an uneasy ceasefire between boarding school and art college, I took myself down to Birmingham in the solitary confines of a compartment carriage, and sought solace in Hudsons Bookshop, a stone's throw from New Street station. Like many an eighteen year old, my taste was in a state of flux, but I returned home with a copy of *Narrow Boat* by someone called L. T. C. Rolt, and a recording of Elgar's 1st Symphony performed by the Philharmonia Orchestra conducted by Sir John Barbirolli. 'Glorious John' was known to me, for I had seen him waving his arms about at the Free Trade Hall with the Halle Orchestra, whilst of Rolt I had no foreknowledge, but I was attracted to Denys Watkins-Pitchford's scraperboard illustrations, whilst Sir Compton Mackenzie's dust-wrapper recommendation - 'an elegy of classic restraint' - was good enough for me; restraint being a virtue I had honed to something approaching perfection towards the end of my teens.

Posterity vindicates I had not purchased impetuously. Both the book and recording remain analogous in my consciousness to this day. So that I cannot hear the symphony's opening movement's second subject without picturing Tom and Angela Rolt's attendance at Market Drayton's 'Dirty Fair', or read of 'The Stour Cut' without hearing the seamless transformation of the scherzo into the adagio which, according to Scott Goddard's eloquent sleeve notes, belongs amongst 'the greatest things in all the history of the exacting and recondite form called symphony'. Something of the same unique quality could be assigned to *Narrow Boat*. No other book, before or since, quite so lyrically captures the intrinsic appeal of the canal system. Rolt was fortunate in his timing. The Second World War was about to sweep a whole way of life away, never mind the sequestered, throw-back enclave of the canals.

Ars longa, vita brevis, Hippocrates never tired of saying - as though it were some comedic catch-phrase - and great works of art are apt to sustain us over the span of a lifetime. My twin acquisitions on 24th August 1970 have never let me down in that respect, though sadly that cannot be said of a good many purchases since. Echoes of Rolt pervade

these pages, and you must take my word that a good deal of Elgar provided whistled accompaniment to my research trips. I suppose what fundamentally attracts me to both of them is their propensity to hark backwards: Rolt, it is generally accepted, went along with the notion of the Inland Waterways Association in the hope that it would succeed in preserving in aspic the practises and traditions of working boats and their crews; Elgar doggedly clung to 19th century musical tropes when all around him, the Stravinskys and Schoenbergs of the 20th century, were forging paths he could not find it in himself to follow.

'I find these guides rather old fashioned,' a critical voice - hiding behind the anonymity of Amazon Customer Reviews - once posted, little suspecting that he could offer me no higher praise. Indeed, why would anyone in their right minds chose to explore the canals if part of them wasn't receptive to the past, if they didn't find it downright addictive? Delving backwards enables us to escape the uncongenial realities of the present, never mind the unimaginable threats of the future.

Fifty years and counting. I don't suppose there have been many of them when I haven't at least dipped into *Narrow Boat*, or listened to 'Elgar One', as we aficionados fondly refer to it. It is vital to have constants in one's life: family, a few well chosen friends, music, books ... a reliable supply of pies and beer. In my characteristically self-effacing manner, I hope that eleven editions of this guide have provided companionship, insight, and a little gentle humour, to all who kindly purchased them along the way.

Contents

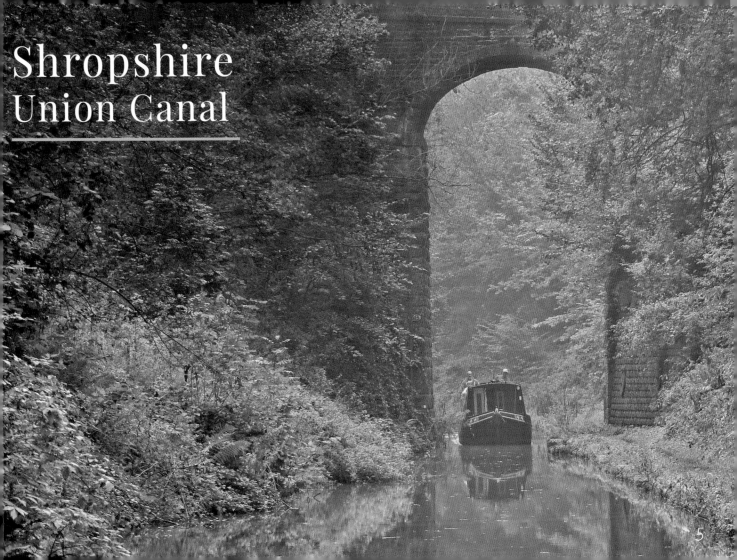

Shropshire
Union Canal

BE the envy of your peers. Begin your holiday beside the sewage works of Wolverhampton. Things can only get better. And they do. Quite quickly as it happens, for the Shropshire Union turns its back on the filter beds, shrugs off the conversational gambits of Pendeford's housing estates, and strides out into open country, never looking back. The beauty, though, of canal travel, is the opportunity it provides to explore the unexplored, and Autherley Junction is not without its moments. Take, for example, Bridge 1, through which boaters from the Staffordshire & Worcestershire Canal must pass to enter the six inch stop lock which separates them from the Shropshire Union. It sets the tone for the confident engineering style of the Birmingham & Liverpool Junction Canal, the original name of Thomas Telford's thirty-nine mile route between Autherley and Nantwich. Napton Narrowboats' hire base currently occupies premises originally erected for the collection of tolls, the stabling of horses, and other ancillary waterway activities.

Known pithily to working boatmen as 'Cut End', this was, until 1970, the dominion of Sam Lomas, an engaging character who had started work on the canals in 1916. A born raconteur, one of his favourite stories concerned how he had reported for his first day of work on the eve of his fourteenth birthday and was told to "sit outside the office and watch the boats go by" because he couldn't legally start until he was actually fourteen: 'And', Sam would gleefully inform anyone prepared to listen, 'That's exactly what I've been doing ever since!' Hard now not to envy so onerous a responsibility. In 1958 he was awarded an MBE for 'meritorious service'.

Old photographs show 'The Shroppie' stretching bleakly away from 'Cut End' across a flat and empty tract of land towards a low and undistinguished horizon. This, however, is no longer the case, for where houses haven't been built, there are swards of open public space, 'landscaped' indiscriminately with trees and vegetation. 'Green is good' the planners will tell you, but not necessarily when the result is so anonymous. From Bridge 2, Reapers Walk leads to a convenience store, fish & chip shop, Indian takeaway, buses into Wolverhampton, and a surprising survival ... a 17th century dovecote, sole remnant of Barnhurst Farm, a sizeable property which had once belonged to wealthy wool merchants, but was demolished in the 1970s.

Map labels:

Kidderminster (see Stourport Ring CC)
62A
63
Aldersley Leisure Village
Aldersley Junction
Wolverhampton Race Course
S&W
21
20
18 19
17
BCN
Wolverhampton (see Stourport Ring CC)
Oxley Park Golf Course
65
sewage works
W. Mids.
1
SHROPSHIRE UNION
Autherley Junction
Pendeford Dovecote
3
2
mp 1/38
3A
Wolverhampton Boat Club
4 stop gates
former Boulton Paul works
Staffs.
P
5
mp 2/37
6
M54 to Telford
NORTH
Monarch's Way
Monarch's Way
River Penk
7
2
mp 3/36
Monarch's Way

1: Oxley Marine
2: Napton Narrowboats

Morrisons
S&W
Great Haywood (see Stourport Ring & Four Counties Ring CCs)

1 One-way working in narrow sections

Wolverhampton Airport was established between the Shropshire Union and Staffordshire & Worcestershire canals on land previously used as a sewage farm. Amy Johnson flew demonstration flights to mark the official opening on 25th June 1938. During the Second World War the aerodrome was employed as an Elementary Flying Training School, and amongst its intake were contingents of Turkish, Iraqi and Iranian pilots. One can't help but wonder if many of the finer points of flying technique were lost in translation. After the war the aerodrome gradually returned to civilian use. In the 1950s, Don Everall Aviation operated scheduled flights to the Isle of Man and Channel Islands. The Ealing feature film, *The Man in the Sky*, staring Jack Hawkins and Elizabeth Sellars, was largely shot on location here in 1956. Closed in 1971, housing now occupies the airport's site.

Cast iron mileposts measure distances between Autherley, Norbury and Nantwich, and by the time you reach the first of these the towpath has changed sides at Bridge 3; a roving, or 'change-line' bridge, somewhat compromised by the presence of the concrete latecomer beside it. Wolverhampton Boat Club built their premises here in 1966, having previously been eponymously based at Autherley; and, by all accounts, a very sociable club it is too. Sam Lomas was once their Commodore.

Industrial units east of the canal - now occupied by furniture makers and a chicken processing plant - once belonged to the aircraft makers, Boulton Paul. Over a thousand WWII Defiant fighters were built here, a design whose reputation for unreliability has been rehabilitated in recent years. During the war a dummy factory was erected on the outskirts of Brewood to mislead enemy planes. One Junkers Ju 88 did manage to attack the Boulton Paul works, however, though the five bombs it dropped hit the neighbouring sewage farm instead. Its mission ended even more ignominiously, being shot down over Nuneaton. Incidentally, the canal still narrows at the site of stop gates, placed beyond Bridge 4 to minimise flooding were the canal to be breached by bomb damage.

An embankment carries the canal over the River Penk as a rural atmosphere is firmly established. A sequence of narrows and widenings ensues as the canal cuts through a band of Keuper Sandstone. Canalside cornfields are woven with a poppy trim. The M54, which links Telford to the M6, spans the canal, on a section completed in 1983. Briefly, the towpath is commandeered by the Monarch's Way, a 615 mile long approximation of King Charles II's convoluted escape route from Worcester to Brighton via Bristol and Yeovil in 1651.

GETTING into its characteristic loping stride, the old Birmingham & Liverpool Junction component of the Shropshire Union Canal forges north in a series of cuttings and embankments, known respectively as 'rockings' and 'valleys' to generations of working boatmen. As originally built - it was opened throughout in 1835 - its course across this agricultural landscape would have resembled an open wound. Long ago, however, absorbed into nature's soothing tapestry, the canal now looks as if it has always been there, especially in this era of reduced maintenance regimes.

Having grown accustomed to the functional lines of Telford's overbridges, Bridge 10's ornamentation comes as a surprise. Known as Avenue Bridge, it was built to carry the carriageway to Chillington Hall. The advent of the canals heralded many similar attempts at ornament- ation and disguise, where powerful landowners would only condescend to permit a waterway to cross their parklands if suitable steps were taken to adorn the otherwise purely functional architecture of the new trade route. Chillington itself lies about a mile and a half to the west in grounds landscaped by Capability Brown. En route you encounter Giffard's Cross, where in the sixteenth century one of the Giffards (who have inhabited the estate for over eight hundred years) shot a marauding panther. Relax, they are more or less extinct in the area now.

'Brood' is one of the prettiest villages on the Shropshire Union, if not the canal system as a whole. This is Mike Webb country: or perhaps that should be, 'Espionage Webb', as he was affectionately known on account of the meticulous records he kept of boat movements during the postwar years, when he was growing up in Brewood and attending the local

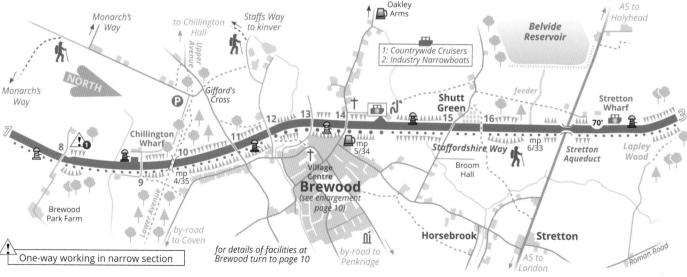

for details of facilities at Brewood turn to page 10

One-way working in narrow section

grammar school, where he and his chums fell into the habit of collecting boat names because there was no nearby railway line at which to trainspot. But Mike's greatest legacy - painstakingly nurtured by his widow, Maria - is the photographs he took of working boats in the late 'fifties and early 'sixties. A retrospective collection of them appears in *The Twilight Years of Narrow Boat Carrying* available from Audlem Mill Canal Shop (Map 9). Mike's funeral took place in Brewood in 2012. Fittingly his coffin arrived by boat. A bench just south of Bridge 14 commemorates this gentle soul together with a suitably illustrated memorial in the churchyard.

Countrywide Cruisers occupy Brewood Wharf. The town's gas works stood here from 1872 until the First World War, supplies thereafter coming from a much larger works in Stafford. Electricity didn't arrive in Brewood until 1928. For two or three miles the towpath is made busier than usual by walkers doing the Staffordshire Way, a long distance footpath which encounters a good many canals between Kinver and Mow Cop. Belvide Reservoir is one of the main sources of water supply for the Shropshire Union Canal. It is also, under the auspices of the West Midland Bird Club, a magnet for ornithologists. Broom Hall, east of Bridge 16, was the home of William Carlos who hid King Charles II in the oak tree at nearby Boscobel after the Battle of Worcester in 1651.

A sturdy, yet elegant aqueduct of iron, brick and stone construction carries the canal over Watling Street, a route intitially forged by ancient Britons between the channel ports and the north-west, which subsequently became one of the most important Roman roads. When road numbering was introduced after the First World War it was designated the A5, linking London with Holyhead.

As a tyro guidebook compiler in the 1980s, the gnarled author of this guide erroneously drew attention to the intriguing juxtaposition at this point of Telford's Birmingham & Liverpool Junction Canal with his Holyhead Road. Fortunately, for the sake of historical accuracy, the truth later dawned on him that Telford had driven his road through the Black Country, leaving the Watling Street at Weedon in Northamptonshire and rejoining it to Oakengates in Shropshire. We live and we learn!

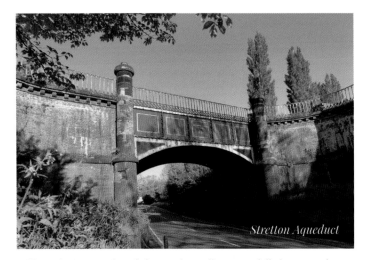

Stretton Aqueduct

From the perspective of the canal traveller - especially boaters - the crossing seems over in a flash. Best, perhaps, to pause, and take the steps leading down to road level to appreciate the structure more fully (though do beware the traffic, hurtling by at speeds the canal builders could scarcely have envisaged). Eight impressive cylindrical pillars - turrets, almost - frame substantial curved retaining walls which support the iron trough that spans the road, bearing Telford's name and dated 1832. Note where the road was lowered in the early 1960s to permit the passage of larger vehicles in modern times. It's long overdue a fresh coat of paint, though one supposes that would entail closing the A5: perish the thought.

Boatbuilding and maintenance is undertaken at Stretton Wharf. Here, until the mid-1950s, stood the Aqueduct Inn, its gable ends signwritten to the effect that 'teas are provided and parties catered for'. Vivian Bird referred to it in passing when journeying northwards in 1953 to load oil at Ellesmere Port with the Thomas Clayton pair, *Towy* and *Kubina*, as described in *By Lock and Pound*, an eminently readable account of The Shroppie being used as a working waterway.

BREWOOD

MAP 2

Probably because it is so close to the county boundary, Brewood feels more like Shropshire; there being a 'west country' richness about it which comes as a surprise considering its proximity to Wolverhampton. Furthermore, there is a timelessness about 'Brood' which seduces you into spending longer here than you might have planned. Winding lanes of gracious houses lead to the old market place, enhancing one corner of which is 'Speedwell Castle', a Gothic fantasy erected in the 18th century on the winnings of a racehorse named Speedwell. The tall spired parish church is notable for its Giffard family tombs. In the south-east side of the churchyard a stone backed by the carved image of a narrow boat pair commemorates Mike Webb, whilst elsewhere lies the grave of Hugh Rose, a Scots engineer who came here to build the canal. A plaque in the Market Place recalls that the contractor, Thomas Andrew Walker, was born in Brewood in 1828. Among his achievements were the Manchester Ship Canal, Severn Tunnel and London's District Line. The Roman Catholic church, by Bridge 14, is the work of no less a Victorian architect than A. W. N. Pugin.

Eating & Drinking

BRIDGE INN - Bridge 14. Tel: 01902 903966. Welcoming former boatmans' pub. Marston's & guest ales. Food from noon. Useful laundry. ST19 9BD
THE CURRY INN - Church Street. Tel: 01902 850989. Eat in or take-away Indian. Opens 5.30pm. ST19 9BT
LAZY DAYS - Stafford Street. Tel: 01902 850038. Cafe open 9am-3pm Tue-Sat, 10am-2pm Sun. ST19 9DX
THE OAKLEY ARMS - Kiddemore Green Road (1 mile west of Bridge 14). Tel: 01902 859800. Brunning & Price pub/restaurant housed in a former country club whose owner's twin daughters both married members of the rock group Deep Purple. Food served

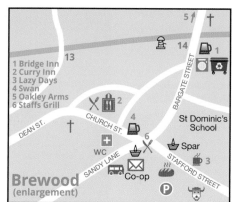

1 Bridge Inn
2 Curry Inn
3 Lazy Days
4 Swan
5 Oakley Arms
6 Staffs Grill

Brewood
(enlargement)

from noon daily throughout. ST19 9BQ
STAFFORDSHIRE GRILL - Market Place. Tel: 01902 850123. Country pub/steak house. Rooms. ST19 9BS
SWAN - Market Place. Tel: 01902 850330. Traditional village local. Opens 11.45am daily. ST19 9BS

Shopping

Spar (with cash machine) and Co-op (inc post office). Try the Village Bakery (Tel: 01902 850196) for cakes and filled baps. Butchers W. Maiden & Son (Tel: 01902 850346) are easily missed at the far end of Stafford Street. Established in 1946, you can see pies being made on the premises and take away that Black Country delicacy, 'gray paes' or Staffordshire oatcakes.

Things to Do

CHILLINGTON HALL - about a mile and a half west of Bridge 10. Tel: 01902 850236. Guided tours on selected dates. Holiday lets. WV8 1RE
BOSCOBEL HOUSE/WHITE LADIES PRIORY - English Heritage properties well worth a detour approximately three miles west of Brewood.

Connections

BUSES - Select services 877/878 trundle back and forth between the market place and Wolverhampton at roughly hourly intervals Mon-Sat, with some services continuing via Wheaton Aston to Stafford.
TAXIS - Codsall & Perton Cars. Tel: 01902 844944.

WHEATON ASTON   MAP 3

Twinned with the sizeable town of Wheaton, Illinois, Wheaton Aston was once a small farming community but is now a somnolent suburban enclave. St Mary's little Victorian church is distinguished with some glass by Charles Eamer Kempe, a prolific manufacturer of stained glass who was inspired by William Morris and trained by George Frederick Bodley. Surprising what treasures await in otherwise unpromising settings.

Eating & Drinking

HARTLEY ARMS - Bridge 19. Tel: 01785 840232. Well appointed canalside pub open from 11am. Food served lunchtimes and evenings (from 5.30pm) Mon-Sat and 12-4pm Suns. ST19 9NF
COACH & HORSES - High Street. Tel: 01785 841048. Village ST19 9NP

Shopping

A Premier convenience store, with post office counter, is just three or four minutes away from the canal and opens 6am-9pm daily. Deeper into the village there's a small pharmacy and the Church Stores Spar which does a nice line in hot snacks too. Turner's quaint canalside garage stocks Calor gas, diesel and boating accessories. Free range eggs from Bridge Farm. (Br.19)

Connections

BUSES - Select services 877/878 run approx half a dozen times Mon-Sat, to/from Wolverhampton (via Brewood) and Stafford.

NOTHING epitomises rural England quite so much as the ripe smell of muck-spreading, and there is plenty of opportunity to savour this fragrant bouquet as the canal traverses a landscape almost entirely given over to agriculture. Wheaton Aston Lock is of a solitary disposition, the only one in twenty-five miles of canal; a telling measure of Telford's advanced engineering techniques. As originally built, the locks on the B&LJC were equipped with mitred pairs of gates at both ends of each chamber. Much extended, one of Telford's trademark tollhouses lurks behind a high hedge alongside the lock.

Dated 1956, a Francis Frith postcard of the canal at Wheaton Aston shows GPO telegraph poles marching purposefully along the towpath - as indeed they once did throughout the course of the Birmingham & Liverpool Junction - and occasionally one comes upon a truncated pole in the undergrowth.

The canal penetrates the deciduous heart of Lapley Wood, and there's another typically bosky Shroppie cutting by Little Onn, but elsewhere the embankments offer wide views eastwards towards Cannock Chase. How astonishingly remote and unpeopled the landscape seems. The West Midlands conurbation is less than a dozen miles to the south,

yet moor for the night between Wheaton Aston and Little Onn, and you'll have only the occasional eerie hoot of a hunting owl, or the distant silent wash of headlights on a country lane, for company. Something of this sense of isolation must explain the survival of Mottey Meadows, alluvial flood meadowlands, unploughed for centuries, whose name apparently derives from the French word for peat - motteux. Sadly, though perhaps understandably, access is by permit only, though there is an annual Haymaking Festival in June at which time more of this fascinating landscape can be explored, encountering such rarities as the Horsetail Weevil and Snake's Head Fritillary, the latter at its most northerly location.

Old maps intriguingly depict the existence of a gunpowder magazine at the point where the canal bears due north beyond Bridge 20, and Jack Roberts references it in *Shropshire Union Flyboats*, of which more anon. One of the canal's lengthy embankments carries it across a sequence of culverts which provide access between neighbouring fields. It also spans a brook which flows eastwards into the River Penk, registering the fact that this is the watershed between the Trent and the Severn. The ghost of a Roman Road bisects the canal at the southern end of Rye Hill Cutting.

Abandoned wartime aerodromes have their ghosts as well, and in decay accumulate a patina of lore and legend, hard to equate with the often mundane use to which they were put after closure. Wheaton Aston was opened in 1941 and became one of the RAF's largest training units,

continued overleaf:

by-road to Bishops Wood

Coach & Horses

Mottey Meadows

Spar

Wheaton Aston

school

Whitehouse Farm

Hartley Arms

70'

stop gate

Shushions Manor

by-road to Marston

resettlement site

Little Onn

St Edith's Well

Lapley Wood Cutting

18

19

mp 8/31

20

20a

aqueducts

stop gate

former WWII aerodrome

Hall

Wheaton Aston Lock 7ft 0ins

17

mp 7/32

20b

20c mp 9/30

21

22

23

mp 24 10/29

by-road to Church Eaton

2

4

NORTH

Roman Road

Rye Hill Cutting

"Staffs Way" to Penkridge

WC

by-road to Penkridge

11

continued from page 11:

operating a squadron of 'Oxfords'. There were at least two canal dramas: on 4th July 1944 an American P-47 'Thunderbolt', having taken off from RAF Atcham near Shrewsbury, lost power at three thousand feet. The pilot attempted an emergency landing at Wheaton Aston aerodrome, but undershot the runway and skidded across a field - killing a pair of cows in the process - before finally ditching in the canal. On Independence Day, Richard M. Dunlap's luck was in, and in the words of a certain compatriot, thirteen years later, was merely 'all shook up'.

Another well remembered wartime incident occurred at the lock when a narrow-boat, carrying an unsheeted cargo of shining aluminium on a moonlit night, was attacked by a German aircraft which unleashed a bomb that exploded less than a hundred yards from the chamber. Wheaton Aston boasted a well-equipped gymnasium, run for a time by Eric Boon, the champion lightweight nicknamed the 'Fen Tiger' on account of his Cambridgeshire origins. An even better known boxer who served here was Freddie Mills, world light heavyweight champion 1948-50.

After the war the aerodrome's somewhat less than hospitable huts were used for some twenty years as a transit depot for displaced persons, primarily Poles. As is often the case with exiles, there was a good deal of adherence to the traditions of their country of origin. The church played a guiding role in the camp's day to day life. Fr. Mieczyslaw Bossowski, the resident priest had escaped the clutches of both the Gestapo and the Soviet NKVD, not being allowed to return to his homeland until shortly before his death in 1994. Gradually the camp's occupants were assimilated into British life. Many found work in the Cannock and North Staffordshire coalfields, or in the latter's pottery industry. The camp closed in 1965 and subsequently became a pig farm. Stroll westwards along the lane from Bridge 24 and you will find poignant remnants of both the camp and the airfield; not least an old control tower.

At Bridge 21 the canal crosses the course of a Roman road which linked Pennocrucium (a settlement on Watling Street, about two miles east of Stretton Aqueduct) with Mediolanum, modern day Whitchurch. Rye Hill Cutting leads to Little Onn. With its elaborately tall chimneys and stepped gables, Little Onn Hall was built on a medieval moated site by a Colonel Ashton in 1875. Following their father's death, the colonel's two unmarried daughters commissioned Thomas Hayton Mawson, author of *The Art & Craft of Garden Making*, to landscape the grounds. Mawson adapted the moat as part of a water feature, but apparently his plans were never completed because the sisters ran out of money. Canal Companion users should make a mental note to pay homage to another of Mawson's schemes next time they're on the Caldon Canal, for it was he who designed Hanley Park in Stoke-on-Trent. St Edith's Well was noted for its healing properties, particularly with regard to failing eyesight. Frustratingly, the well is on private land. Obviously, you 'should have gone to Specsavers' after all.

Boat & Bike, Wheaton Aston

PERSISTING in its self-absorbed hike across the empty landscapes of west Staffordshire, The Shroppie even attempts to shun the little town of Gnosall, the name of which recalls to mind that old comic song by Flanders & Swann about The Gnu. In this case, you don't say Ger-no-sall, you say No-zull, or Knows-all.

Near High Onn, the buildings of two wharves remain intact. One - now converted into a most desirable home - belonged to Cadbury's, the other to a local landowner, suggesting that there was once a degree of agricultural traffic on the canal. Logs, kindling and coal are on sale at the latter and winding permitted courtesy of the owner. Bridge 26 is of the 'turnover' type, where the towpath changes sides,

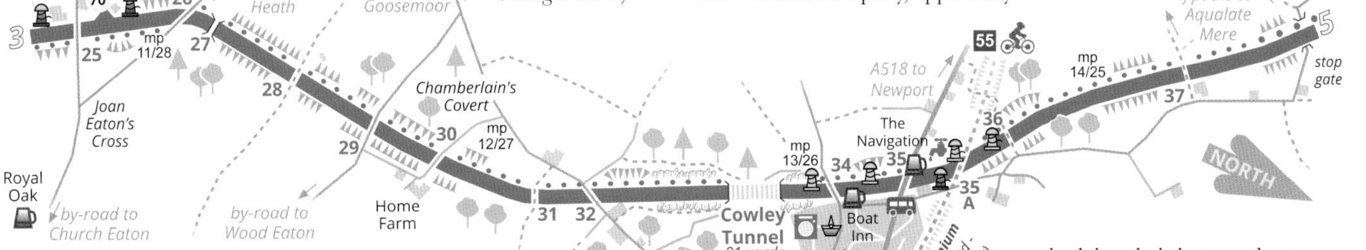

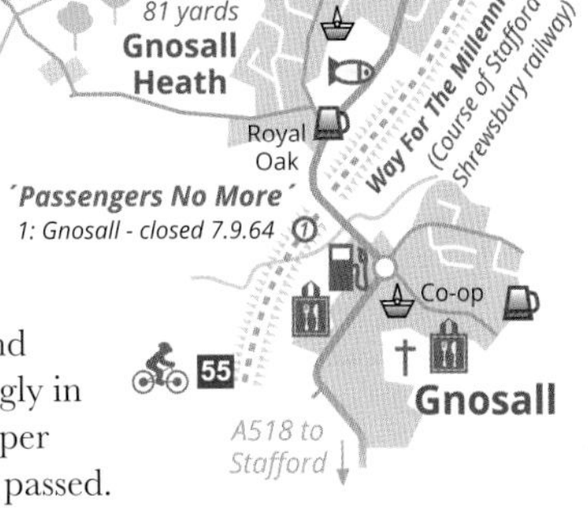

Gnosall's canal environment is zealously cared for by its Parish Council. There are several visitor moorings of 48 hour duration, plus a generous 5 days beyond Bridge 35A. A small holding, inhabited by goats and ducks and chickens (kept in order by a noisy cockerel), adds bucolically to the scene.

Bridge 35A - curiously rectangular and reminiscent of the one at Welton on the Leicester Section of the GUC - used to carry a railway over the canal, but now forms the course of the Stafford & Newport Greenway, part of The Way For The Millennium, a forty mile long distance footpath connecting two extremities of Staffordshire, Newport to the west and Burton-on-Trent to the east. Historically, the railway was unusual in that it was actually built by the Shropshire Union Canal Company, apparently

[map area: labels include]
former milk depot
by-road to High Onn
Lord Talbot's Wharf
70' 26
25 mp 11/28 27
by-road to Bromstead Heath
by-road to Goosemoor
28
Joan Eaton's Cross
Chamberlain's Covert
29 30 mp 12/27
Royal Oak
by-road to Church Eaton
by-road to Wood Eaton
Home Farm
31 32
Cowley Tunnel 81 yards
Gnosall Heath
Royal Oak
55
A518 to Newport
The Navigation
34 35
35A
Boat Inn
55
mp 13/26
mp 14/25
36 37
fpaths to Aqualate Mere
aq.
stop gate
NORTH
Way For The Millennium (Course of Stafford - Shrewsbury railway)
'Passengers No More'
1: Gnosall - closed 7.9.64
Co-op
Gnosall
55
A518 to Stafford

uniquely, on this occasion, bearing a public road as well. Bridge 31 is equally unusual in that it carries two farm tracks separated by a central stone wall. Deep shadowy sandstone cuttings, spanned - like leaping squirrels - by lichened red or grey stone bridges of simple balance and unaffected dignity, lead to the eighty-one unlined yards of Cowley Tunnel (No.33); the only one on the Shropshire Union. Cuttings such as this are apt to play aural and olfactory tricks. The blended aromas of bacon and diesel hang enticingly in the air and voices carry further than you'd think: so be inclined to temper your remarks concerning the odd looking couple on that boat you just passed.

hedging their bets on the transport mode of the future. When, in 1847, they leased themselves to the London & North Western Railway, few shareholders would have backed the canal to outlast the railway. Now it forms a nice, traffic-free route for a run before or after boating. In his detailed history of the line, *The Shropshire Union Railway*, Bob Yate alludes to Gnosall's timber built station *continued overleaf:*

continued from page 13:

buildings, likening them to a barn: 'the platforms boasted some of the finest station gardens in the country for many years'. The last Station Master, Stanley Griffiths, was only twenty-one when Beeching and Marples conspired to close the line on 7th September 1964. A couple of miles west of the canal at Bridge 37 lies Aqualate Mere which, at about a mile long, is the most extensive natural lake in the region. For its size it is remarkably shallow, having been scoured by retreating glaciers, and is notable in geological circles for its rare Esker deposits. Bitterns are regular visitors to its extensive reedbeds. Footpaths and bridleways provide access to the site which is managed as a National Nature Reserve by Natural England.

On a clear day the embankments north of Gnosall reveal that famous Shropshire landmark, The Wrekin, 15 miles to the south-west; a slumbering hunchback of a summit, 1335ft high. A. E. Housman celebrated it in *A Shropshire Lad* - 'his forest fleece the Wrekin heaves' - and Salopians raise their glasses to: "All friends around the Wrekin".

CHURCH EATON (MAP 4)

Eating & Drinking

ROYAL OAK - High Street (approx 15 mins walk east of Bridge 25). Tel: 01785 823078. Community-owned pub offering Woods Shropshire Lad and guests. Food Wed-Fri from 5pm, Sat & Sun from noon. ST20 0AJ

GNOSALL MAP 4

Gnosall Heath thrived with the coming of the canal and the railway not long afterwards, Gnosall stood back and watched with alarm, the onset of Progress. Two pubs slaked the thirst of passing boatmen, a steam powered flour mill, a saw mill, and a smithy took advantage of the new transport mode, whilst an Ebenezer Chapel kept a sense of proportion amidst all the excitement. Nowadays the pubs pander to pleasure boaters and passing motorists and the flour mill and chapel have become private residences. Half a mile east of the canal, Gnosall slumbers on its hilltop, the substantial parish church of St Lawrence (clerestoried nave and Norman pillars) being its most notable (though invariably locked) landmark.

Eating & Drinking

THE BOAT - Wharf Road (Bridge 34). Tel: 01785 822208. Marston's/Banks's pub with curved wall abutting the bridge. Open from noon daily. Meals served lunchtimes and evenings (from 5.30pm) Tue-Sat and from noon until 4pm on Sundays. ST20 0DA
THE NAVIGATION - Newport Road (Bridge 35). Tel: 01785 824562. Cosy pub open from noon daily. Food served weekdays lunchtime and evenings (from 5pm), throughout at weekends. ST20 0BN

Three more pubs to chose from in the village. Fish & chips on A518 open daily (except Sundays), both sessions. Tel: 01785 822806. No less than three takeaways: Bengal Spice (Tel: 01785 823248); Gnosall Kitchen (Tel: 01785 823388); and Jia Jin Chinese/English (Tel: 01785 824388).

Shopping

Convenience store (with cash point) by Bridge 34. Another convenience store on way into Gnosall and Co-op in village itself. Gnosall Laundry Services (Tel: 0794 300 6222) provide handy launderette services, plus ironing and dry cleaning, close to Bridge 34.

Connections

BUSES - Arriva service 5 half-hourly (hourly Sun) to/from Stafford and Telford. Tel: 0871 200 2233.

NORBURY JNCT. MAP 5

Just as much a magnet for motorists as boaters. The tall boiler room chimney; a bell on the roof of the workshop, rung at the commencement of each working day; three pairs of staff cottages; and the Section Inspector's villa, *Ferndale*, retain much of the magic of Norbury Junction's heritage. BIFoR, the Birmingham Institute of Forest Research has a facility in nearby Shelmore Wood studying the effect of carbon dioxide emissions on woodland. Sworn adversaries, Pevsner and Thorold, nevertheless shared an enthusiasm for St Peter's, Norbury, half a mile to the north-west; notably its effigy of a cross-legged knight.

Eating & Drinking

OLD WHARF TEA ROOMS - canalside Bridge 38. All-day, all year licensed cafe; sizeable portions of homely cooking. Tel: 01785 284292. B&B and s/c accommodation also available. ST20 0PN
JUNCTION INN - canalside Bridge 38. Tel: 01785 284288. Opens noon. Food lunch and evenings (from 5.30pm) Wed-Fri, and from noon Sat & Sun. ST20 0PN

Shopping

Excellent boatyard shop: provisions, off-licence, gifts, chandlery and a wide choice of canal books.

HIGH OFFLEY MAP 5

ANCHOR INN - canalside Bridge 42. Tel: 01785 284569. Famously unspoilt boatman's pub which has been in the same family for generations. Devizes-brewed Wadworth 6X from the jug. Catering is restricted to sandwiches, but what delightfully innocent and simple sandwiches they are. Real pub, real ale, real treasure! Camping/caravans. ST20 0NB.

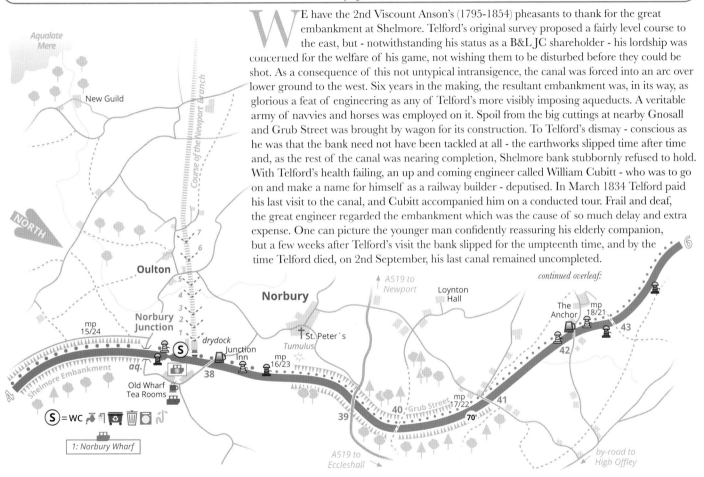

WE have the 2nd Viscount Anson's (1795-1854) pheasants to thank for the great embankment at Shelmore. Telford's original survey proposed a fairly level course to the east, but - notwithstanding his status as a B&LJC shareholder - his lordship was concerned for the welfare of his game, not wishing them to be disturbed before they could be shot. As a consequence of this not untypical intransigence, the canal was forced into an arc over lower ground to the west. Six years in the making, the resultant embankment was, in its way, as glorious a feat of engineering as any of Telford's more visibly imposing aqueducts. A veritable army of navvies and horses was employed on it. Spoil from the big cuttings at nearby Gnosall and Grub Street was brought by wagon for its construction. To Telford's dismay - conscious as he was that the bank need not have been tackled at all - the earthworks slipped time after time and, as the rest of the canal was nearing completion, Shelmore bank stubbornly refused to hold. With Telford's health failing, an up and coming engineer called William Cubitt - who was to go on and make a name for himself as a railway builder - deputised. In March 1834 Telford paid his last visit to the canal, and Cubitt accompanied him on a conducted tour. Frail and deaf, the great engineer regarded the embankment which was the cause of so much delay and extra expense. One can picture the younger man confidently reassuring his elderly companion, but a few weeks after Telford's visit the bank slipped for the umpteenth time, and by the time Telford died, on 2nd September, his last canal remained uncompleted.

continued overleaf:

Aqualate Mere

New Guild

NORTH

Oulton

Norbury

A519 to Newport

Loynton Hall

The Anchor

mp 18/21

43

42

Norbury Junction

mp 15/24

drydock

Junction Inn

St. Peter's

Tumulus

mp 16/23

38

aq.

Course of the Newport Branch

Shelmore Embankment

Old Wharf Tea Rooms

40   Grub Street

mp 17/22

41

39   70'

Ⓢ = WC

1: Norbury Wharf

A519 to Eccleshall

by-road to High Offley

continued from page 15:

Not until the following January was Shelmore Bank considered solid enough for the canal to be put in water and for the first boat to gingerly proceed across. Tall trees mask the immensity of the embankment nowadays, curtailing what would otherwise be panoramic views. The bank slipped in 2003 and remedial work had to be undertaken to the tune of nearly two million pounds: fivefold now, one imagines.

Sadly - for all abandoned routes tug at the heartstrings of true canal travellers - Norbury is no longer a junction, though the name lives on, and a roving bridge spanning an arm which leads to a drydock at least sustains the illusion of another canal heading off into the unknown. The Newport Branch was abandoned by the LMS Railway in 1944, yet exploration of the country roads west of the canal will reveal overbridges and the poignant remains of lock chambers. Vivid descriptions of the canal can be found in Jack Roberts' book of working boat memories: *Shropshire Union Fly-Boats*, published by Canal Book Shop and available from Audlem Mill (Map 9).

Formed in 2000, the Shrewsbury and Newport Canals Trust aim to 'protect, conserve and improve' the route and its branches with the ultimate goal of restoring a continuous navigable waterway linking Norbury Junction with Shrewsbury. Several short sections of the canal remain in water at Newport, some five miles to the south-west of Norbury, and the Trust are restoring Wappenshall Wharf on the outskirts of Telford. John Hillaby walked along the towpath from Newport to Norbury on his epic trek from Land's End to John o' Groats, described in the 1968 book *Journey Through Britain*; a masterpiece of travel and nature writing, unbelievably out of print.

Even without a proper junction to its name, Norbury remains a busy canal location, popular with day-trippers of all persuasions. The Local History Group published an excellent book describing the development of this canal community in 2012, and it should still be obtainable from the well-stocked shop at the wharf. When the first Canal Companions appeared in 1982, British Waterways had a Section Office and maintenance yard here providing employment for thirty men engaged in the day to day upkeep of the canal. Now the yard appears moribund, even the enterprising carpentry firm who occupied it recently have apparently decamped to Stoke on Trent.

As the canal's raison d'etre morphed from goods into leisure in the 1960s, Norbury became home to a number of subsequently well-known canal stalwarts: John Stothert, Harry Arnold, David Piper, Tony Lewery, Steve Rees-Jones et al. John Stothert founded Shropshire Union Cruises in 1962, initially consisting of a fleet of plywood, outboard powered hire cruisers. Proving too fragile for canal use, these were gradually super-seded by steel boats. Shropshire Union Cruises sold out to Dartline who were themselves taken over by Anglo-Welsh. Nowadays, Norbury Wharf continues to operate a hire fleet in the tradition of its illustrious predecessors. Like a canal supergroup, the rest forged their own careers: Harry Arnold went on to become a doyen of inland waterway journalism; David Piper a boat-builder; Tony Lewery an expert in the history and application of roses & castles; and Steve Rees-Jones the operator of horsedrawn trip boats. There must have been something empowering about the Norbury air, or maybe it was just the ale on tap in the Junction Inn.

Leaving Norbury astern, lines of moored boats usher the canal into a cutting. Staffordshire's Grub Street is not synonymous with the lower echelons of the literary trade. No, this Grub Street is known in canal circles as the location of another of the Shroppie's trademark cuttings. For over a mile the canal is wrapped in a thick coat of vegetation, again, like Shelmore, hiding the sheer size of the eighty foot deep cutting, whose most unusual feature is the double-arched bridge which carries the A519 across the canal. The tiny telegraph pole is a survivor from the line which once marched beside the Shroppie. Appropriately, canals are again being used as lines of communication with the burying of optical fibres beneath selected lengths of towpath. A black, monkey-like creature is reputed to have haunted Bridge 39 ever since a boatman was killed here in the 19th century. Working boatmen referred to haunted places as 'frightenings'.

CROSSING the border between Staffordshire and Shropshire, the canal continues to traverse an uncluttered countryside almost entirely given over to agriculture. A newish crop conspicuous in neighbouring fields is elephant grass. It can come as a surprise to find so remote a landscape in the 'crowded' middle of England. One is tempted to categorise the area as 'lost' but for the obvious truth that it has never been 'found' in the first place.

South-west of Shebdon Wharf, Batchacre Hall was home to - in the words of Henry Thorold - the 'eccentric bachelor politician' Richard Whitworth (1734-1811), an early advocate of canals. Such was his enthusiasm for all things watery, he constructed a lake in the grounds on which historic naval battles were re-enacted, together with a trial length of canal. Batchacre Hall is now a farmhouse and livery stable.

Blithely we pleasure boaters sail across embankments and through cuttings with no more thought for their construction than if we were driving down the M6. But imagine the impact of Telford's brash new canal on the surrounding early nineteenth century landscape. Put yourself in the position of the occupant of Batchacre Park. Up until 1830 dawn rose across the open pasturelands throwing light through his east-facing windows. A year later his view of the rising sun was cut off forever by an embankment twice the height of the farmhouse. No wonder the landowners of this rural corner of Staffordshire had their misgivings, and the canal company paid dearly in compensation for the land they acquired. A series of leaks in the vicinity of Shebdon brought about closure of the canal in 2009, but soil-blending techniques have consolidated the bank for the foreseeable future, hopefully.

West of the canal, there are good views of The Wrekin, with the Clee and Breidden hills prominent on the far horizon. You wouldn't expect to encounter a factory in the midst of otherwise empty countryside, but you do! It was opened by Cadbury, the chocolate manufacturers, in 1911 as a centre for processing milk collected from the dairy farming hinterland of the Shropshire Union Canal. Canal transport was used exclusively to bring countless churns gathered from numerous wharves along the canal; from simple wooden stages at the foot of fields, to

continued overleaf:

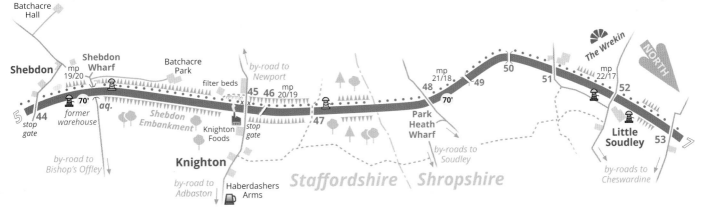

Former Cadbury's works, Knighton

the sophistication of Cadbury's own milk concentration depot at High Onn. Typically a boat could carry a hundred 10 gallon churns. Cadbury owned a distinctive fleet of narrowboats, being one of the first operators to experiment with motorised craft. Cocoa and sugar crumb were also brought by boat to Knighton and blended with milk to make raw chocolate, which was subsequently returned by boat to Bournville to complete the manufacturing process. Sugar and coal were other commodities transported by boat to Knighton. Cadbury's fleet was disbanded in 1928 and the contract passed to FMC until nationalisation in 1948. The last boatman to trade to Knighton was Charlie Atkins senior; eponymously nicknamed 'Chocolate Charlie'. He carried the final cargo from Knighton to Bournville in 1961, but some fine examples

of historic craft are sometimes to be seen moored here. These days the works trades under the name of Knighton Foods and produces dry powdered ingredients for drinks, desserts and baking products.

Bisected by the county boundary, Knighton Reservoir lies to the east of the canal, just off the edge of our map. It was built to feed the canal but, being unlined, had a pronounced tendency to leak, and whilst it remains in water, doesn't contribute to the canal's supply. In common with Belvide (Map 2) however, it's popular with bird-watchers, and several rare visitors - red-necked phalarope, snow bunting, common scoter for example - have been recorded. Park Heath Wharf consists of a winding-hole and little else other than the footprint of a former weighbridge.

THE Shroppie flirts with the county boundary as Staffordshire gives Shropshire a subtle dig in the ribs. The landscape, however, is impervious to the machinations of local government, remaining aloof and typically inscrutable: a tall, dark, silent canal, this Shropshire Union; much given, punningly, to 'brooding'.

Woodseaves is another prodigious cutting: almost a hundred feet deep in places. These cuttings proved just as troublesome to Telford and his contractors as the embankments. In its raw, newly completed state, it must have corresponded to the canal at Corinth. Brittle at best, frequent rock falls were a fact of life, and indeed still are, as occasional lumps of fragmented rock imply. The towpath had been impassible for the best part of a year while we were researching this edition, whilst boaters occasionally feel their craft encountering submerged debris as well. Speed, in any case, is restricted to 2mph. Too fast, one imagines, for any botanists in your party, anxious to identify the huge variety of species on view. A feature of Woodseaves is its pair of high bridges, spanning the canal as if they are portals to the mysterious chasms of another world. They carry farm tracks and you are occasionally treated to a surreal encounter with a tractor passing loftily overhead, almost helicopter like in the context of the setting.

Tyrley (pronounced 'Turley') Wharf was a point of discharge and collection for the local estate at Peatswood and the dwellings provided for its workforce. The buildings date from 1837 and were erected by Thomas Twemlow of nearby Peatswood Hall in a graceful Tudor style, far more architecturally ambitious than the utilitarian nature of most contemporary wharfage. At one time one of the cottages was licensed for the sale of ales and liquors. In the 1980s - a period now nostalgically viewed as one of much enterprise on the canals - Lancastrians, Ken and Lillias Greenhalgh, ran a marvellous craft shop in the end cottage, whilst their neighbours, Misses Picken and Dale, charmed passers-by with home-made cooking, garden-fresh vegetables, and tales of daring-do, for they were both former Wrens.

Between 1917 and 1932 Cadbury's used to collect milk from here and take it by boat to their works at Knighton. On the end wall of the northernmost cottage, a poignant little memorial remembers five local men who didn't return from the First World War. Up the lane towards the A529, a former chapel - erected in 1902 in thanksgiving for the safe return of a Twemlow from the Boer War - serves as a workshop for the restoration and manufacture of rocking horses. This delightful enterprise belongs to a lady called Alison Smith, who led a peripatetic life on the canals, before settling

continued overleaf:

Four Alls

A529

Goldstone Wharf
mp 23/16 55
70'
Wharf Tavern
54
6
by-road to Cheswardine

mp 24/15
56
Bridge Farm
57
Woodseaves Cutting
58

NORTH

Shropshire

Staffordshire

Tyrley Grange
P

Rocking Horse Works

Tyrley Cutting
mp 25/14
59 Tyrley Wharf
70'
60
Tyrley Locks
33ft 0ins

1 2 3 4 5
mp 26/13
61
R. Tern
MD
aq.

Peatswood Estate

for details of facilities at Cheswardine & Tyrley
turn to page 23

down in Tyrley. The wooden boat she acquired in 1989 was none other than *Heather Bell*, built by Nursers of Braunston in 1937 for Christopher March, the son of a wealthy Worcester solicitor. During the Second World War, *Heather Bell* contributed to the war effort by being employed as a working boat crewed by Christopher's sister, Daphne (an Oxford graduate) together with Eily 'Kit' Gayford, who was later instrumental in training the 'Idle Women' who crewed working pairs on the Grand Union.

In the early 20th century northbound boats, tug-hauled up from Wolverhampton, would be taken forward by horse from Tyrley, and extensive stabling was provided on either side of the canal: Jack Roberts describes changing horses here in *Shropshire Union Fly-Boats*. The short pound between locks 1 and 2 is overlooked by a fine example of a Telford lock-keeper's cottage. This, incidentally, has been Alison Smith's home for a number of years. Furthermore, she has it on good authority that Telford himself dropped in for a cup of tea on one of his surveying trips to the fledgeling canal - Darjeeling if you must know!

Seventeen lock-free miles come to an abrupt end for northbound boaters at Tyrley where a flight of five carry the canal down into Market Drayton. The lower chambers are dramatically located in a shadowy sandstone cutting across which branches intertwine to form a tunnel of trees. Chiaroscuro lighting effects challenge photographers. Damp, and rarely touched by sunlight, all manner of mosses and ferns flourish in this conducive environment. After dusk bats leave their tree bole roosts to hunt for insects, acrobatically twisting and turning over the luminous pounds between the locks. Fishing rights are under the auspices of Palethorpes Angling Society. We cheerily asked one angler if he'd caught anything: 'Not a sausage,' came the lugubrious reply.

Peatswood estate - including an erstwhile boating lake - lies to the east of the canal - its hall demolished in 1979, though a substantial Queen Anne Revival style Clockhouse survives and can be rented by self-catering groups. Apparently a short canal of sorts once led to a marl pit. Bridge 61 is known as Tyrley Castle in deference to an 11th century fortification recalled now solely by the name of a farm to the west. Berrisford Aqueduct carries the canal over a by-road on the approach to Market Drayton. We can recommend descending the steps from its southern end to appreciate the imposing nature of this sandstone structure from below.

MARKET DRAYTON was the largest, in fact the only, town encountered by the old Birmingham & Liverpool Junction Canal on its route from Autherley to Nantwich. Naturally, a sizeable wharf was provided for dealing with local cargoes; though the canal's monopoly on local trade lasted only thirty years before the railway reached the town. It is sometimes difficult, in these days of the ubiquitous juggernaut, to appreciate the importance of the canal wharf and the railway goods yard to the past prosperity of small towns like 'Drayton. They must have been the hub of local life, few businesses would have been able to carry out their trade without regular recourse to the wharfinger and the stationmaster. From the opening of the canal until the First World War no commodity, apart from local agricultural produce, could have arrived at Market Drayton, or been dispatched, without the involvement of these important gentlemen. Apparently, one of the wharf's earliest tenants was William Hazledine, the ironmaster affectionately nicknamed 'Merlin' by Telford.

The wharf remains a busy place, with boating facilities on the towpath side and a basin opposite. The boatyard (Talbot Wharf) is still in the Machin family who for many years ran their Holidays Afloat hire fleet from here. Some of the wharf's buildings are rather dilapidated, but at the northern end of the basin the attractive, if oddly shaped Betton Mill is now occupied by offices and apartments. When first erected in 1906 it was used for the storage of cheese, before subsequently becoming a corn mill. The canal widens north of Bridge 63, being overlooked, on the offside, by a housing development with private moorings. This was the site of Ladyline, one of the leading lights of the 1960/70s expansion in canal leisure boating: why they even published a series of guide books researched by Hugh McKnight, highly respected author of *The Shell Book of Inland Waterways*.

The canal makes a quick getaway north of 'Drayton. Proposals were announced in 2020 for a new marina and housing development at Victoria Wharf, but the pandemic intervened. Note the substantial stone abutments where the North Staffordshire Railway once crossed the canal. Opened in 1870, it linked Market Drayton with Newcastle under Lyme and Stoke on Trent until 1956, being considered 'surplus to requirements' long before Beeching raised his ugly head.

A burgeoning business park is encroaching upon the canal, though the high hedge mitigates the intrusion. The town's livestock market is also near at hand, close enough to hear the auctioneer on Mondays and Wednesdays if the wind is in the right direction. *continued overleaf:*

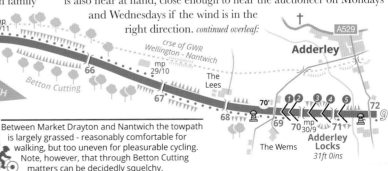

'Passengers No More'
1: M. Drayton - csd 9.9.63

Market Drayton Town FC

A53 to Shrewsbury

A529 to Nantwich

old corn mills

Town Centre

Aldi

cattle market

Morrisons

Lidl

Red Lion Joules Brewery

Asda

Palethorpes

Market Drayton

Brownhills Farm

site for marina

65

sch

63

64 mp 27/12

62

Betton Mill

Talbot Wharf

S = WC

7

North Staffordshire Railway Stoke Branch

course of former

NORTH

Betton Cutting

mp 28/11

crse of GWR Wellington - Nantwich

66

mp 29/10

The Lees

67

68

69

70

mp 30/9

71

Adderley

A529

Adderley Locks
31ft 0ins

The Wems

70'

72

> Between Market Drayton and Nantwich the towpath is largely grassed - reasonably comfortable for walking, but too uneven for pleasurable cycling. Note, however, that through Betton Cutting matters can be decidedly squelchy.

continued from page 21:

Betton Cutting lacks the impressive height of Grub Street and Woodseaves to the south, though it is said that a shrieking ghost haunts it, and that working boatmen would avoid lingering here in the old days. Reluctant debunkers of myth at the best of times, we can't help wondering, however, if that unnerving association emanates from *Narrow Boat*. L. T. C. Rolt was a connoisseur of ghost stories and a fan of M. R. James, doyen of that genre. Indeed, he alludes to 'that which walks in Betton Wood knows why it walks or why it cries' from James's short story *A Neighbour's Landmark* in *Narrow Boat*, noting that the fictitious wood had been 'grubbed up' in any case. Besides, no boatman worth his salt would have dreamt of overnighting so far from an ale house. That said, there is something of a fey quality about the B&LJC throughout its length, a blurring of the homespun and outlandish liable to send shivers down susceptible spines.

The now much overgrown and obliterated course of the Nantwich & Market Drayton Railway - opened in 1863 and subsequently amalgamated with the Great Western Railway - accompanies the canal. Delve into the trees near milepost 28/11 and you'll come upon its trackbed, and the opportunity, if you're so minded, to pocket a piece of ballast as a souvenir. A significant secondary route (leading to Crewe) in its heyday, its passenger services failed by just a few weeks to see out their centenary.

Briefly, in the early 1960s, the 'Pines Express' from Manchester to Bournemouth used this route, but primarily it was a goods line. Bob Yate - in his book *By Great Western to Crewe* - alludes to the unofficial names bestowed on the line's crack goods trains: 'The Early Riser' (Manchester to Wolverhampton); 'The Grocer' (Southall to Crewe); 'The Lancashire Lad' (Westbury to Manchester); and 'The Sparagrass' (Worcester to Crewe). At its zenith, something in the region of twenty important goods trains per day passed each way. Once a good proportion of this trade would have used the canal. Now, inevitably, it all goes by road; and one can't quite help but wonder if this really constitutes progress? How nice it would be to see one of the GWR's quintessential 'Hall' class locomotives hurry past on a heavy goods: why it might even be number 4901 itself: *Adderley Hall* !

When we first became familiar with Adderley Locks in the early 1980s, they ran to a resident lock-keeper - who went by the delightfully bucolic name of Frank Butter - and were so beautifully maintained and manicured that they won first prize in the National Lock & Bridge Competition. Not so lovingly tended now, they are nevertheless a pleasure to work through. A privet hedge beside the third lock down indicates the site of a demolished lock-keeper's cottage, whilst a bench by Lock 4 commemorates the canal stalwart Ike Argent.

Market Drayton Wharf

CHESWARDINE (Map 7)

Cheswardine lies a country mile to the east - say 25 minutes on foot - of the canal and can be accessed from bridges 52-55. High Street ascends to the parish church of St Swithin's much rebuilt by the Gothic Revival architect John Loughborough Pearson, best known for Truro Cathedral. 'Stately ... but not specially distinguished' was Pevsner's put down regarding the former. Now a care home, neo Elizabethan Cheswardine Hall was erected in 1875 for Newcastle-under-Lyme MP, Charles Donaldson-Hudson.

Eating & Drinking

FOX & HOUNDS - High Street. Tel: 01630 661244. Nicely furnished Joule's house. Food served 6-8.30pm Tue-Fri, and from noon Sat & Sun until 8.30 and 4.30pm respectively. TF9 2RS
WHARF TAVERN - Goldstone Wharf (Bridge 55). Tel: 01630 661226. A popular port of call throughout the boating season for good pub grub. Caravan and camp site, self-catering and spacious garden. TF9 2LP. *Quaint community pub called the Red Lion also on High Street - Tel: 01630 661234.*

Shopping

A delightful and welcoming community shop adjoins the Fox & Hounds. Open Mon-Fri 7.30am-10am and 3pm-5pm; Sat 9am-11am; Sun 9am-10.30am.

TYRLEY   Map 7

Eating & Drinking

THE FOUR ALLS - Woodseaves (10 minutes walk west of Tyrley Wharf). Tel: 01630 652995. Pub with accommodation. Food served Mon-Fri 12-3pm and 5-8.30pm, Sat 12-8.30pm and Sun 12-5pm. TF9 2AG
The Rocking Horse Works can be contacted on 01630 653194.

MARKET DRAYTON Map 8

'Drayton is best visited on a Wednesday when the ancient market is in full swing and country folk gather to seek out a bargain and a gossip. Though perhaps not quite as bucolic as of yore, this remains the town's real strength, along with its half-timbered houses which mostly date from the aftermath of a fire that swept through the place in 1651. Drayton's most famous son was Robert Clive, best remembered here for scaling the sturdy tower of St Mary's and for blackmailing local shopkeepers - ideal escapades in preparation for a career in diplomacy and military leadership. He established British rule in the Sub Continent and became known as 'Clive of India'. Betjeman and Piper's Shell Guide of 1951 recalls that the district was once terrorised by a murderous gang known as 'The Bravoes of Market Drayton' - shades of the Peaky Blinders! Two busy food factories, Palethorpes and Muller, provide employment.

Eating & Drinking

BUTTERCROSS BISTRO - Cheshire Street. Tel: 01630 317377. Smartly refurbished eaterie open Mon-Sat 8.30am-4pm, plus Fri & Sat evenings 5-9pm and Sun 9am-4pm. TF9 1PF
CLIVE & COFFYNE - Shropshire Street. Tel: 01630 657523. Cosy pub featuring Hobsons and Hancocks ales. Coffynes are mutton pies! TF9 3BY
JONES'S - High Street. Tel: 01630 652042 Well appointed coffee shop open 9am to 4pm ex Sun. Sister establishment in Whitchurch. TF9 1QB
FOODSHION - Cheshire Street. Tel: 01630 658382. Chinese, Asian & Thai cuisine to eat in or take-away from 4.30pm daily ex Tue. TF9 1PD
RED LION - Great Hales Street. Tel: 01630 652602. Joule's Brewery was originally in Stone but closed in 1974. The name, happily, was revived in 2010 and their beers are brewed here in Drayton using local mineral water. The Red Lion is the 'brewery tap' and a fine establishment it is too. Opens 11am, food served throughout daily from noon. TF9 1JP

Shopping

'It comes to something when even the charity shops are closing down' we overheard one local bemoaning, and it can't be easy for small market towns to compete these days, let alone small independent shops. Yet Market Drayton tries hard and looks its best on a Wednesday, market day. Drayton Deli is a good food shop beside the handsome Buttercross. The Fields Kitchen on High Street is another excellent provisions shop. Asda, Lidl, Aldi and Morrisons supermarkets compete for boaters' general requirements.

Things to Do

MUSEUM & RESOURCE CENTRE - Shropshire Street. Open Tue, Wed, Fri, & Sat mornings from April to October. Admission free. Local history nostalgically displayed in an old shop. TF9 3DA
SWIMMING CENTRE - Phoenix Bank. Tel: 0345 000 7004. Indoor and outdoor (May-Sep) pools. TF9 1JT

Connections

BUSES - Arriva service 64 operates approximately hourly Mon-Sat to/from Shrewsbury and Hanley (Stoke-on-Trent) via Newcastle-under-Lyme.
TAXIS - Drayton Cabs. Tel: 01630 803015.

ADDERLEY   Map 8

Scattered village forgetful of the fact that it once boasted a railway station. The isolated church largely dates from 1800 and is under the care of the Churches Conservation Trust. Lovely ironwork tracery on clear glass windows and a mounting block.

RESPLENDENT in trademark 'Shroppie' grey and white paint, the Audlem flight is a pleasure: whether you are working up or down it, or simply spectating; and how often can you say that! Thirty-one miles out from Autherley, northbound travellers encounter Cheshire for the first time. Then fifteen locks, snuggled in a brackeny cutting of larch and Scots pine, drop the canal the best part of a hundred feet. Needless to say, the flight can be busy, and at such times patience, courtesy and good humour have their rewards. To paraphrase some old advice: be nice to people when you're working up lock flights, because you might meet the same people coming down. One or two of the lock chambers have retained their keeper's cottages, others have lost them, though at Lock 8 you can still smell the scents of garden flowers. Back in the present day, cakes and other morale-boosting edibles are often available at Kinsell Farm; ditto vegetables and fruit from an honesty box by Lock 9.

The barrel-roofed building by Lock 10 was used by stonemasons, blacksmiths and carpenters engaged in maintenance. Towards the foot of the flight - known to old boatmen as the Audlem "Thick" - you pass Audlem Wharf, one of the prettiest ports of call on the Shropshire Union, with a former warehouse restored as a popular pub and the adjacent lofty Kingbur Mill converted into a superb craft shop. The mill was built during the First World War by H. Kingsley Burton, hence the name. It produced animal feeds; boats brought in raw materials and took away sacks of feed. Old photographs depict a covered gantry which spanned the roadway and jutted out over the canal to facilitate loading and unloading. The mill ceased working in the nineteen-sixties and was converted into a canal shop in the 'seventies by the late John Stothert, much of its internal fittings and machinery being atmospherically retained.

Shadowing the Shropshire Union - which belonged to the London & North Western Railway by the time the railway age was in full swing - the rival Great Western company's Wellington to Nantwich and Crewe route was a useful means of competition. The crane which adorns the wharf outside the Shroppie Fly pub belonged at the railway station before it was resited. Audlem station closed in 1963, but not before it had been immortalised by Flanders & Swann in their melancholy elegy to the Beeching axe, *Slow Train*. George Dow, the railway public relations officer, historian and early designer and advocate of diagrammatic maps, lived in Audlem for many years, his close friend Hamilton Ellis being a regular visitor. What a shame the latter wasn't

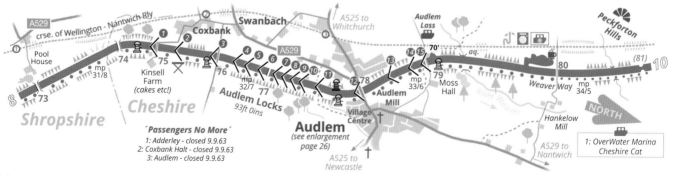

A529   crse. of Wellington - Nantwich Rly   Swanbach   A525 to Whitchurch   Audlem Lass   Peckforton Hills

Pool House   Coxbank   A529   70'   aq.   80   (81)   10

74   75   76   77   78   79

Kinsell Farm (cakes etc!)   mp 31/8   mp 32/7   Audlem Locks 93ft 0ins   mp 33/6   Moss Hall   Weaver Way   mp 34/5   NORTH

73   Audlem Mill   River Weaver   Hankelow Mill

Shropshire   **Cheshire**   Village Centre   **Audlem** (see enlargement page 26)

'Passengers No More'
1: Adderley - closed 9.9.63
2: Coxbank Halt - closed 9.9.63
3: Audlem - closed 9.9.63

A525 to Newcastle   A529 to Nantwich

1: OverWater Marina
Cheshire Cat

cajoled into portraying the flight in one of his inimitable oil paintings, after all it was in railway ownership for a century.

The handsome building which houses the Shroppie Fly pub - whose distinctive bar is formed from an old BCN day boat - originally provided warehouse space and canal employee accommodation. Delightful sepia photographs of it appear in Peter Silvester's book *Audlem Locks*, an informative guide to the flight, well worth obtaining from Audlem Mill. Alongside Lock 13 is another of Telford's lock-keeper's cottages, albeit of two storeys on this occasion. Below the bottom lock the canal widens into a winding hole overlooked by a well preserved stable block. Jane Marshall, of the Daystar Theatre Group, runs Roses & Castles workshops here. Previously it had been home to the pioneer hotel boat operators, Tom and Doris Whitely. Throughout the 1950s their pair *Prince* and *Mafeking* toured the canals under the Waterborne Tours banner.

The canal, wide with concrete banking but deceptively shallow, bounds across the strippling River Weaver on Moss Hall aqueduct, followed by a high embankment. One of the more outlandish notions of the Ministry of War Transport during the Second World War (and there were plenty to chose from) was to make the Weaver navigable by 100 ton barges to this point, beyond which a lift would carry them up to the level of the Shropshire Union, upgraded sufficiently for them to travel as far south as Wolverhampton. However, as Peter Brown points out in *The Shropshire Union Canal* - a substantial tome devoted to the history of all the SUC system's component parts - barges of that increased capacity were unlikely to have proved viable in the longer term, water supply on a much widened canal would have been problematical, and time-consuming transhipment would still have been demanded at Wolverhampton.

OverWater is one of the new breed of 'farmland' marinas. A waterbus service links the marina with Audlem on summer weekends. Bridge 80 retains its early British Waterways era blue and yellow number plate, whilst immediately to the south, a drainage paddle is embossed 'SUC Ellesmere 1928'; minor artefacts of enduring value.

Audlem

Audlem — Map 9

Gorgeous Audlem has grown in confidence and commerce in the six decades we've known it, and its annual Festival of Transport and Gathering of Historic Boats in July only serves to put it even more firmly on the map. Yet the village seems comfortable with its burgeoning popularity, and assimilates visitors without descending into self-conscious pomposity. Canal apart, high points include the ancient buttermarket and parish church of St James ('on a turfed eminence', as Pevsner put it when he finally got around to surveying Cheshire in 1970) in photogenic propinquity. Not to be outshone, the nonconformist Methodist and Baptist chapels are equally impressive.

Eating & Drinking

AYAAN'S - Tel: 01270 812226. Shropshire Street. Open daily (ex Tue) from 5pm for take-away: kebabs, burgers, chickens. CW3 0AE

THE BRIDGE - canalside Bridge 78. Tel: 01270 812928. Marston's, food daily 12pm-8pm (6.30pm Sun). Nice etched windows pertaining to Marston & Thompson ... who remembers Thompson now? CW3 0DX

LINDEN STORES - Shropshire Street. Tel: 01270 812258. Stylish restaurant serving seasonal, locally sourced food. Open Thur-Sun for lunch and Thur-Sat for dinner from 5.30pm. Alcohol outsales. CW3 0AE

THE LORD COMBERMERE - The Square. Tel: 01270 812277. Refurbished village centre pub. CW3 0AQ

THE OLD PRIEST HOUSE - The Square. Tel: 01270 811749. All day breakfasts, coffees, teas and light lunches. 10am-3pm daily ex Mon & Tue. CW3 0AH

THE SHROPPIE FLY - canalside Lock 13. Tel: 01270 748898. Warehouse conversion of fluctuating fortunes. Canalside seating. CW3 0DX

VILLAGE CHIPPY - Cheshire Street. Fish & chips. Tel: 01270 811777. CW3 0AH

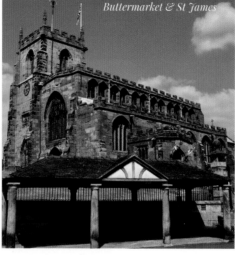
Buttermarket & St James

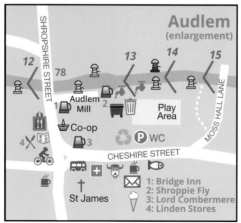
Audlem (enlargement)

1: Bridge Inn
2: Shroppie Fly
3: Lord Combermere
4: Linden Stores

Shopping

Amazing to find a village with so many outlets. Indeed, shopping here is a pleasure rather than a stressful chore. Oxtail & Trotter's butchery (Tel: 01270 811793) on Cheshire Street is excellent, but there's also a well-stocked Co-op (ATM) open daily 7am-10pm, a Boots pharmacy, and a bicycle shop (Tel: 01270 811333) should you need running repairs. Post office services, chocolates and ice cream (ex Wed & Sun) from Lllovely on Cheshire Street. Laundry facilities and cafe at OverWater Marina by Bridge 80.

Things to Do

AUDLEM MILL CANAL SHOP - Tel: 01270 811059. Christine and Peter Silvester operate one of the best canal shops on the system and are congenial mines of local information to boot. As well as a wide range of gifts, crafts and needlework, the mill stocks an unrivalled range of canal books, and a growing list of self-published titles of historical canal importance. Events are held throughout the year. CW3 0DX

SECRET BUNKER - Hack Green, Map 10. Tel: 01270 629219. Open 10.00-5.00 daily during summer season - telephone for other times. Admission charge. Refreshments. "Experience a real four minute warning and view original TV broadcasts to be transmitted in event of a nuclear strike." Authentic equipment in its original macabre setting brings home the power of nuclear weapons and the government's state of readiness. Chilling stuff! CW5 8AQ

Connections

BUSES - D&G service 72 to/from Nantwich roughly half a dozen times per day Mon-Sat. Sadly, the Wednesdays only mid-morning link with Market Drayton, once a boon for would-be towpath walkers, has had its cross-county funding withdrawn.

GRUB Street, Hack Green: is the Shroppie scoring literary points? Itinerant canal writers apart, there are two isolated locks and the remnants of a stable at Hack Green, recalling the practice of frequent changing of horses on the 'fly' boats which travelled day and night with urgent, perishable cargoes, the sort of canal age equivalent of a lorry pull-in now.

This is the Cheshire Plain and dairy farming has long been a vital part of the area's economy - though for how much longer one might wonder, given the precarious state of agriculture in the 21st century. Making a profit from milk is notoriously difficult these days, no wonder farmers are being encouraged to replace cows with canal boats as demonstrated by a growing number of new marinas in the area.

When we first explored this canal in the early Eighties we were blissfully unaware of Hack Green's nuclear bunker, a Second World War radar station secretly designated to play a role as a Regional Government Headquarters in the event of a nuclear war. Deemed redundant at the end of the Cold War, it has somewhat bizarrely become a tourist attraction.

Adroitly changing the subject, let us recall how trade survived on this canal until the 1960s; which must be some sort of testimony to the viability of canal carrying. Perhaps in the final analysis attitudes rather than economics prevailed. One of the most celebrated traffics on the Shroppie in latter years was Thomas Clayton's oil run from Stanlow on the banks of the Mersey to Langley Green, near Oldbury in the Black Country. The contract commenced in 1924 and the Clayton boats, with their characteristic decked holds, and river names, were a mainstay of trade on the canal for thirty years. Even post-war, a thousand boat-loads per annum were being despatched from Stanlow, some remaining horse-drawn until the early Fifties. But, in common with other canals, the Shropshire Union lost its final freights to the motor lorry; then, for many, with the disappearance of its working boats, something died on the Shroppie, some intangible component of canal heritage that no amount of preservation, nor hectic holiday trade, can ever quite compensate for. On the outskirts of Nantwich the canal passes beneath the Crewe to Shrewsbury (and South Wales) railway.

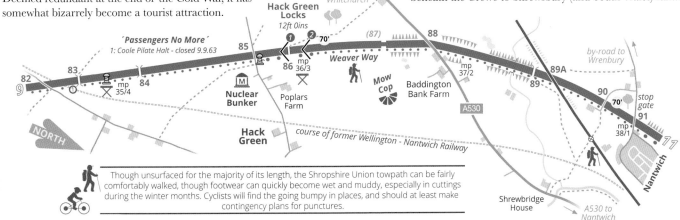

Though unsurfaced for the majority of its length, the Shropshire Union towpath can be fairly comfortably walked, though footwear can quickly become wet and muddy, especially in cuttings during the winter months. Cyclists will find the going bumpy in places, and should at least make contingency plans for punctures.

Smoky Approach to Cowley Tunnel (Map 4)

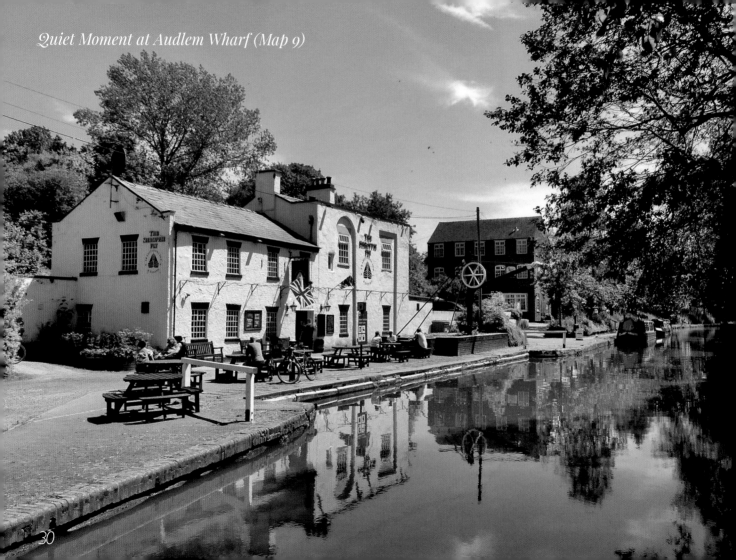

Quiet Moment at Audlem Wharf (Map 9)

Brief Encounter at Adderley Locks (Map 8)

Lord Talbot's Wharf (Map 4)

Widebeam Staircase at Bunbury Wharf (Map 12)

JUNCTIONS past and junctions present stimulate interest throughout this length of what has long been commonly known as the Shropshire Union Canal. The junction *past* lay at Nantwich, where Telford's narrow Birmingham & Liverpool Junction Canal - upon which work began at this end in 1827 - met the SUC's earlier constituent, the broad Chester Canal, opened as far as its terminal basin at Nantwich in 1779. The junctions *present* are at Hurleston - where the hugely popular Llangollen Canal commences its 44 mile, 21 lock journey into the mountainous heart of North Wales - and at Barbridge - where the Middlewich Branch of the Shropshire Union Canal provides a strategic link with the Trent & Mersey Canal. A broad embankment elevates the canal above the housing, back gardens and allotments which constitute the periphery of Nantwich. Ironically, these earthworks, together with a cast iron aqueduct over the Chester road, could have been avoided if the owners of Dorfold Hall had not objected to the passage of the canal across their land. The aqueduct

Industrial park

Wardle

102

12

17

Bache House

Llangollen Canal

Olde Barbridge Inn

2

101 Barbridge Junction

Snugburys Ice Cream
(see p. 65)

fresh eggs!

1A

A51

100

1

Middlewich Branch

11D

reservoir

Hurleston Locks
34ft 3ins

99

Acton

B5341

NORTH

98

Dorfold Hall

94 95

70'

97

96 Hurleston Junction

NBCYC

93

1: Nantwich Canal Centre (ABC)
2: Barbridge Marine/Midway Boats

10

S 92
mp
39/0

S

WC

A534

Nantwich Town FC

Town Centre

R. Weaver

Nantwich
(see enlargement on page 38)

was refurbished in 2015.
A Sculpture Trail has been laid out beside the embankment's refurbished towpath, the main exhibit being in the form of a boat horse built out of reclaimed lock gates. Nearby, stands a B&LJC milepost indicating that it's 39 miles to Autherley on the outskirts of Wolverhampton. Visitor moorings are provided along the length of the embankment, and they make for a pleasant overnight stay with easy access to the town centre, an enjoyable ten minutes stroll to the east.

The basin, former terminus of the Chester Canal, hints at the more expedient route to the south which Telford would have liked to have used; in the event it took him five years to complete the not strictly necessary earthworks. Nowadays the basin - still boasting a former cheese warehouse - is pretty choc-a-bloc with boats, all a far cry from 1939 when Tom and Angela Rolt couldn't get *Cressy* into the basin because a bar of silt, built up by the passage of motor boats, prevented their entry. Adjoining the basin are the premises of the Nantwich & Border Counties Yachting Club, an organisation whose founder members were early advocates of the use of the canal system for leisure. The Leisure Age has impacted on the canal's agricultural hinterland as well. The Friesian milking herds which characterised these Cheshire pasturelands are not so prevalent now. Some farm buildings have been converted into domestic dwellings other farm businesses, such as the Sadlers at Park Farm, have had to diversify, in this case into ice cream. You could say farming is not quite as black and white as it once was, more chocolate and vanilla.

Hurleston and Barbridge are the 'Clapham Junctions' of the inland waterways. At the height of the cruising season the section between them is often frenetic with boats converging from and diverging to all points of the canal compass. Lucky, then, that the old Chester Canal was built for use by 14ft beam barges known as 'Mersey Flats' and that there is

Barbridge

plenty of room to manoeuvre. Both junctions have suffered casualties in their infrastructure. There was a substantial junction house at Hurleston adjoining Bridge 97. Its dereliction (and subsequent demolition by British Waterways) so 'maddened' the financier, Sir John Smith (1923-2007), that he founded the Landmark Trust in 1962, a body dedicated to reviving old buildings for use as holiday homes. But perhaps even more regrettable was the loss in 1958/9 of the warehouse and transhipment shed which spanned the main line at Barbridge, the sole remaining evidence of which is a narrowing in the canal to the south of the roving bridge over the Middlewich Branch. Should you want to see what it looked like, a fine painting of it by Brian Collings appeared in Tom Foxon's *Anderton for Orders*, reproduced in full colour in the first edition of 1988. An Edwin Shearing photograph, showing the working boats *Ferret* and *Grantham* moored alongside, can be found in both *The Old Chester*

Canal edited by Gordon Emery and *The Shropshire Union Canal* by Peter Brown. The Jolly Tar public house, which once stood prominently - not to say garishly - opposite the junction, has disappeared beneath a housing development. One day, in the not too distant future, the whole of England will have disappeared beneath a housing development.

At Wardle there's an old roadside 'pinfold' where stray cattle would have been penned. Nearby, the canal wriggles beneath Bridge 102 which carries the busy A51, a road that encounters a fair few canals on its desultory course between Tamworth and Chester. This stretch of the road can trace its origins back to the Middle Ages, when it linked Nantwich with Chester, and was known as Watfield Pavement. It plays host to a slightly different cast of travellers now compared to the merchants, pedlars and drovers of the misty past.

A recently inserted roundabout leads to the burgeoning Cheshire Green industrial park. What a knack developers have of making their sprawls sound so mendaciously bucolic. This one occupies the site of RAF Calveley, originally built in 1941 as a fighter base concerned with the defence of the Manchester and Liverpool areas. But as the threat of bombing in those areas reduced, Calveley shifted its focus to pilot training. After the war it continued as a maintenance base until the Air Ministry sold off the land in 1960. A memorial commemorates twenty seven airmen who lost their lives whilst stationed here. Even training could be a deadly business.

NANTWICH 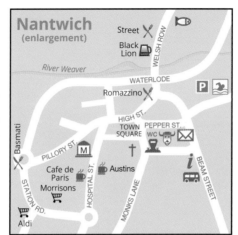MAP 11

North or south, there are few English towns of this size nicer than Nantwich. The octagonal tower of St Mary's church, glimpsed across freshly-built rooftops from the high canal embankment, tempts you to moor and get to know Nantwich better. Walking in from the basin, the aqueduct forms an appropriate portcullis, and the appeal of the town increases as the centre is reached. Welsh Row is a handsome thoroughfare: keep your eyes peeled for the Tollemache Almshouses, Cheshire Constabulary police houses, Primitive Methodist chapel and Town Well House (No.52). In medieval times Nantwich was the chief salt producing town in the county.

Eating & Drinking

AUSTINS - Hospital Street. Tel: 01270 625491. Consciously old fashioned coffee house which transcends kitsch by virtue of its range of comfort food including their very own bangers and mash, cottage pie, omelettes, cakes. Open Tue, Thur, Fri & Sat 10am to 3.30pm. CW5 5RL

BASMATI - Pillory Street. Tel: 01270 620600. Indian restaurant/take-away housed in railway station booking hall. Open 5.30pm daily (ex Tue). CW5 5SS

BLACK LION - Welsh Row. Tel: 01270 628711. 17th century half-timbered pub on way into town. Ales from Cheshire brewer Weetwood. Meals served Fri-Sun lunchtimes and Thur-Sat evenings. CW5 5ED

CAFE DE PARIS - Hospital Street. Tel: 01270 627562. Charming cafe under authentic French ownership, open from 9am to 4pm daily ex Sun. CW5 5RP

CHURCHE'S MANSION - Hospital Street. Tel: 01270 627311. Modern British restaurant housed in famous 16th century half-timbered house. Lunch and dinner (from 5pm) Wed-Sat, Sunday lunch from noon. Afternoon teas Wed-Sun. CW5 5RY

ROMAZZINO - High Street. Tel: 01270 619100. Italian open from noon daily. CW5 5AR

STREET - Welsh Row. Tel: 01270 625539. Open daily from noon for eat in or take-away burgers, burritos, noodles & curries: i.e. 'street food'. CW5 5ED

WATERSIDE CAFE - Nantwich Basin. Tel: 01270 748283. 9am-3pm daily. CW5 8LB

Shopping

Nantwich's antique shops and boutiques emphasise its position at the centre of a Gucci-heeled hinterland. Keep a tight rein on your womenfolk, without firm male guidance they will run amok in the town's fine clothes, shoes, and household goods outlets. But it is the food sellers that are most satisfying: butchers like Clewlows (in our top five canal-connected purveyors of pork pies), bakers like Chatwins (whose headquarters are in the town) and fishmongers like Sea Breezes all of whom have outlets in Pepper Street.

On Hospital Street are A. T. Welch's surprisingly narrow yet deep premises housing butcher, grocer, delicatessen and coffee merchant counters. The indoor market hall is open on Tuesdays, Thursdays and Saturdays. Laundry facilities are available at the canal basin.

Things to Do

TOURIST INFORMATION - Civic Hall. Tel: 01270 303150 or 628633. CW5 5DG

NANTWICH MUSEUM - Pillory Street. Tel: 01270 627104. Well presented displays of local history. Free admission. Small gift shop. CW5 5BQ

Connections

BUSES - Arriva service 84 connects every 20 minutes Mon-Sat (hourly Sun) with Crewe in one direction and hourly with Chester in the other, with useful stops at Barbridge and Calveley for towpath walkers.

TRAINS - services to/from Crewe, and Shrewsbury via Wrenbury and Whitchurch.

TAXIS - Direct. Tel: 01270 585000.

ACTON MAP 11

A short walk across the fields from Bridge 93 leads to this village whose imposing church repays investigation, for amongst the gravestones you'll come upon that of A. N. Hornby, the English cricket captain whose one-off defeat to Australia at The Oval in 1882 brought about a spoof obituary which referred to the cremated 'remains' of the English game being sent to Australia, hence the origin of 'The Ashes'.

BARBRIDGE MAP 11

Eating & Drinking

OLDE BARBRIDGE INN - Old Chester Road (adjacent Bridge 100). Tel: 01270 528327. Comfortable canalside pub serving Weetwood ales. Food served throughout from noon daily. CW5 6AY

BRICK WORKS and tileries once bordered the canal between Wardle and Calveley. Nowadays it's distribution hubs. NWF and Boughey are part of the same group, the former can trace their roots back to a 19th century farming co-operative. J. S. Bailey, cheese factors, occupy the site of Calveley Corn Mills. The Canal & River Trust make use of a former canal/railway transhipment shed as a boating facilities block. The canalside canopy would have afforded protection from the elements for boats being discharged or loaded. A railway siding ran through the opposite side of the building. Jack Roberts and his father (q.v.) delivered bales of wool here, loaded at Newtown (Map 34) in 1904, for onward transport by rail to Huddersfield.

The towpath changes sides at Bridge 104, and the canal passes the site of an old brickworks, whose winding hole remains usefully extant. Bunbury is a fascinating canal environment. The wide-beam staircase locks providing an obvious centrepiece. Alongside them is a fine stable block, recalling the practice of exchanging fresh horses for tired ones on the fast 'fly boats' which covered the 80 miles between the Mersey ports and the Black

Country factories in just over 24 hours. These premises are now occupied by Anglo Welsh, their offices and shop being accommodated in an adjacent warehouse still displaying the faded legend 'Shropshire Union Railways & Canal Co' on its north facing gable end.

Tilstone Lock lies in a gorgeous setting. Beside it a former mill stands astride the Gowy, dating from 1838 and restored for residential use. A curious circular structure overlooks the head of the lock chamber. There are others at Beeston and Tarvin locks and they were once used by lengthsmen to store maintenance equipment.

On the hillside to the south stand the melancholy and increasingly vandalised ruins of Beeston Towers, an

continued overleaf:

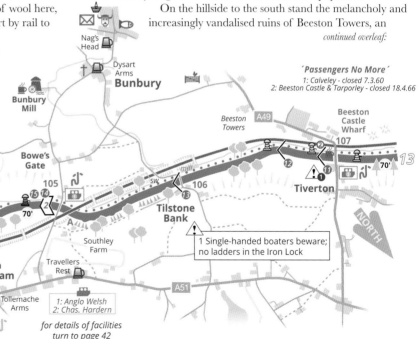

'Passengers No More'
1: Calveley - closed 7.3.60
2: Beeston Castle & Tarporley - closed 18.4.66

1 Single-handed boaters beware; no ladders in the Iron Lock

Locks
15 & 14 Bunbury Staircase Locks 15ft 7ins
13 Tilstone Lock 9ft 8ins
12 Beeston Stone Lock 8ft 6ins
11 Beeston Iron Lock 7ft 0ins

1: Anglo Welsh
2: Chas. Hardern

for details of facilities turn to page 42

continued from page 39:

ostentatious half-timbered mansion erected in 1886 for a wealthy Warrington timber merchant, John Naylor. Naylor achieved fame in 1916 by co-authoring, along with his brother Robert, *From John O'Groats to Land's End*, a lengthy - in more senses than one - account of a 1,372 miles walk between those two extremities of the British Isles; all 659 pages of it. In the 1930s Beeston Towers became a girls boarding school, whilst more recently an hotel. Now, despite Grade II listing, its fate is in the lap of the gods, and we all know how callous they can be.

As the canal approaches the two Beeston locks, it crosses the Vyrnwy Aqueduct, a 68 mile pipeline constructed in the 1880s from a dam in mid-Wales to Liverpool - see also Map 23. As originally built, the locks at Beeston formed a two chambered staircase on an alignment slightly to the north. Instabilities in the quicksand upon which it stood, however, brought about its collapse a dozen years after the canal was opened. Lacking sufficient capital to effect a repair, the canal remained effectively severed, goods being inconveniently transhipped along a tramway in the interim. Unsuccessful attempts were made to find a solution to the

Lock 12, Beeston

problem before Thomas Telford was consulted in 1827. He recommended replacement of the staircase by two single chambers, the lower being constructed of iron plates. An effective solution, proven by time, but the ground didn't give up easily, and down the years the chamber has become distorted, precluding its use by two narrowboats simultaneously.

The cattle mart by Beeston Castle Wharf closed in 2019. We always used to enjoy wandering up to see if an auction was taking place, momentarily exchanging the personna of boaters for that of farmers. Somewhat inevitably, the site is being redeveloped as housing. The neighbouring hillside conceals Second World War oil storage tanks. A signal box perches on the railway embankment, still bearing the closed station's appellation - Beeston Castle & Tarporley. Chas. Hardern's boatyard is centred on a whitewashed building which originally provided stabling for boat horses, complete with first floor hay loft. The house by the bridge on the towpath side was formerly the Railway & Canal Inn.

Bunbury Stables

BEESTON Castle (which appeared on the Chester Canal Company's seal) dominates the landscape, like a visitor from another planet, an upturned plum pudding of an outcrop, a geological afterthought commandeered by medieval man for a fortress. Behind it the Peckforton Hills ride the horizon like surfers on an Atlantic beach. This is good hiking country. The Sandstone Trail, a 34 mile footpath across Cheshire's backbone from Frodsham to Whitchurch (see Map 19), crosses the canal at Wharton's Lock and may be conveniently linked with the towpath and other public footpaths to form a number of circular walks. Actually, Beeston isn't the only 'medieval' castle on view. Behind it stands Peckforton Castle, a Victorian gothic interloper used these days as an 'hotel, spa, team building and wedding venue'. Incidentally, the lock-keeper's cottage at Wharton's Lock was destroyed by a stray German bomb during the Second World War, perhaps on the same occasion as Bunbury village was bombed.

By Bridge 109, Bate's Mill survives as an enviable private residence; still, apparently employing water power as a source of electricity. A country road swoops down to cross the millstream and an adjacent expanse of water is the haunt of wildfowl. Beyond Bridge 111 the canal is carried over the Gowy on an embankment framed with larch trees. A public footpath passes through a culvert beneath the embankment. Trains rattle and hum across the middle distance, but otherwise the world seems undisturbed, and in the long pound between Wharton's and Christleton locks the boater has time for reflection and communing with nature.

A large marina adds considerably to boat movements in the vicinity and contrasts in approach to the lengthy linear moorings to be found on the following map. Various commercial enterprises cluster beside Crows Nest Bridge, No.113, but in times gone by there was a brick works and a bone mill here, the latter notorious for its evil-smelling processing of animal bones into glue and other by-products; though at least it brought traffic to the canal: coal in to fire its boilers, and finished products out.

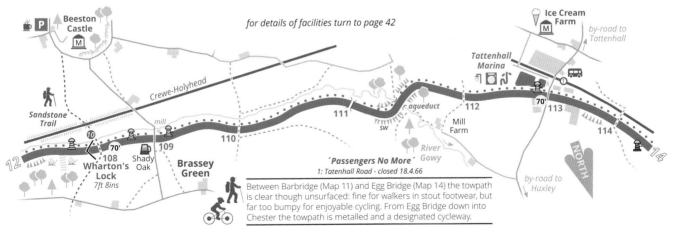

for details of facilities turn to page 42

'Passengers No More'
1: Tatenhall Road - closed 18.4.66

Between Barbridge (Map 11) and Egg Bridge (Map 14) the towpath is clear though unsurfaced: fine for walkers in stout footwear, but far too bumpy for enjoyable cycling. From Egg Bridge down into Chester the towpath is metalled and a designated cycleway.

41

CALVELEY   MAP 12

Eating & Drinking

J. S. BAILEY - Nantwich Road. Tel: 01829 262900. Suppliers of cheese to the catering industry, Bailey's run a shop and cafe at their Calveley Mill premises open from 8am-5pm Mon-Fri, 4pm Sat. In addition to a wide range of cheese, the shop deals in everyday essentials (such as wine and beer), whilst the cafe does breakfasts and daily specials along with lighter fare. CW6 9JW

Connections

BUSES - Arriva service 84 operates hourly, daily to/from Nantwich and Chester.

ALPRAHAM   MAP 12

Eating & Drinking

TOLLEMACHE ARMS - Chester Road. Tel: 01829 261716. Well appointed Robinson's pub/restaurant open all day and offering accommodation. Breakfasts served, then meals from noon. CW6 9JE
TRAVELLERS REST - Chester Road. Tel: 01829 260523. Traditional pub on CAMRA's 'National Inventory of unspoilt pub interiors'. Open from 6.30pm weekdays and both lunchtimes/evenings at weekends. CW6 9JA

TIVERTON   MAP 12

LOCKGATE COFFEE HOUSE - adjacent Bridge 107. Tel: 01829 730592. Charming timber built coffee shop: for breakfasts, lunches and teas. CW6 9NJ

BUNBURY   MAP 12

Masquerading as 'Great Paxford' in ITV's 2015/6 Second World War drama *Home Fires*, Bunbury suffered in wartime for real when the Luftwaffe, returning from a raid on Liverpool, jettisoned bombs, destroying several houses and damaging the parish church of St Boniface. One of Cheshire's finest churches, it contains many notable effigies and tombs.

Eating & Drinking

DYSART ARMS - Bowe's Gate Road. Tel: 01829 260183. Inimitable Brunning & Price country inn open from 10am daily; well worth the walk! CW9 9PH
Fish & Chips in village centre open 11.30am-1.30pm and 5-8pm Tuesdays to Saturdays. Try also Tilly's Coffee Shop.

Shopping

Well stocked Co-op convenience store with post office counter in the centre of the village about 20 minutes walk from the canal at bridges 105 or 106.

Things to Do

BUNBURY MILL - Bowe's Gate Road. Tel: 01829 733244. Open Sunday & Bank Hol Mon afternoons 1-5pm, April to October. Enchanting watermill with additional delight of a tearoom. CW9 9PY

BEESTON   MAPS 12 & 13

Eating & Drinking

SHADY OAK - Bate's Mill Lane (canalside Bridge 109). Tel: 01829 730581 Open from noon Thur-Sun. Food served lunch and evening (from 5pm) Thur-Fri and throughout at weekends. CW6 9UE

Things to Do

BEESTON CASTLE - Chapel Lane (one mile south of Wharton's Lock along the Sandstone Trail). Tel: 0370 333 1181. Open daily under the aegis of English Heritage: 10am-6pm summer, 10am-4pm winter. Admission charge. Captured at least three times during its turbulent history - by Simon de Montfort in his revolt against Henry III, and by both the Roundheads and Cavaliers during the Civil War - this 13th century fortress commands a wonderful panorama from its upper keep, the canal being discernible all the way to Egg Bridge. Shop, cafe, woodland walks. CW6 9TX

TATTENHALL   MAP 13

Picturesque village tucked under the skirts of the Peckforton Hills. Some of its houses were designed by Sir Clough Williams-Ellis of Portmeirion fame. Spar shop, pubs/cafes. Buses from Bridge 113.

Things to Do

ICE CREAM FARM - Newton Lane. Tel: 0800 133 7000. Huge family orientated visitor attraction offering indoor and outdoor activities, not to mention fifty flavours of ice cream made by the Fell family on site. Open daily 9am-6pm. CH3 9NE

WAVERTON   MAP 14

Quaint estate village with handsome sandstone church. At Common Farm is the Spitting Feathers Brewery (Tel: 01244 332052) whose output can be sampled at the Brewery Tap in Chester - see page 50.

EGG BRIDGE   MAP 14

Egg Bridge offers useful facilities east of Bridge 119. They include a post office/pharmacy; 'One Stop' convenience store (with cash machine), a deli/sandwich bar, and Pizza Guy (Tel: 01244 336006) which does baguettes, pizzas, kebabs and fish & chips. CH3 7NB. Bus service 41 runs hourly (ex Sun) to Chester.

CHRISTLETON   MAP 14

CHESHIRE CAT - canalside between bridges 120 and 121. Tel: 01244 332200. Vintage Inns restaurant/pub open throughout the day. Accommodation. CH3 6AE
RING O' BELLS - village centre. Tel: 01244 335422. Smartly refurbished gastro-pub which regularly wins awards. Closed Mons. Village store opposite. CH3 7AS

AN impecunious affair, the Chester Canal struggled to make ends meet throughout its independent existence. It hardly helped matters that its southern end went unconnected to the rest of the canal system for over thirty years. Consequently working capital was in short supply. Money had to be borrowed to pay wages. Subscribers forfeited their shares. Workmen were laid off, barges laid up. What cargoes were carried were subject to theft. Vandalism is not exclusively a modern phenomenon: in 1778 magistrates ordered a Chester man to be 'whipped from Northgate to Cow Lane Bridge' for tampering with canal company property. We've obviously become too soft with miscreants.

Although the countryside is conspicuously flat, the Peckforton Hills to the south and Delamere Forest to the north-east give your gaze something to linger over; whilst, if the elements have blessed you with a clear day, the brooding summits of Celtic Wales are to be discerned on the western rim of the world, and Helsby Hill, overlooking the Mersey estuary, to the north. Long lines of moored craft make the considerate boater's progress irritatingly slow in the vicinity of Hargrave. Thankfully, the provision of traffic lights on the road above Bridge 115, has

effectively ceased the irritating tendency of motorists to honk their horns like excitable Mediterraneans at a fiesta.

The canal skirts Waverton, a Victorian estate village, largely constructed at the behest of the Dukes of Westminster. Egg Bridge introduces the suburban fringes of Chester. In the 1920s, T. W. Cubbon, wrote an account (*Only a Little Cockboat*) of a voyage, in a canvas covered boat powered by a petrol engine, from Chester along the Shropshire Union and Staffs & Worcs canals to the rivers Severn and Avon. In the book he relates his first night on the canal at Egg Bridge moored abreast a widebeam barge, but being forced to move on in the small hours of the morning because rats from the barge had boarded his boat. The barges and the rats may have gone, but signs of former commerce remain at Egg Bridge in the form of a canalside mill converted into housing. When the first edition of this guide was published forty years ago there were hire bases either side of Bridge 119: Welsh Border Cruises favouring representation by Blakes; Eggbridge Marina by Hoseasons - how the face of hire boating has changed! The Civil War Battle of Rowton Moor took place on 24th September 1645. Fighting began at six o'clock in the morning, and continued sporadically throughout the day, largely by opposing forces of cavalry. Participants numbered roughly four thousand on each side. But, in what would seem on paper like an even contest, the Parliamentarians, lead by Sydenham Poyntz, secured a comparatively easy victory over the Royalists commanded by Marmaduke Langdale. What colourful names military men

continued overleaf

43

Bridge 115 and poplars, Hargrave

had back then: modern British commanders tend to be called Ted, Brian or Dave. Six hundred Cavaliers were killed. The victorious Roundheads were presumably too puritanical to party.

Brief associate of many a canal on its way from London to Birkenhead - and Telford's chosen route through the Black Country for his Holyhead Road - the A41 draws alongside the canal. The curious, cast iron columned, hexagonal timber topped structure overlooking the road's passage through Christleton is an old hydraulic sewage lift, manufactured by Adams of York circa 1900. Probably the very earliest hire cruisers on the canal system were available from a boatyard at Christleton. Inland Hire Cruisers began providing boats for intrepid holidaymakers way back in 1935. In those days you could hire a small cruiser for £4 a week, though you also had to fork out ten shillings in

tolls to the LMS Railway who owned the canal prior to Nationalisation in 1947. As is often the way of the world, a competitor sprang up nearby; a thwarted former employee perhaps, it does happen! IHC requested prospective hirers to send 6 pence for an illustrated brochure. Downmarket Dean's required two threepenny stamps.

Between bridge 121 and 122 stands Butler's Mill, converted into apartments now, but still manufacturing animal feeds on site until the mid 1970s. The cantilevered lucam remains an attractive feature. A system of pulleys enabled boat horses to hoist bags of grain into the mill by dint of simply walking them along the towpath. At Christleton the canal commences its descent to Chester and the surface of the towpath is well maintained, all the way to Ellesmere Port. The sense of anticipation accelerates, an adrenalin surge ensues!

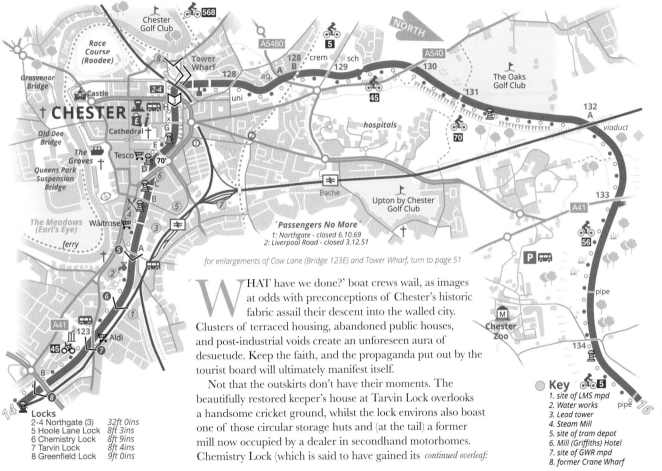

North

Chester Golf Club

Race Course (Roodee)

Grosvenor Bridge

R. DEE

Castle

† CHESTER

Old Dee Bridge

Cathedral †

Tesco

The Groves

Queens Park Suspension Bridge

The Meadows (Earl's Eye)

ferry

Waitrose

Tower Wharf

uni

aq.

crem

sch

The Oaks Golf Club

hospitals

Bache

Upton by Chester Golf Club

viaduct

Chester Zoo

pipe

A41

123

Aldi

pipe

'Passengers No More'
1: Northgate - closed 6.10.69
2: Liverpool Road - closed 3.12.51

for enlargements of Cow Lane (Bridge 123E) and Tower Wharf, turn to page 51

W HAT have we done?' boat crews wail, as images at odds with preconceptions of Chester's historic fabric assail their descent into the walled city. Clusters of terraced housing, abandoned public houses, and post-industrial voids create an unforeseen aura of desuetude. Keep the faith, and the propaganda put out by the tourist board will ultimately manifest itself.

Not that the outskirts don't have their moments. The beautifully restored keeper's house at Tarvin Lock overlooks a handsome cricket ground, whilst the lock environs also boast one of those circular storage huts and (at the tail) a former mill now occupied by a dealer in secondhand motorhomes. Chemistry Lock (which is said to have gained its *continued overleaf:*

Locks

2-4 Northgate (3)	32ft 0ins
5 Hoole Lane Lock	8ft 3ins
6 Chemistry Lock	8ft 9ins
7 Tarvin Lock	8ft 4ins
8 Greenfield Lock	9ft 0ins

Key

1. site of LMS mpd
2. Water works
3. Lead tower
4. Steam Mill
5. site of tram depot
6. Mill (Griffiths) Hotel
7. site of GWR mpd
8. former Crane Wharf

continued from page 45:

unusual name from the proximity of a works producing gallic acid for use in the tanning industry) is overlooked by Boughton Waterworks, itself dominated by an impressively cylindrical water tower dating from the 1850s. The city's domestic water supplies are pumped up from the River Dee, only a few hundred yards away at this point. The terraced houses on the opposite bank of the canal front onto a street prosaically named Watertower View; shades of Railway Cuttings, East Cheam. Indeed, its neighbour is Railway Terrace, a reminder that Chester's LMS motive power depot, 6A, stood nearby. In the immortal words of R. S. Grimsley - who heroically compiled a complete guide to the location of all the main locomotive sheds and works in Great Britain - the depot lay 'at the end of a cinder path' off Hoole Lane. Didn't they all!

Such scenes contextualise this once heavily industrialised quarter of Chester. Further evidence coming in the lofty shape of a lead shot tower (originally used for making musket shot during the Napoleonic Wars) and numerous warehouses, timber yards, chemical works and mills (now converted into flats and pubs and clubs) which shoulder-barge the canal as it passes through an area of the city once vital to the coffers of the Shropshire Union. All that's missing are the cargo vessels which thronged the canal. Their crews would rub their eyes in surprise at holidaymaking boaters emerging from Waitrose laden with delicacies for dinner, or diners aboard the Mill Hotel's restaurant boat, which at least maintains a widebeam tradition more in keeping with the Chester Canal's working past than the ubiquitous narrow boats of the present day.

Tarvin Lock

Beyond Tarvin Road Bridge, No.123, the numbering sequence turns to alphabetical suffixes, a sure sign that the bridges were erected after the canal was originally completed, illustrating the rapid growth of Chester in the 19th century. Either side of Cow Lane Bridge (123E - a popular mooring zone whose name recalls the site of a cattle market), side arms extended into covered basins in the heyday of the canal; the approach to a side-bridge spanning the westernmost of these may still be discerned where the council have attractively landscaped the area between the canal and the wall to create a pleasant sward known as King Charles Tower Garden.

It is the canal's juxtaposition with Chester's cathedral and its largely medieval but occasionally Roman wall, however, which is arguably its most memorable gesture. The round tower from which King Charles I despondently witnessed his Cavaliers retreating raggedly from Rowton Moor looms out over the water so dramatically that the canal resembles a moat, which is exactly what it once was, and the canal builders took good advantage of this defensive channel. Canyon-like, the canal parallels the city wall and proceeds beneath Northgate spanned by a slender footbridge across which condemned prisoners were lead from the city's gaol to the Bluecoat Chapel to receive their last rites.

Some boaters may be feeling almost as nervous at the prospect of Northgate Locks as prisoners facing eternity. A gargantuan staircase, hewn out of solid sandstone and noisily bookended by the inner ring road (opened - doubtless with a pretty shake of her strawberry blonde bouffant hairdo - by Barbara Castle on 22nd April 1966) and the railway,

Three Men and a Boat

they are ponderous in operation, but quietly satisfying to complete. The flight's three massive, and intrinsically gaol-like chambers lower the canal over thirty feet. Originally there were five of them, leading direct to the Dee. Volunteer lock-keepers are often on hand to help these days, but don't necessarily bank on one being there. If you're new to staircases, remember the golden rule: going down ensure that the chamber below is empty; going up that the chamber above is full.

Tower Wharf rewards those who have persevered through Northgate Locks with a canalscape overlooked by apartment blocks yet still brimming with interest: Telford's warehouse (now an eponymous and justifiably popular pub) with its arched loading bay; the adjoining Raymond (previously Harvest) House, erstwhile offices of the Chester Canal Co. and departure point of packet boats to Ellesmere Port; an elegantly canopied drydock; a large boatyard, where the Shropshire Union carrying fleet was once built and maintained; and the rare fascination of two adjacent canal levels side by side. The former North Basin - callously infilled in the Fifties - has been re-dug and re-watered as part of a redevelopment scheme: though the 'retail opportunities' prominently advertised, seem reluctantly slow to accrue. A plaque on Bridge 126 appropriately commemorates Lionel Thomas Caswell Rolt's championing of the canals, for he was born across the Dee, in the Handbridge suburb of the city, in 1910. He passed the first four years of his life on Eaton Road, a period vividly described in the first chapter of *Landscape With Machines*.

Canal boaters have long harboured covetous thoughts concerning the River Dee. True, it has always been theoretically feasible to negotiate the Dee Branch from Tower Wharf and, with the help of a high spring tide, negotiate Chester Weir to reach the calmer waters of the Upper Dee, explorable for a dozen picturesque miles upstream to Farndon. But that has always been a hazardous passage, reliant on experienced boating skills and the stamina to deal with the bureaucracy of two navigational authorities. Little wonder, then, that in recent years the final lock into the

continued from page 47:

river has become semi-derelict.

From time to time, inland waterway activists advocate a revitalised link between the canal and the non-tidal Dee, key to which is the provision of a new lock in a former mill race adjoining the weir. An ambitious, yet praiseworthy scheme, eminently achievable were engineering the only challenge. Eminently desirable too, for, the Dee is undeniably picturesque: witness the resort-like Groves, which does a passable imitation of Henley on a hot summer afternoon.

Meanwhile, in the event of a tedious hiatus between promotion and realisation, we would advocate perambulation of the excellent Riverside Promenade Trail which will give you a willow-framed flavour of the river between the Dee Branch and The Groves. En route you will be introduced to Crane Wharf, which flourished in the 18th century before the river began silting up, and which in latter years was the base of Crosville, the much mourned independent operator of bus services throughout North Wales and Cheshire; to Chester Race Course, one of Britain's oldest and shortest, an anti-clockwise flat course graced by an elegant grandstand; a railway bridge designed by Robert Stephenson which once fell down; to the Grosvenor Bridge of 1832 which briefly boasted the widest arch in the world; to the Old Dee Bridge which dates from the 14th century; and to the aforementioned Groves, a pleasure resort par excellence which, when it isn't acting like it's on the Thames, imagines it's on the Seine. Who wouldn't relish boating past such treasures!

Downstream, it is another matter, the tidal Dee surges to and fro along a channel dug in the 18th century in an ultimately futile attempt to prolong Chester's role as a port. In the Middle Ages it rivalled Bristol, but had fallen into decline, hence opening of the Wirral Line of the Ellesmere Canal in 1795. Sadly, the practise of conveying Airbus A380 wings by barge from Broughton to Mostyn for transhipment onto a sea-going vessel for transport to France, ceased with the mothballing of the works in 2020.

Photogenically framed by a drydock and a graceful, curving footbridge (No.126) what is generally known as Taylor's Boatyard was originally the Shropshire Union's extensive boatbuilding and maintenance yard. Facilities included three covered slipways (of which one remains), a sawmill, smithy, and paintshop. In excess of seventy men were employed in the construction and repair of both wide beam flats

Tower Wharf, Chester

Sunrise over the River Dee

and narrowboats, among the latter being *Saturn*, the restored flyboat, built here in 1906. Under London & North Western Railway ownership, the Shropshire Union's fleet of over five hundred vessels appeared secure. Yet in 1921, a sudden decision was made to cease carrying and disband the fleet. Determination, by the Government, for a 56 hour working week (effectively a maximum of 8 hours a day) rendered boat operation unviable overnight. The yard was acquired by a local boatbuilding family called Taylor, who operated the business for the next fifty years. Taylors turned their hand to a wide range of vessels, commercial, leisure and even military. Of particular appeal was a series of classic wooden cabin cruisers, one of which, *Amaryllis*, is on display at the National Waterways Museum, Ellesmere Port. Taylors sold out to Bithells in the 1970s and subsequently the yard was taken over by David Jones. These days it belongs to the Askey family, the yard's historic buildings have acquired listed status, and a firm sense of tradition continues.

The Wirral Line of the Ellesmere Canal, a constituent of the Shropshire Union, wriggles out of the city's suburbs. Girls come giggling out of Chester University's Parkgate Road Campus as if auditioning for extras in Channel 4's Chester based soap *Hollyoaks*. Bridge 128A carries the canal over the A5480 link road: in more ways than one, it is an elevating experience to glide on water over queueing road traffic. Bridge 128B bears National Cycle Route 5, formerly the Great Central Railway's line from Chester Northgate to Wrexham. Chester's crematorium lies alongside Bridge 129. The towpath is popular with cyclists, and soon the landscape opens out, though not necessarily agriculturally, much of the offside being bounded by a golf course.

A fine sandstone viaduct (132A) conveys the railway between Chester and Birkenhead, the preserve of scurrying third-rail electric units now, but once the route of Great Western expresses and sleeper trains carrying passengers to catch Transatlantic liners from the Mersey. Up on the neighbouring hillside stands a neo-classical house called Friars Park; perhaps designed by Lutyens, but more likely inspired by him. Visitor moorings by Bridge 134 offer the opportunity to visit Chester Zoo.

Timing is everything in Chester. Venture into the city centre on a hot summer's afternoon, and the frenetic free-for-all of tourists and shoppers will send you scurrying back to your boat for refuge. Take an early morning perambulation around the walls, when Chester is still breathing like a sleeping child, and you'll be so entranced, you'll be reluctant to leave. Yet in all of Britain's inland waterways, only York can vie with Chester when it comes to antiquity, and the city wall, which kept enemies at bay down the centuries, now keeps 21st century reality in its place. Once through the ancient gateways you are wrapped in a medieval time warp which makes Chester the most agreeable of places to saunter in and absorb the atmosphere.

It was the Romans who founded the city, seeing it as a likely place to build a port and keep a weather eye on the troublesome Marches; they called it Deva. In the Dark Ages the Anglo Saxons undid much of their predecessors' civilisation, but by the Middle Ages Chester was flourishing again and a 12th century writer noted ships from Aquitaine, Germany and Spain berthed in the shadow of the city wall. Chester's celebrated 'Rows' are thought to have had their origins during this period. These covered galleries above street level are quite unique, and elevate window-shopping into a pleasurable experience for all and sundry.

During the Civil War the city supported King Charles, but it did him little good for it was from the walls of Chester that he saw his bedraggled cavalry retreat from Rowton Moor. Victorian Chester grew up outside the city wall, beyond the canal and out towards the railway. What the Victorians did inside the wall is best overlooked by those romantics who like to think that all that black and white half timbering is original.

With time at your disposal, we can recommend a circular walk encompassing both of the road bridges over the Dee. Descend Bridge Street to the Old Dee Bridge, which dates from 1387. From the iron-railed pavement side you can admire the view upstream beyond the weir which holds back all but the highest spring tides at bay. The half-timbered upper storeys of a suburban row of shops lead uphill on a thoroughfare simply known as Handbridge to the lofty spire of St Mary Without-the-Walls. Proceed along Overleigh Road until you reach the gates of the Old Cemetery on your right. Follow the path through the cemetery. Many poignant memorials catch one's eye. We were particularly moved by one marking the last resting place of Walter and Ellen Jones, who died in 1923 and 1942 respectively, whose baby son Austin had lived just three weeks in 1895, and whose other son, another Walter, had been killed in action in France in 1915: rather an unfair share of sorrow to burden one family with, wouldn't you concur? The cemetery path ascends to Grosvenor Road. Turn right to cross Grosvenor Bridge, designed by Thomas Harrison (1744-1820), and opened by Princess Victoria in 1832. There are elevated views in either direction up and down the tidal reaches of the river: an opportunity, perhaps, to picture King Edgar the Peaceful being rowed along the river in AD 973 by eight Tributary Princes, all previously kings in their own right. Return to the city centre, pausing to admire the equestrian statue of Field Marshal Viscount Combermere (1773-1865), veteran of a lengthy list of campaigns, as the plinth attests. Opposite him stands The Propylaeum, gateway to Chester Castle designed in the Greek Revival style by Thomas Harrison. Other examples of Harrison's work include the Northgate archway; the Wesleyan Methodist Church on St John Street; and the east wing of Chirk Castle (Map 24).

Eating & Drinking

THE ARCHITECT - Nicholas Street. Tel: 01244 353070. Brunning & Price restaurant pub housed in Thomas Harrison's former residence, hence the name. CH1 2NX

ARTICHOKE - Steam Mill Street. (Bridge 123B) Tel: 01244 329229. Bar & bistro adjacent canal. Kitchen from 4pm weekdays, 12.30pm weekends. CH3 5AN

BEAR & BILLET - Lower Bridge Street. Tel: 01244 311886. Half-timbered inn built in 1644 to replace a building destroyed during the Civil War siege. John Lennon's grandmother was born here. Nowadays run by the Market Town Taverns group who have establishments in the north-west and Yorkshire. Open daily from noon. Food served throughout. Okell's ales from the Isle of Man. CH1 1RU

BLACKSTOCKS - Northgate Street. Tel: 01244 325822. Eat in or take-away fish & chips open daily from 11.30am. CH1 2HQ

THE BREWERY TAP - Lower Bridge Street. Tel: 01244 340999. Good food (noon to 9pm daily) and locally brewed ales (plus guests) from Waverton in ancient high-ceilinged house. CH1 1RU

CHEZ JULES - Northgate Street. Tel: 01244 400014. French restaurant with emphasis on seasonal produce. Tempting Wednesday soiree cinema. CH1 2HQ

THE HANDBRIDGE - Handbridge. Tel: 0772 906 2902. Attractive red brick pub across the Dee in the suburb where L. T. C. Rolt was born. Open Wed-Sun from noon. CH4 7JF

MARMALADE - Northgate Street. Tel: 01244 314565. Licensed cafe open from 9am daily (10am Sun) for breakfasts, lunches and afternoon teas. CH1 2HQ

MILL HOTEL - Milton St. (Bridge 123C). Tel: 01244 350035. Restaurant, bar food and real ales. The amusingly named *L'eau-t Cuisine* broad beam restaurant boat does lunch /evening cruises. CH1 3NF

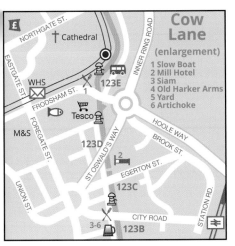

Cow Lane
(enlargement)

1 Slow Boat
2 Mill Hotel
3 Siam
4 Old Harker Arms
5 Yard
6 Artichoke

123E
123D
123C
123B
3-6

Cathedral
WHS
Tesco
M&S

OLD HARKER ARMS - City Road (Bridge 123B). Tel: 01244 344525. Well-appointed Brunning & Price warehouse conversion. Wide range of real ales and good choice of food. CH3 5AL. Up the steps on City Road stand a plethora of ethnic restaurants.

OLIVE TREE - Watergate. Tel: 01244 956643. Greek brasserie. Open daily from 11am. CH1 2LE

PORTA - Northgate Street. Tel: 01244 401178. Quaint tapas bar open from noon daily. CH1 2HT

SIAM - City Road. (Bridge 123B). Tel: 01244 403222. Thai and Teppan-yaki restaurant. CH1 3AE

SLOW BOAT - Frodsham Street (Bridge 123E). Tel: 01244 317873. Canalside Asian fusion. Open from 5pm (1pm Sun). CH1 3JJ

TELFORD'S WAREHOUSE - Tower Wharf (Bridge 123L). Tel: 01244 390090. Eat and drink in Telford's handsome canal warehouse - what would the immortal Scottish engineer make of it now? CH1 4EZ

THE YARD - City Road (Bridge 123B). Tel: 01244 325199. Modern Italian Dining. CH1 3AE

Shopping

One of the most amenable shopping centres in Britain. The Rows contain some of the most up-market shops in the city within their fascinating galleries, whilst St Michael's Arcade is a Victorian confection of soaring iron and glass reached off Bridge Street Row. At the opposite end of the retail spectrum is Chester's fine indoor market, open Mon-Sat, 8am-5pm, where stalls specialise in fresh Cheshire produce. Don't miss the marvellous Cheese Shop (Tel: 01244 346240 - CH1 2HT) on Northgate. There's a Waitrose supermarket canalside between bridges 123A & B, and a Tesco on Frodsham Street adjoining Bridge 123E. Finally, if you're moored at Tower Wharf, useful facilities on nearby Garden Lane (access via Bridge 126E) include a convenience store, several fast food outlets, and a launderette.

Things to Do

VISITOR INFORMATION CENTRE - Town Hall, Northgate. Tel: 01244 405340. CH1 2HJ

CHESTER CATHEDRAL - One of England's ecclesiastical masterpieces. Tel: 01244 324756. Gift shop and cafe. CH1 2HU

DEWA ROMAN EXPERIENCE - Pierpoint Lane. Tel: 01244 343407. Open daily 9am-5pm. Roman remains. CH1 1NL

GROSVENOR MUSEUM - Grosvenor Street. Museum of local history. Admission free, open daily. Tel: 01244 972197. CH1 2DD

CITY SIGHTSEEING - open-top bus tours.

CHESTER BOAT - from the boating station on The Groves aboard Bithells launches. Tel: 01244 325394. CH1 1SD

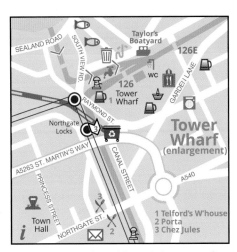

Tower Wharf
(enlargement)

Taylor's Boatyard
126E
126 Tower Wharf
Northgate Locks
WC

1 Telford's W'house
2 Porta
3 Chez Jules

Town Hall

CHESTER ZOO - One of Europe's finest zoos. Open daily. Best reached from the canal via Bridge 134. Tel: 01244 380280. CH2 1EU

MILITARY MUSEUM - Chester Castle. Tel: 01244 327617. CH1 2DN

Connections

BUSES - bus station on George Street off Northgate. Service 1 runs every 20 minutes (hourly Sun) to Ellesmere Port, a 35 minute ride away. Service 84 (hourly, daily) shadows the Shropshire Union most of the way down to Nantwich.

TRAINS - major railhead. Railway station on City Road, reached from Bridge 123B. Through trains to Ruabon (for Llangollen) and Chirk. Ditto Crewe, Cardiff, Manchester, Liverpool, Birmingham and London. Free bus link to city centre for rail ticket holders.

TAXIS - Chester Radio Taxis. Tel: 01244 372372.

LEAVING Chester and its tourist throng behind, you are entitled to feel ever so slightly smug as you steer along a broad-beam canal in the historic wake of steam powered flats hastening back across the Mersey to Liverpool for another cargo of imported grain. Or you may prefer to be driving the horse of a flyboat across the Wirral's wrist to Ellesmere Port with Walsall manufactured spurs for export to Argentina. Your fantasies can be further indulged at the admirable (if sadly under funded) National Waterways Museum, or Boat Museum as diehards continue to call it ... well, some of your fantasies, anyway.

But first comes a salutary reminder, in the shape of a complex motorway intersection, that this is the age of the car and the juggernaut lorry and that water as a mode of transport has, by and large, been irrationally consigned to the past. All but throttled by sliproads, the village of Stoak seems understandably traumatised by the cacophony on its doorstep, the crenellated tower of St Lawrence's church offering up a prayer for survival. Incidentally, a hire boat called *The Rambler*, based at Stoak in the 1930s, may even have predated those available at Christleton on Map 14.

With the jagged, Iron Age fort topped outline of Helsby Hill prominent to the north-east, the gleaming refineries of Stanlow define themselves on the horizon. Stanlow, opened in the 1920s, is second only to Fawley on The Solent in output, and provides a sixth of Britain's petroleum requirements. In the 12th century there was an abbey on

Boaters may shun this length of waterway, but the towpath is metalled throughout and popular with walkers and cyclists alike: disparate life forms who appear to co-exist fairly harmoniously up this way.

Key ○
1 site of Wolverhampton
Corrugated Iron Works

*two locks leading to Lower Basin

for enlargement Ellesmere Port turn to page 54

the banks of the Mersey. But life there was too bleak for even its hair-shirted inhabitants, and they moved to new premises near Clitheroe in Lancashire in 1287.

Car showrooms either side of Bridge 140A run the gamut from Skoda to Mazda, with Harley-Davidson motorbikes thrown in for good measure. Visitor moorings offer the opportunity for you to step out of the 19th century straight into the 21st in the form of Cheshire Oaks, Europe's first designer outlet village and still the largest in the UK. After Bridge 145 a huge wasteground is all that remains of the once gargantuan Wolverhampton Corrugated Iron Works. The company moved here in 1905, and it is said that some of its two thousand strong workforce simply walked up the Shropshire Union Canal's towpath to their new abode.

For boaters intending to stay just a short time in the vicinity, limited mooring space is usually available between the motorway bridge and the National Waterways Museum. Preferable though, in our opinion, are the spacious moorings in the lower basin reached through the locks. To access them you will have to report to the museum's reception desk and pay, but in with the price comes the novel feeling that, temporarily at least, you and your boat have become one of the prize exhibits.

Ellesmere Port, the 'port' of the Ellesmere Canal, dates from the last decade of the 18th century. The Wirral Line of the Ellesmere Canal met the Mersey here at what had, until then, been simply the small village of Netherpool. The opening of the Birmingham & Liverpool Junction Canal and later the Manchester Ship Canal turned these docks into a transhipment complex of almost unique significance. Abandoned in 1958 and suffering neglect typical of the 1960s, Ellesmere Port's darkest hour came in 1970 when Telford's superb 'Winged Warehouses' - three blocks of four storey structures which spanned the lower basin - were destroyed by fire. The Holiday Inn which occupies the location now provides a pale replacement.

Twinned locks leading to the Lower Basin at Ellesmere Port

STOAK   MAP 16

Soporific rural community despite presence of motorways on its doorstep.

Eating & Drinking

BUNBURY ARMS - village centre, access via bridges 136 or 137. Tel: 01244 951833. Food served 12-3pm/5-8pm Mon-Fri; 12-8pm weekends. CH2 4HW

Connections

BUSES - service No. 26 runs three or four times per day Mon-Fri to/from Chester & Ellesmere Port.

ELLESMERE PORT   MAP 16

A 'cup tie' town of two halves, with a bit of extra time bolted on. Terraced streets fan out from the canal, still backing onto cobbled alleyways. Strung out along Station Road are tattoo parlours, tanning studios, pawnbrokers and accident claim solicitors. Selwyn Lloyd, Chancellor of the Exchequer (and a Wirral lad, to boot) unveiled Westminster Bridge in 1961. It carries you across the railway into a second half of unconsidered concrete and a 'time-wasting' shopping mall. Extra time takes place out by Junction 10, where The Coliseum retail park boasts the biggest Marks & Spencer outside of London. Follow the money!

Eating & Drinking

ESSENCE OF SPICE - Whitby Road. Tel: 0151 355 9596. If in doubt, eat Indian! Open from 5pm Mon-Sat and 1pm Sun. CH65 8AB

PORT & ANCHOR - South Pier Road. Tel: 0151 355 9307. Cafe/restaurant Tue-Sun from 9am; early close Tue at 4pm, but dinners served otherwise. CH65 4FL

WATERSIDE CAFE - National Waterways Museum.

Cheshire Oaks plays host to a wide range of restaurants: Cafe Rouge, Carluccio's, Miller & Carter, Nandos, Prezzo, Wagamama, Zizzi etc.

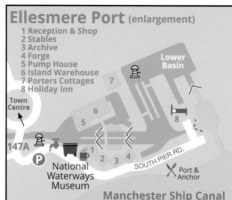

Ellesmere Port (enlargement)

1 Reception & Shop
2 Stables
3 Archive
4 Forge
5 Pump House
6 Island Warehouse
7 Porters Cottages
8 Holiday Inn

Lower Basin

Town Centre

147A

National Waterways Museum

SOUTH PIER RD.

Port & Anchor

Manchester Ship Canal

Shopping

Five minutes walk (through a seedy underpass) takes you to a convenience store. Ten minutes and you'll reach the Market Hall (closed Weds), an Aldi and a large Asda. From the visitor moorings between bridges 140A and 141 Sainsbury's is easily reached.

Things to Do

THE NATIONAL WATERWAYS MUSEUM - South Pier Road. Tel: 0151 355 5017. Open daily 10am-4pm. Admission charge. Along with Gloucester and Stoke Bruerne in Northamptonshire, this is one of three Canal & River Trust operated museum sites. Each has its own unique atmosphere. Here, a dockland setting hosts a collection of narrow and widebeam inland waterway craft, though the sad truth that not all of them are in a good state of health only serves to illustrate the time-consuming and expensive challenge of keeping such invaluable examples of waterway heritage afloat. Exhibition Hall, Engine House, Historic Cottages, Stables and Forge. Cafe and shop. Boat trips along the Shropshire Union. Secure moorings, water and refuse facilities provided for visiting boaters. CH65 4FW

BLUE PLANET AQUARIUM - Cheshire Oaks. Tel: 0151 357 8804. Deepwater antidote to the inherent shallowness of all canals. CH65 9LF

Connections

BUSES - Service 1 links Ellesmere Port with Liverpool and Chester every 20 minutes Mon-Sat (hourly Sun) calling usefully en route at Cheshire Oaks Designer Outlet, the Blue Planet Aquarium, and Chester Zoo.

TRAINS - frequent Merseyrail services to/from Liverpool (via Birkenhead) and Chester (change at Hooton).

TAXIS - King Kabs. Tel: 0151 355 1122.

Middlewich
& Anderton

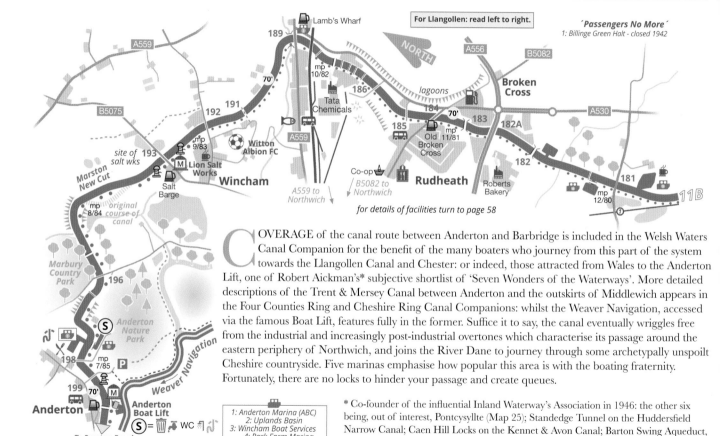

For Llangollen: read left to right.

Lamb's Wharf

'Passengers No More'
1: Billinge Green Halt - closed 1942

NORTH

Broken Cross

Tata Chemicals

lagoons

Witton Albion FC

Lion Salt Works

Wincham

Old Broken Cross

Rudheath

Co-op
B5082 to Northwich

Roberts Bakery

Salt Barge

site of salt wks

Marston New Cut

original course of canal

A559 to Northwich

for details of facilities turn to page 58

11B

Marbury Country Park

Anderton Nature Park

Weaver Navigation

Anderton

Anderton Boat Lift

To Preston Brook
(use Four Counties Ring/
Cheshire Ring CCs)

S = 🗑 ⚓ WC

1: Anderton Marina (ABC)
2: Uplands Basin
3: Wincham Boat Services
4: Park Farm Marina
5: Oakwood Marina

COVERAGE of the canal route between Anderton and Barbridge is included in the Welsh Waters Canal Companion for the benefit of the many boaters who journey from this part of the system towards the Llangollen Canal and Chester: or indeed, those attracted from Wales to the Anderton Lift, one of Robert Aickman's* subjective shortlist of 'Seven Wonders of the Waterways'. More detailed descriptions of the Trent & Mersey Canal between Anderton and the outskirts of Middlewich appears in the Four Counties Ring and Cheshire Ring Canal Companions: whilst the Weaver Navigation, accessed via the famous Boat Lift, features fully in the former. Suffice it to say, the canal eventually wriggles free from the industrial and increasingly post-industrial overtones which characterise its passage around the eastern periphery of Northwich, and joins the River Dane to journey through some archetypally unspoilt Cheshire countryside. Five marinas emphasise how popular this area is with the boating fraternity. Fortunately, there are no locks to hinder your passage and create queues.

* Co-founder of the influential Inland Waterway's Association in 1946: the other six being, out of interest, Pontcysyllte (Map 25); Standedge Tunnel on the Huddersfield Narrow Canal; Caen Hill Locks on the Kennet & Avon Canal; Barton Swing Aqueduct, which carries the Bridgewater Canal across the Manchester Ship Canal; Bingley Five-rise Locks and Burnley Embankment, both on the Leeds & Liverpool Canal.

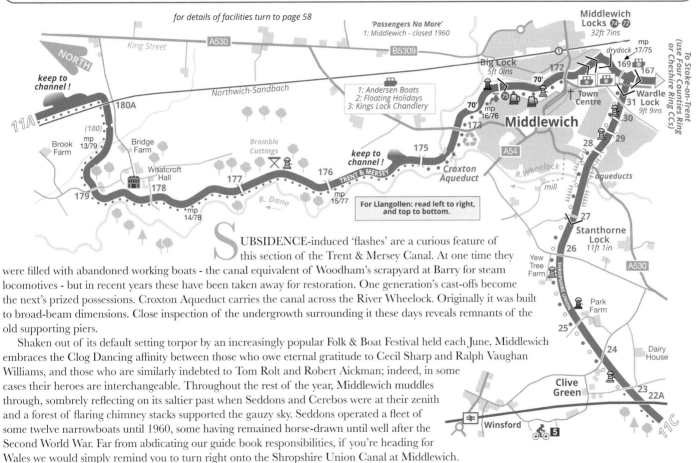

for details of facilities turn to page 58

NORTH

King Street

A530

B5309

Northwich-Sandbach

'Passengers No More'
1: Middlewich - closed 1960

Middlewich Locks 74-72
32ft 7ins

keep to channel !

11A

180A

(180)
mp 13/79

Brook Farm

Bridge Farm

Whatcroft Hall

179

178

177

176

mp 14/78

mp 15/77

R. Dane

Bramble Cuttings

175

keep to channel !

TRENT & MERSEY

1: Andersen Boats
2: Floating Holidays
3: Kings Lock Chandlery

Big Lock *5ft 0ins*

70'

172

70'

mp 16/76

173

Middlewich

Croxton Aqueduct

A54

Town Centre

drydock
mp 17/75

169

167

Wardle Lock *9ft 9ins*

31

30

29

28

27

Stanthorne Lock *11ft 1in*

26

25

24

23 22A

R. Wheelock

mill

aqueducts

To Stoke-on-Trent
(use Four Counties Ring
or Cheshire Ring CCS)

Yew Tree Farm

Park Farm

Clive Green

Dairy House

Winsford

5

11C

SHROPSHIRE UNION

For Llangollen: read left to right, and top to bottom.

S UBSIDENCE-induced 'flashes' are a curious feature of this section of the Trent & Mersey Canal. At one time they were filled with abandoned working boats - the canal equivalent of Woodham's scrapyard at Barry for steam locomotives - but in recent years these have been taken away for restoration. One generation's cast-offs become the next's prized possessions. Croxton Aqueduct carries the canal across the River Wheelock. Originally it was built to broad-beam dimensions. Close inspection of the undergrowth surrounding it these days reveals remnants of the old supporting piers.

Shaken out of its default setting torpor by an increasingly popular Folk & Boat Festival held each June, Middlewich embraces the Clog Dancing affinity between those who owe eternal gratitude to Cecil Sharp and Ralph Vaughan Williams, and those who are similarly indebted to Tom Rolt and Robert Aickman; indeed, in some cases their heroes are interchangeable. Throughout the rest of the year, Middlewich muddles through, sombrely reflecting on its saltier past when Seddons and Cerebos were at their zenith and a forest of flaring chimney stacks supported the gauzy sky. Seddons operated a fleet of some twelve narrowboats until 1960, some having remained horse-drawn until well after the Second World War. Far from abdicating our guide book responsibilities, if you're heading for Wales we would simply remind you to turn right onto the Shropshire Union Canal at Middlewich.

ANDERTON   MAP 11A

It's nice to linger by The Lift and watch it perform its conjuring trick. Good visitor moorings provide every excuse to do so, whilst the adjoining country park gives you an opportunity to stretch your legs.

Eating & Drinking

THE MOORINGS - restaurant and coffee shop at Anderton Marina. Tel: 01606 79789. CW9 6AJ
STANLEY ARMS - canalside opposite Anderton Lift. Tel: 01606 77661. Greene King ales. Offside customer moorings. CW9 6AG
LIFT CAFETERIA - canalside, integral to Lift Visitor Centre. Tel: 01606 786777. CW9 6FW

Things to Do

ANDERTON BOAT LIFT - Tel: 01606 786777. Canalside Visitor Centre celebrating the Lift and local canals in all their historic glory. CW9 6FW A widebeam trip boat named *Edwin Clark* after the Lift's designer offers trips up or down the Lift. River trips to Northwich and back are also usually available.
ANDERTON NATURE PARK - waymarked trails through reclaimed wasteland where many plants usually confined to coastal environments thrive.

Connections

BUSES - Network Warrington service 9A runs to Northwich approximately bi-hourly Mon-Sat.
TAXIS - Cheshire Executive. Tel: 01606 41111.

MARSTON   MAP 11A

Eating & Drinking

SALT BARGE - Ollershaw Lane (Bridge 193). Tel: 01606 212525. Cosy local serving food from noon daily. Nice choice of locally brewed ales. CW9 6ES
Nicho's cafe/sandwich bar (Tel: 01606 48623) 2 mins west of Bridge 192.

Things to Do

LION SALT WORKS - Ollershaw Lane (Bridge 193) Tel: 01606 275066. £10m well-spent on restoring and interpreting an open-pan salt manufactory. Open daily (ex Mon) 10.30am-5pm. Cafe & shop. CW9 6ES

WINCHAM WHARF   MAP 11A

Eating & Drinking

LAMB'S WHARF - Manchester Road (adjacent Bridge 189). Tel: 01606 514053. Re-opened pub in former mill. Open from 5pm Tue-Fri and from noon at weekends. No food. CW9 7NT
THE CODFATHER - Manchester Road. Tel: 01606 42342. Excellent fish & chips. CW9 7NE

BROKEN CROSS   MAP 11A

Eating & Drinking

OLD BROKEN CROSS - Rudheath (Bridge 184). Tel: 01606 333111. Refurbished canalside pub open from noon daily. Food served throughout. Sky TV. CW9 7EB.

MIDDLEWICH   MAP 11B

A salt making town since the days of the Roman occupation, Middlewich's most interesting building is probably the parish church of St Michael whose tower remains visibly wounded by missiles unleashed during the Civil War. Leaflets are obtainable from the library to guide you around some of the known sites of Roman history.

Eating & Drinking

BIG LOCK - Webb's Lane (Lock 75). Tel: 01606 836983. Re-opened after extensive refurbishment in 2020. Open from noon daily, food served throughout. Incorporates a coffee shop. CW10 9DN

KING'S LOCK INN - Booth Lane (Lock 71). Tel: 01606 836894. Popular canalside pub originally constructed on two levels to provide stabling for boat horses below. Features a narrowboat-shaped bar. CW10 0JJ
THE NARROWBOAT - Lewin Street. Tel: 01606 738087. Town centre pub with a well-appointed dining room. Bed & Breakfast. CW10 9AS
WHITE BEAR - Wheelock Street. Tel: 01606 837666. Welcoming pub/restaurant. CW10 9AG

Shopping

There are Lidl and Morrisons supermarkets. A small market is held every Tuesday. Correspondents recommend Broads Bakery on Lewin Street (adjacent Bridge 169). Dave's, on Lewin Street, is an 'angling supercentre'.

Connections

BUSES - Arriva service 37A links Middlewich with Northwich (via Winsford Rly Sta) and Sandbach half-hourly (ex Sun). D&G service 42 runs to/from Congleton and Crewe, hourly Mon-Fri, bi-hourly Sat.

CHURCH MINSHULL MAP 11C

A pretty village boasting some handsome half-timbered houses, though the walk downhill from Bridge 14 can be fraught with unyielding traffic. Tom and Angela Rolt enjoyed an extended stay here in the fateful autumn of 1939 while Tom worked for Rolls-Royce at Crewe. In those days electricity was generated by the village's watermill - would that it still were!

Eating & Drinking

THE BADGER - Cross Lane (village centre). Tel: 01270 522348. Comfortable country pub open from 11am daily and serving food throughout until 9pm. Accommodation. CW5 6DY

RELEGATING the Middlewich Branch subconsciously to the back of your mind as an unspectacular but necessary link in the waterways of the North-west would be unjust, for this is a rumbustious canal, carrying you loftily above the snaking valley of the River Weaver, and presenting you with expansive views towards an horizon bounded by Delamere Forest and the Peckforton Hills. Designed by Thomas Telford, the route reflects his confidence and expertise, slicing across the grain of the countryside in a sequence of deep cuttings and high embankments. Its locks (see Maps 11B and 11D) have a significantly greater rise/fall than most narrow equivalents.

Church Minshull looks - from the canal's elevated position between bridges 12 and 13 - like a toy village embracing the river's luxuriant banks.

Several sizeable farms border the canal, their fields filled with Cheshire's trademark black and white milking herds or cut red by the plough in a ruddy shade of corduroy. Near Bridge 22, woods partially obscure the Top Flash, a subsidence induced lake beside the Weaver. The West Coast Main Line adjoins the canal. Moor overnight hereabouts, and the roar of the Caledonian Sleeper will invade your dreams. Chances are, its cosseted occupants will be decanted bleary-eyed in Fort William, Aberdeen or Inverness before you can get to Nantwich. Between bridges 18 and 19 former canal horse stables have been fetchingly refurbished as living quarters after years lying derelict. Note how the adjoining canal cottage boasts three storeys to the rear. Keep your eyes peeled for the Jacobean style house alongside Bridge 14. Old maps refer to this as Minshullhill Wharf.

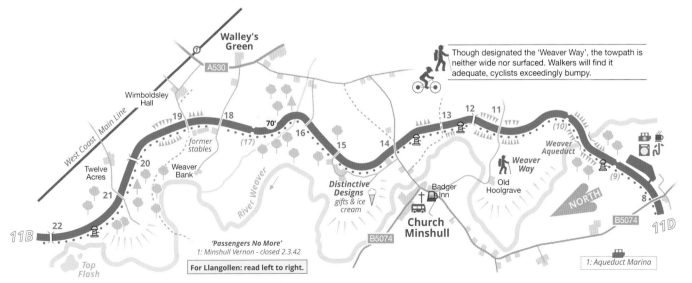

Though designated the 'Weaver Way', the towpath is neither wide nor surfaced. Walkers will find it adequate, cyclists exceedingly bumpy.

'Passengers No More'
1: Minshull Vernon - closed 2.3.42

For Llangollen: read left to right.

1: Aqueduct Marina

CANAL junctions invariably provoke an adrenalin rush, and there are two here to contend with in quick succession if, like a lot of boaters, you're using the Middlewich Branch to get to the Llangollen Canal. Minshull and Cholmondeston locks are deep and heavy-gated, and with two busy marinas between Middlewich and Barbridge queues can form at times. Relax and enjoy the countryside, which has an air of remoteness about it, despite being only three miles from the urban periphery of Crewe.

The Middlewich Branch was a latecomer in the context of the canal network as a whole, opening in 1833, only seven years before the Crewe to Chester railway. Nevertheless, under the auspices of the Shropshire Union it thrived, becoming the preferred route between the industrial centres of the Black Country and the North-west. Trade also developed between Ellesmere Port, on the banks of the Mersey, and The Potteries: Cornish china clay in one direction, finished crockery in the other; traffics which continued right up until the 1960s. By the middle of the 19th century, both the canal and the railway were effectively owned by the same company, the powerful London & North Western Railway, and in 1888 a curious experiment was undertaken. A narrow gauge railway was laid along the towpath, along which a small locomotive steamed up and down hauling strings of narrowboats. The concept didn't catch on here, though it was adopted abroad, especially in France. *Groceries avilable at Venetian Marina.*

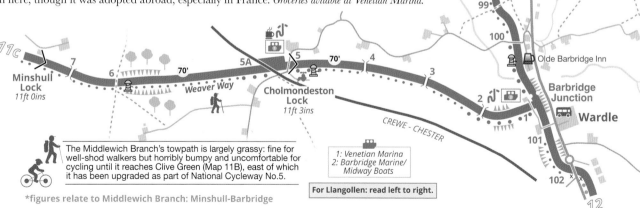

The Middlewich Branch's towpath is largely grassy: fine for well-shod walkers but horribly bumpy and uncomfortable for cycling until it reaches Clive Green (Map 11B), east of which it has been upgraded as part of National Cycleway No.5.

*figures relate to Middlewich Branch: Minshull-Barbridge

1: Venetian Marina
2: Barbridge Marine/
Midway Boats

For Llangollen: read left to right.

Llangollen Canal

'PLEASE Lift Your Fenders' urge the signs, as you enter the bottom lock of the Hurleston flight. Sound advice - if a tad risqué - as a couple of its chambers have bowed outwards down the years, and anything over 6ft 10ins beam has to proceed with caution; though what self-respecting boater would cruise with their fenders down is another matter. Boats may pass in the short and deceptively shallow intervening pounds, but a certain degree of unwritten protocol and etiquette should be displayed if tempers aren't to fray. Fortunately, volunteer lock-keepers are usually on hand in healthy numbers throughout the season, both to help with the work and to offer friendly, and, for the most part cogent advice.

Adjoining the locks, a reservoir stores water which has flowed down the canal from the River Dee at Horseshoe Falls above Llangollen, before being treated and piped to the kitchen sinks of Crewe. Thank your lucky stars for this water; without it, the London Midland & Scottish Railway would have closed the canal during the Second World War, when they thought no one would be looking. In fact, technically the canal was 'abandoned' and it was only its use as a water channel that saved it from the dereliction suffered by other LMS owned waterways

under an infamous Act of 1944. Gradually, a new traffic of pleasure boats began using the canal, and under the 1968 Transport Act the Llangollen Canal (as the section of the old Ellesmere Canal between Hurleston and Llangollen had become known) was classified a 'cruiseway', its position as one of the premier canal holiday routes assured for posterity.

Wherein lies the Llangollen's appeal? Well it doesn't do it any harm that it never gets suburban, let alone urban or industrialised, and there can't be many canal routes which can lay claim to that. Furthermore the fact that it sets off from England in search of Wales gives it a sense of purpose ironically at odds with its ad hoc origins. Crusty old canal salts will tell you it's overrated, but we'll let you be the judge of that! What is noticeable, is a preponderance of hire boats over privately owned craft. Intuitively, one expects to be travelling East to West, but, initially the canal runs, disconcertingly, on a North-South axis. A rural atmosphere is rapidly established. Big farms like Bache House hint at an intensity of agriculture past its zenith.

At Burland, an old estate village on the Nantwich to Wrexham main road, a rectangle of water denotes a former wharf. But the canal's

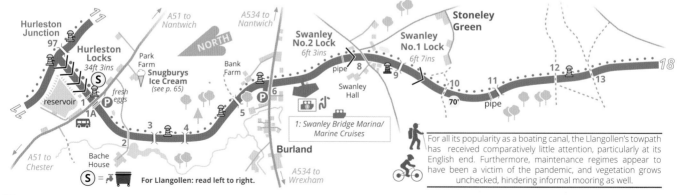

1: Swanley Bridge Marina/ Marine Cruises

For all its popularity as a boating canal, the Llangollen's towpath has received comparatively little attention, particularly at its English end. Furthermore, maintenance regimes appear to have been a victim of the pandemic, and vegetation grows unchecked, hindering informal mooring as well.

For Llangollen: read left to right.

Locking Down Hurleston

prosperity these days comes from the berthing of boats, as at Swanley Marina, rather than the delivery and despatch of goods. Interestingly, though we tend to think of narrowboats carrying single cargoes of mostly bulky commodities such as coal, chemicals or minerals, up until the sudden demise of the Shropshire Union fleet in 1921 hundreds of horse-drawn boats plied the system bearing a huge variety of daily necessities; the ubiquitous DHL and UPS logistics vans of their day: all delivered - albeit scarcely credible - without the aid of GPS. Swanley Hall is another substantial farm. Like Hurleston, the locks at Swanley and Baddiley (Map 18) can become congested at busy times.

Bridge 11 features brickwork embossed with the manufacturer's name: 'Wood & Ivery, Albion Brick Works, West Bromwich'. The flow of water down the Llangollen Canal increases the running of the by-washes, causing a gush of water to run across the canal at the foot of locks. To compensate, steer slightly into the overflow. Going downhill, avoid being drawn over to the cill of the by-weir. Also bear in mind that - like a river with a current - your boat will travel slightly faster on its way back down the canal. The times quoted at the top of each map are averaged out. Add a bit when going towards Wales, subtract a bit on the way back, and you should be there or thereabouts.

WRENBURY is one of the most picturesque ports of call at the English end of the Llangollen Canal. Bridge 20, rebuilt in timber and electrified (operated with a CRT Yale key), is equipped with less than discreet traffic lights but it would take more than these to spoil the attractive scene presented by the canal wharf and its old mills, now used as a pub and boatyard. The older of the two buildings dates back to the opening of the canal,

though its site was used for a mill as early as the 16th century, power coming from the adjoining waters of the stripling Weaver. On the opposite bank, the more modern mill belongs to the 20th century, being constructed in a surprisingly effective combination of corrugated iron and mellow brick. The former miller, Arthur Sumner, once operated a small fleet of narrowboats, acquired out of necessity when the Shropshire Union ceased carrying in 1921. Sumner's boats were immaculately turned out with red cabin sides, Tuscan lettering and a profusion of roses and castles. When lorries inevitably took over from the boats, their livery was equally attractive, if somewhat less ornate. Descendants of Arthur Sumner were landlords at the Dusty Miller until 2011. Nowadays, appropriately enough, the younger mill serves as a hire fleet base, canal shop, and self-catering apartment.

Wrenbury Hall's history goes back to Domesday but the present mock Elizabethan mansion dates from 1919. In living memory it has been used to rehabilitate tuberculosis sufferers and as a training centre for ambulance personnel, but now it promotes itself as 'South Cheshire's most desirable wedding venue'. The residing family's motto was Riget Otio Virtus. Fluency in Latin being taken for granted where Canal Companion users are concerned, it is hardly necessary to translate this as 'virtue becomes stiff with idleness' - rather like some paddle gear we could mention.

Either side of Wrenbury, the Llangollen Canal wends its way through peaceful countryside of considerable charm. About a mile and a half or so to the south-east stands an obelisk in the landscaped grounds of Combermere Abbey, a substantial house developed on the site of a Cistercian monastery abandoned at the time of The Dissolution. The monument commemorates one Stapleton Cotton, a distinguished soldier who served under the Duke of Wellington who visited the house in 1820. Amongst other recreational activities, Combermere is now used as a venue for - how did you guess? - weddings!

by-road to Audlem

Wrenbury Heath

River Weaver

NORTH

15 16 17

14

Baddiley Locks
19ft 8ins

17

Wrenbury Hall

18

Wrenbury

19

Wrenbury Mill

20

nursery

21

1: ABC Boat Hire

22

70'

Combermere Abbey monument

1 Blind bend
2 CRT facilities Yale key required for Bridge 20

Ryebank

Barn Books

Gauntons Bank

23

19

by-road to Marbury

Marbury Lock
6ft 0ins

Bridge 20, Wrenbury

WRENBURY MAP 18

Named one of England's fifty best villages to live in by a *Sunday Times* survey, this straggling village lies in the civil parish of Wrenbury-cum-Frith. What centre there is adjoins a green bordered by black & white cottages redolent of Cheshire. The church (whose mellifluous chimes can be heard from the canal) and school are its most notable buildings. There was once a third pub known as the Hawk & Buckle.

Eating & Drinking

COTTON ARMS - adjacent Bridge 20. Tel: 01270 780377. A favourite with boaters, campers and caravanners. Food (ex Mon/Tue) and real ale. CW5 8HG

DUSTY MILLER - Cholmondeley Road (Bridge 20). Tel: 01270 780537. Comfortably furnished canalside pub occupying a converted mill. No food on Weds. Robinsons ales from Stockport.

NO.18 THE PARK - Nantwich Road. Tel: 01270 781026. Coffee shop open Wed-Sun from 10am-4pm; closes 2.30 pm Sundays. CW5 8EW

Shopping

Post office stores five minutes walk from the canal. Open from 7.30am to 8pm Mon-Sat and 8.30am to 8pm Sun. Hot take-away food counter.

Things to Do

SNUGBURYS - Park Farm. (Maps 11, 11D & 17) Tel: 01270 624830. Ice cream parlour. Open daily 10am-5pm. Time was canallers could thread their way safely across the fields from bridges 3 and 4, but permissive access has been rescinded, and now you must go from Bridge 1, which involves trudging along a busy main road, only partially pavemented, and not child - friendly. Nice ice cream though! CW5 6BU

Self-Catering

ABC offer self-catering for up to four people in an apartment in Wrenbury Mill - Tel: 0330 333 0590.

Connections

TRAINS - roughly bi-hourly Transport for Wales services to/from Crewe and Shrewsbury via Whitchurch and Nantwich.

BUSES - D&G service 72 operates half a dozen times daily (ex Sun) to/from Nantwich (via Audlem, Map 9).

MARBURY MAP 19

The church lych-gate celebrates "Ye who live mid English pastures green", and there's a secluded bench in the graveyard from which you can watch the antics of the wildfowl on the Big Mere. Two centuries old oak tree on the green whose trunk is surrounded by a circular seat.

Eating & Drinking

THE SWAN INN - village centre. Tel: 01948 522860. Refurbished country pub 5 minutes walk from Bridges 23 or 24. Food served throughout from noon daily. Up to four local ales. SY13 4LS

GRINDLEY BROOK is the focal point of this part of the Llangollen Canal. Here are six locks in close proximity, three of them forming a substantial 'staircase' overlooked by a splendid round-bayed lock-keeper's house typical of Telford's architectural style. In fact, the interest at Grindley Brook starts below the bottom lock where a fine skew bridge of blue engineering bricks baked in Rowley Regis still carries the trackbed of the old Chester to Whitchurch railway over the canal. A trio of single chambers precedes the staircase, the bottom of which is spanned by the Chester road, and bordered by old mill buildings.

The activity at Grindley Brook on a Bank Holiday weekend or busy summer's day provides wonderful entertainment for the spectator, if not the imperturbable lock-keeper who is on duty daily from 8.30am April to October. The staircase locks, in particular, cause considerable congestion: Sundays and Mondays are busiest for ascending boats; Thursdays and Fridays for descending boats. Delays in excess of two hours are not unheard of, though it is worth bearing in mind that mornings are less busy than afternoons, from which one can only conclude that modern day boaters are a load of lazy lie-ins.

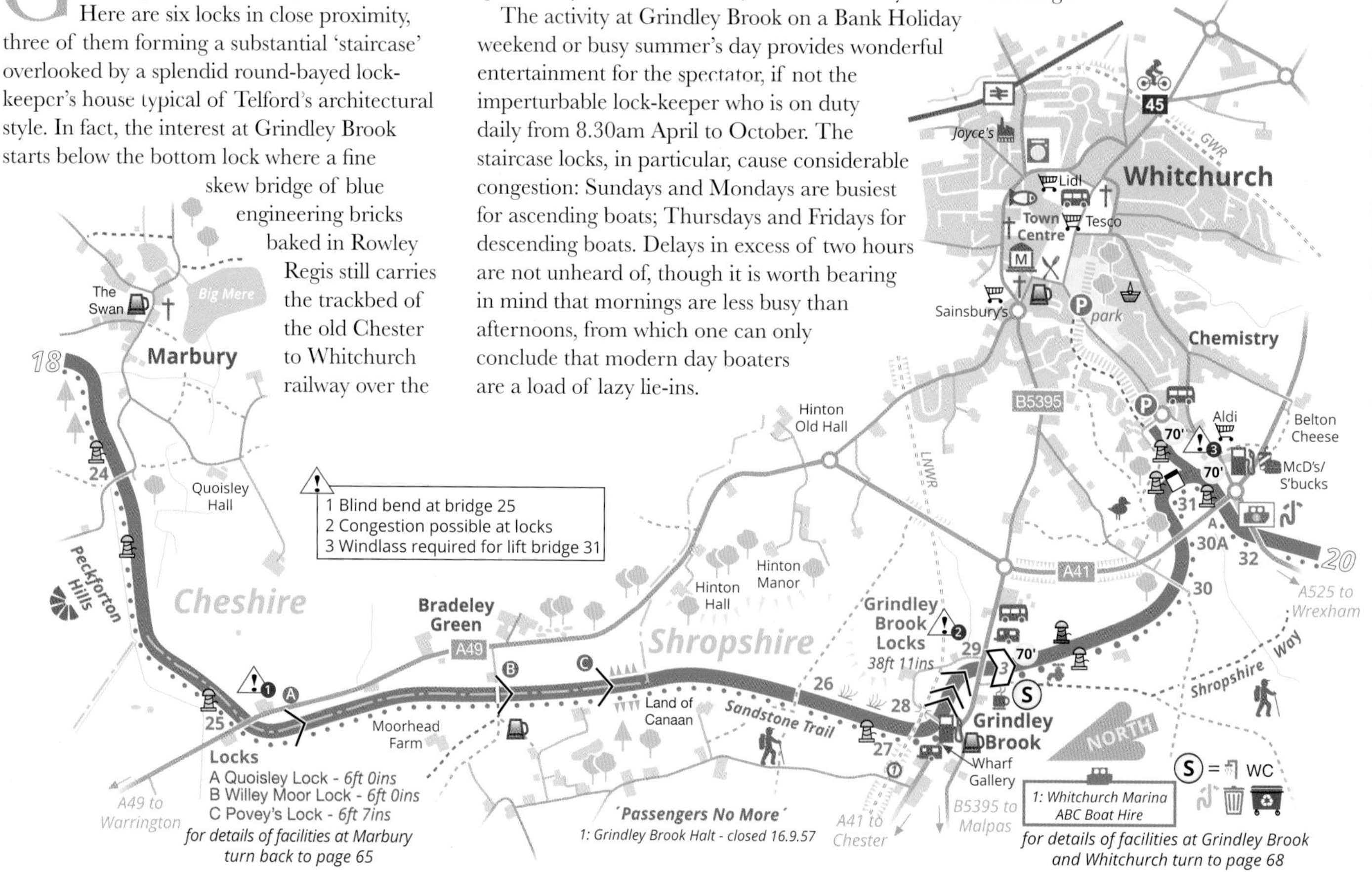

1 Blind bend at bridge 25
2 Congestion possible at locks
3 Windlass required for lift bridge 31

Locks
A Quoisley Lock - 6ft 0ins
B Willey Moor Lock - 6ft 0ins
C Povey's Lock - 6ft 7ins
for details of facilities at Marbury turn back to page 65

'Passengers No More'
1: Grindley Brook Halt - closed 16.9.57

1: Whitchurch Marina
ABC Boat Hire

for details of facilities at Grindley Brook and Whitchurch turn to page 68

Grindley Brook Locks 38ft 11ins

S = WC

of Marbury is shunned and the general atmosphere is one of isolation. South of Grindley Brook the canal makes as if to call at the old Shropshire market town of Whitchurch, but then seems to think better of it. A short branch terminated in the centre of town but was abandoned in 1944 and was subsequently, to the town's regret, filled in. In 1993, however, a start was made in reclaiming the arm by restoring the first few hundred yards of it to provide moorings for visitors to the town. After toying with an ambitious scheme to construct an inclined plane to take the arm much nearer to the town centre, Whitchurch Canal Trust are now proposing a more modest terminal basin within the town's country park. Pending this, the former wharf is still obvious at the far end of Jubilee Park. Up until the 1920s cheese fly-boats journeyed from Whitchurch wharf (and a number of other cheese-making towns in the district) to Manchester or Ellesmere Port (for Liverpool), the cheeses being stored on shelves in a hold covered with white canvas to deflect the sun's rays.

Telford lock-house, Grindley Brook

People react to the hold ups in different ways: some with frustration, some with saintly resignation. The secret, of course, is to remember that you are on holiday and supposed to be enjoying yourself. The westbound boater, having climbed some forty feet through the six locks, does at least have twenty lock-free miles to look forward to. But before you leave Grindley Brook, pause a moment and admire the splendid round-bayed house beside the top lock and, directly opposite, the keepers' cabin which still retains its blue & yellow British Waterways nameplate; a precious survivor.

North of Grindley Brook the canal forms the county boundary between Cheshire and Shropshire for a short distance. The 'Sandstone Trail' swells the ranks of towpath walkers on this section. Reeds form a soothing curtain between the path and the water. The picturesque village

The Whitchurch Arm

GRINDLEY BROOK   MAP 19

Canalside community on the A41, the old road from London to Birkenhead. Oily aromas emanate from Robert's canalside fuel depot.

Eating & Drinking

HORSE & JOCKEY - adjacent Bridge 28. Tel: 01948 662723. Renovated pub offering a good choice of food from noon daily. Up to eight ales on tap. SY13 4QJ

LOCKSIDE CAFE - canalside by staircase locks. Tel: 01948 663385. Popular family run cafe open 9am-5pm daily. Wi-fi and gluten-free options. SY13 4QH

WILLEY MOOR LOCK TAVERN - beside the lock. Tel: 01948 663274. Picturesque - and justifiably popular - free house (once a lock-keeper's cottage) reached by motorists via a track off the A49. Good home cooked food served daily at lunchtime (ex Mon) and from 6pm in the evening, plus an interesting and ever changing range of ales; many locally sourced. Pleasant garden with children's play area. SY13 4HF

Shopping

WHARF GALLERY - canalside between bridges 27 & 28. Long established outlet for Buffy Robinson (*www.buffyrobinson.co.uk*) who specialises in batik, wax-resist dyeing. Please email to book a visit: buffy@buffyrobinson.co.uk SY13 4QJ

Grindley Brook also boasts a petrol station with shop backing onto the bottom lock by Bridge 28.

Connections

BUSES - service 41 runs approximately bi-hourly Mon-Sat to Whitchurch in one direction and to Chester in the other.

WHITCHURCH   MAP 19

'The most handsome town in north Shropshire' enthused Messrs Betjeman and Piper in their collaborative Shell Guide of 1951, and the seventy years which have elapsed since have been untypically tactful when compared to many a much spoilt market town. Architecturally, the substantial parish church of St Alkmund's leads the way, but handsome buildings are sprinkled liberally throughout. Cheese and clocks are Whitchurch's gifts to civilisation. Blue Cheshire cheese is characterised by a marbled effect and is one of the great, tangy blue cheeses in the world. Joyce Clocks can be found as far away as Sydney, Shanghai and Tredegar. They commenced clock making in the neighbourhood in the 17th century. Their handsome redbrick premises on Station Road were in use between 1904 and 2012, but now house the antiques and fine arts showroom of Trevanion (Tel: 01948 800202). Christina Trevanion is a frequent, not to say effervescent, guest on television antiques shows.

Eating & Drinking

ALFRESCO KITCHEN - Hadley Park (Bridge 34, Map 20). Tel: 01948 780170). Open Wed-Sun 9am-2pm.

ETZIO - 60 High Street. Tel: 01948 662248. Italian Kitchen just down from St Alkmund's church. Well appointed interior and al fresco decking to rear. Open for lunch and dinner. SY13 1BB

DOCKET No.33 - High Street. Tel: 01948 665553. Michelin listed restaurant specialising in tasting menu, Sat lunch and Thur, Fri & Sat from 7pm. SY13 1AZ

JONES'S - Green End. Tel: 01948 666108. Coffee shop open daily (ex Sun) 9am-4pm. Sister establishment in Market Drayton. SY13 1AA

OLD TOWN HALL VAULTS - St Mary's Street. Tel: 01948 664682. Cosy Joule's (of Market Drayton) pub which was the birthplace of Sir Edward German, composer of Merrie England, Tom Jones, and other light operatic works. Listed Gents loo! SY13 1QU

SPICE HEAVEN - Station Road. Tel 01948 665959. Indian open daily (ex Tue) from 5pm. SY13 1RE

WALKERS - High Street. Tel: 01948 664687. Old fashioned comfort food in first-floor cafe above a bakery: infinitely maternal waitresses. SY13 1AX

WILD SHROPSHIRE - Green End. Tel 0776 668 5076. James Sherwin's Michelin listed 'field to fork' restaurant open for tasting menu dinners Thur-Sat. SY13 1A

There are McDonald's and Starbucks outlets on the A41 opposite Whitchurch Marina accessible via Bridge 32.

Shopping

All services in the town centre, one mile east of the canal. Friday is market day, Wednesday early closing, Farmers Market on the first Saturday in the month. Tesco supermarket by the bus station, Sainsbury's on London Road, Lidl on Bridgewater Street. Benjamin's at the foot of High Street, is a nice deli, cafe and patisserie. Nearby, on Green End, there's a small independent bookshop punningly named Bookshrop Bubbles launderette (ex Wed/Sun) on Station Road. There are a growing number of dealers in antiques in the town. Several food shops stock locally produced Belton's cheeses. Annual Food Festival in late May. Aldi supermarket on Wrexham Road at Chemistry.

Things to Do

HERITAGE & TOURIST INFORMATION CENTRE St Mary's Street. Tel: 01948 664577. Excellent exhibitions of local history and personalities such as Edward German and the Victorian illustrator Randolph Caldecott. Open Tue, Thur & Fri 11am-4pm SY13 1QY

Connections

BUSES - Service 41 links Whitchurch with Chester bi-hourly and calls at Grindley Brook en route. Service 72 runs six times daily (ex Sun) to/from Nantwich via Wrenbury. Service 205 offers a fairly frequent Mon-Sat link between the canal arm at Chemistry and the town centre bus park beside Tesco.

TRAINS - approx bi-hourly Transport for Wales services to Crewe (via Wrenbury and Nantwich) and Shrewsbury.

TAXIS - Whitchurch Taxis. Tel: 01948 509100.

BETWEEN Whitchurch (Map 19) and Ellesmere (Map 22) the Llangollen Canal encounters three distinct types of landscape: farmland, mosses, and meres. Plenty of variety, then, for those displaying withdrawal symptoms from what most would consider the blessed absence of locks. Furthermore, apart from the occasional windlass-operated lift bridge, the unencumbered boater has 'the best seat in the house' from which to enjoy the countryside's subtle scene changes.

Enjoyably undulating, the farmland appears for the most part lush and well husbanded, though burgeoning crops of maize strike an alien chord. The dynastical business of agriculture is undertaken from sizeable farmhouses bolstered by the appurtenances of different eras: handsome brick milking parlours; Dutch barns of a curious corrugated iron kind of charm; and modern day excrescences which wouldn't look out of place on an industrial estate.

Through all this the canal glides serenely: occasionally in cuttings, occasionally on embankments; always with an impenetrably opaque hawthorn hedge on the towpath side. The utilitarian ranks of soil-sapping maize are relieved, here and there, by conversation-provoking points of interest.

Pan Castle marks the enigmatic remains of a motte & bailey structure which - Derrick Pratt speculates in his notes accompanying the Godfrey Edition Ordnance Survey map of Whitchurch dated 1899 - may have been erected circa 1102 by the Pandolfs of Wem. Blackoe Cottages, we *do* know, were built to provide accommodation for canal lengthsmen, and there was stabling here for boat horses as well. Metal footbridge 35 carries a branch of the Shropshire Way over the canal. The flat concrete span of Bridge 39 remains surprisingly in place, as if some benign ferroequinological deity plans to reinstate the Cambrian Railways route from Whitchurch to Oswestry. Prior to closure of the railway in 1965, Whitchurch and Ellesmere were twenty-five minutes away from each other by train. Thereafter buses, crammed with garrulous market day pensioners, took twice as long but maintained the semblance of a link. Nowadays, motorists apart - and Pearson's have never knowingly pandered to that lamentable strata of society - *continued overleaf:*

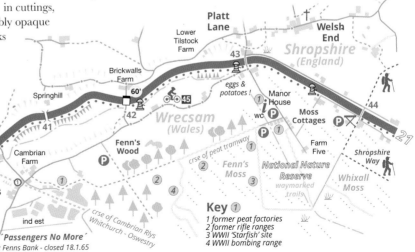

Key ①
1 former peat factories
2 former rifle ranges
3 WWII 'Starfish' site
4 WWII bombing range

'Passengers No More'
1: Fenns Bank - closed 18.1.65

69

continued from page 69:

transport between the two market towns, barely a dozen miles apart, has regressed to the 19th century heyday of the canal.

Not all the variations are nature's, for the canal finds itself paralleling (and briefly crossing on Map 21) the border between England and Wales, the latter being part of what used to be known as the English Maelor, or Flintshire Detached. This curious little pocket of Welshness dates back to Edward I's carving up of the Welsh principalities and Henry VIII's subsequent suppression of the Marcher Lords. Such tinkering continues, for, latterly part of Clwyd, this part of Flintshire is now administered by the County Borough of Wrexham. However life's organizers want to carve it up, though, it remains demonstrably exciting to feel oneself on the cusp of the Celtic country, as if noticing for the first time, the presence of someone you are destined to become much more intimate with. There are limekilns in the spacious garden of the house beside Bridge 42. A lifting structure of dubious reliability, it is painted a dull green; though at least it is spared the blotchy, flaking and frankly disgraceful paintwork that characterizes many of its supposedly black and white cousins.

At Platt Lane the eerie, other-worldly atmosphere of the mosses begins to impinge itself upon the canal. At over two thousand acres, they represent the third largest raised bog, or mire in lowland Britain; only Thorne Moors and Hatfield Chase near Doncaster in Yorkshire are larger. Peat began to form in the vicinity circa BC 8500 and had perhaps created its fully formed 'dome' by AD 500. Picture it as a giant blister, which remained effectively unpunctured until peat extraction for use as fuel began tentatively in the 16th century. This began an ongoing process of drainage which caused the dome to gradually subside. Prior to that

Whixall Moss

the surface of the mosses would have been some thirty feet higher than now. Construction of the canal and railway in the 19th century hastened the speed of change, particularly as the transport they offered encouraged commercial peat cutting to increase. The gradual mechanisation of the process from the day when hand cut turves (measuring roughly 9 by 7 by 4 inches) were eloquently known by their size and colour as 'Whixall Bibles', to the arrival in the late 1960s of peat cutting machinery from Germany exacerbated the decline of the mosses as a natural phenomenon, for they were being pretty much destroyed for commercial gain. Moreover, not content with exploiting the mosses for fuel, horticultural products and as an unlikely source of inedible bedding for horses, use was found for them in both world wars, initially as rifle ranges and subsequently for bomb practice and as a decoy site which could be set ablaze to mislead enemy aircraft crews that they were really over Merseyside.

Now, saner policies pertain, and the mosses are conspicuously empty of human activity; almost, if one dare say it, to the point where it is missed. Under the stewardship of Natural England and Natural Resources Wales the mosses are being restored and cherished as a wetland site of international significance. Often, such scientific credentials sound ever so slightly uninspiring but, trust us, the mosses exude a character all their own, and a network of signposted trails centred on the Manor House National Nature Reserve base near Bridge 43 encourages closer exploration and appreciation. We commend to you *A Peat Cutter's Life*, a book published in 2012 in which Bill Allmark relates to Jeff Beard his vivid experiences of a working life on the mosses. It is obtainable (while stocks last) from the Manor House price £10.

BATTING its eyelids demurely, the Prees Branch tempts all but the most determinedly chaste of main line passers-by into exploration of its reedy, if foreshortened charms. No, you can no longer emulate the antics of that illustrious old boatman Jack (*Shropshire Union Fly-Boats*) Roberts and his father who, on shovelling eighteen tons of North Staffordshire coal from the hold of their boat *Times* at Edstaston Wharf on a hot June day in 1908, flung off their clothes and dived into the canal in a dual attempt to clean up and cool off.

Even that long ago, the branch was silting up; it had taken their horse two hours to drag the boat the last mile. Subsequently the far three miles were abandoned, navigable status remaining just as far as the 'clay hole' from whence much of the 'puddle' for lining the bed of the Ellesmere Canal emanated. Towards the end of his working life in the 1960s, Jack was employed by British Waterways to convey Whixall clay to where it was required aboard the horse-drawn boat *Antwerp*. Latterly, the clay hole was developed into a marina which, to this day, offers a legitimate excuse for a detour up the arm, and a chance to negotiate its two charming timber lift-bridges.

Surprisingly, considering that the much larger town of Wem might have been a more profitable objective, the branch was intended to reach Prees but fell short by a couple of miles. Wharves were provided at Waterloo and Edstaston, together with a bank of lime burning kilns at Quina Brook; burnt lime being an important farming commodity in the innocent days before chemical fertilizers. An unusual three-storey canal house *continued overleaf:*

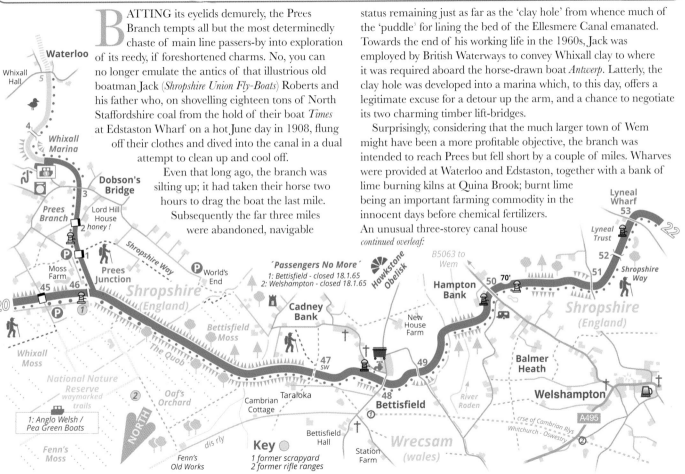

Waterloo
Whixall Hall
Whixall Marina
Dobson's Bridge
Prees Branch
Lord Hill House *2 honey !*
Moss Farm
Prees Junction
Shropshire Way
Shropshire (England)
World's End
Passengers No More
1: Bettisfield - closed 18.1.65
2: Welshampton - closed 18.1.65
Hawkstone Obelisk
B5063 to Wem
Lyneal Wharf
Lyneal Trust
Shropshire Way
Shropshire (England)
Hampton Bank
Balmer Heath
Welshampton
Cadney Bank
New House Farm
Bettisfield Moss
Whixall Moss
National Nature Reserve waymarked trails
Oaf's Orchard
The Quob
Taraloka
Cambrian Cottage
Bettisfield
Bettisfield Hall
River Roden
Wrecsam (wales)
crse of Cambrian Rlys Whitchurch - Oswestry
A495
Station Farm
Fenn's Moss
Fenn's Old Works
dis rly

1: Anglo Welsh / Pea Green Boats

Key
1 former scrapyard
2 former rifle ranges

watches over Prees Junction, its ground floor lying below the level of the embanked canal. Intriguingly, the Tricolour was flying last time we passed, and the grounds contained an fascinating array of outbuildings.

West of the junction, a long straight mile, known colloquially as 'The Quob' - possibly because mires tend to quiver and throb when walked upon - extends across the mosses, evoking an aura every bit as eerie as its nickname. It was not an easy length of canal to cut. Drainage of the peat caused subsidence and the canal company employed a permanent Moss Gang responsible for raising oak-piled clay embankments. Similarly the railway builders, sixty years later, had to lay their track on rafts of faggots and larch poles. Progress rended the gang redundant when steel-piling was introduced in the 1960s, but you can still see how the towpath lies lower than the water, suggesting that instabilities in the landscape remain. A slender timber post, part of the Mosses Trail, marks the boundary between England and Wales, but the canal's familiarity with the latter is shortlived on this occasion.

Though there are no facilities as such, Bettisfield repays closer examination. Uphill to the north stands the quaintly Victorian church, designed by G. E. Street in 1874: the stone was quarried on Grinshill, the stained glass is by Clayton & Bell, the tiles Minton, the bells from Taylor's foundry in Loughborough. The buildings at Bettisfield's Beechinged station have at least derived tender loving care from their domestic occupants, the goods shed being an especially attractive conversion. The railway's trackbed can be explored in an easterly direction to the skeletal remains of a former peat works. A mile to the north, Bettisfield Park (or Hall), seat of the Hanmer family saw use as a military camp during both world wars, bringing many troop trains to the line. Taraloka - formerly a farmhouse called Cornhill - is a Buddhist retreat for women.

Hampton Bank is one of the Llangollen Canal's lesser sung engineering achievements; it carries the canal perhaps thirty feet above a headwater of the River Roden, a tributary of the Tern which joins the Severn below Shrewsbury. Larches mask the bank from the prevailing wind. To the south-east, beyond Wem, stands obelisk-topped Grotto Hill in Hawkstone Park; to the north-west the mountains of Wales. Hampton was another place where lime burning for agriculture took place. L. T. C. Rolt moored at Hampton aboard *Cressy* for a month in the summer of 1947, having been thwarted in an attempt to reach Pontcysyllte.

ENCHANTING Ellesmere embraces the canal which it once gave its name to with the enthusiasm of a doting aunt, a perfume-bosomed response to the commerce it continues to bring to the community coffers two centuries after its conception. Yes, it's worth recalling that what we know glibly as the Llangollen Canal is a term which would be unfamiliar to the canal's promoters. For historically this was the Ellesmere Canal, an ambitious attempt to link the rivers Mersey, Dee and Severn with a main line from Chester to Shrewsbury. In the event, only the Pontcysyllte-Weston Lullingfields section was ever built with, from Welsh Frankton (Map 23), branches to Llanymynech and Ellesmere itself. As it became apparent that the intended main line of the canal would never reach the Dee or Severn, the Ellesmere Canal Company cut a canal eastwards from Ellesmere

to meet the Chester Canal near Nantwich. Hurleston was reached in the year of Trafalgar: two things to celebrate!

Forty years later the Ellesmere Canal amalgamated with the Chester Canal and the new Birmingham & Liverpool Junction Canal to form the Shropshire Union Railways & Canal Company. The route from Hurleston to Llangollen was known as the 'Welsh Section'.

continued overleaf:

Key ◯
1 former rennet works
2 canal warehouse
3 site of cheese factory
4 site of munitions dump
'Passengers No More'
1: Ellesmere - closed 18.1.65

1: Blackwater Marina
ABC Boat Hire

Colemere
Colemere Country Park
Cole Mere
Clarepool Moss
Newton Mere
Welshampton
Newton
Oteley Hall
Moscow Island
The Mere
Town Centre
Ellesmere (see enlargement - page 76)
Castle Mound
Tesco
school
business park
Ellesmere College
Birch Hall
The Lyth
Ellesmere Tunnel 87 yards
Blake Mere
monastery
canal w'shops
Tetchill
Winston Lodges
Val Hill
Grinshill
The Wrekin
Broome Farm
Breiddens
Shropshire Way
Newnes

A528 to Shrewsbury
A528 to Wrexham
A495 to Oswestry
A495 to Whitchurch
A495
B5068 to St Martin's

(S) = 🗑 ♨ 🚽 WC for details of facilities at Ellesmere turn to page 76

54 55 56 58 59 60 61 62 63 64 65 66 67 70' 70'

NORTH

21

23

Blake Mere

Canal Workshops, Ellesmere

The term 'Llangollen Canal' didn't gain general currency until the Canal & River Trust's nationalised predecessors, British Waterways, published a quaint little cruising guide under that title in 1956.

Ellesmere became the headquarters of the canal and the company built imposing offices, which became known as Beech House, quite possibly on account of the copper beech trees either side of the entrance drive was Edward Wilson's eminently plausible theory in his seminal book of 1975, *The Ellesmere and Llangollen Canal*. These premises still preside over the canal junction, though used residentially for many years now, CRT being confined to the charmingly higgledy-piggledy maintenance base next door. Much of the infrastructure of this facility dates back to the earliest years of the canal. Particularly notable is the handsome stone drydock with distinctive weathervane in the shape of a narrowboat atop its slate roof. Workshops of timber and stone construction include a joiner's shop, blacksmith's forge and pattern store where wooden templates used for making accurate moulds for iron castings are kept; though, alas, rarely if ever used. Lock gate manufacture ceased at Ellesmere in 1961. An illuminating account of one man's working life at the yard appeared in *Narrow Boat* magazine's Winter 2011/12 issue.

Opposite Beech House a short arm leads to the town wharf. Just under the cast iron footbridge which spans the arm a boathouse stood at an oblique angle on the off-side. Of two storeys, with a hay loft, it's exact significance has been lost in the mists of time, and it was regrettably demolished in 1951.

For most of its life the arm was overlooked by industrial premises that had originally been opened as an ironworks, but which later became a dairy. Housing has replaced all that lost industry, and together with a Tesco supermarket, the feel is faintly suburban. In the midst of this transformation a Shropshire Union warehouse stands disorientated, like a pensioner attending a rave. Plans have been submitted for a complex of retirement homes bordering the offside of the arm. Thankfully, they include refurbishment of the warehouse. Moorings are at a premium on the arm in summer.

East of Ellesmere the Llangollen Canal undertakes a hauntingly lovely journey through Shropshire's own 'lakeland'. There are seven lakes, or meres in the neighbourhood of Ellesmere without inflow or outflow. They were formed at the end of the Ice Age, 10,000 years ago, as the great glaciers retreated and melted waters collected in cups of the land. The meres support a resident population of birds including kingfishers, herons, grebe, Canada geese, coots and moorhens. In winter there's an influx of wildfowl. On hot late summer evenings the phenomenon of 'breaking' occurs, as algae rise from the depths to spread a deep blue green veil upon the surface. Cole Mere (used by a sailing club, and the only place in England where the rare Least Water Lily grows wild) and Blake Mere both lie beside the canal, the latter only separated from the waterway by a narrow belt of trees which provide shade for picnics on warm summer days. Forget the helter-skelter rush towards Llangollen, this is one of the true highlights of the canal, a place to linger, unwind and find a real sense of peace. The unique charm of the meres was evoked in Mary Webb's 1926 novel *Precious Bane*. The little Monastery of Our Lady & St Joseph by Ellesmere Tunnel is home to an order of Poor Clare Colettines.

Westwards, the canal rapidly escapes into empty countryside, skirting the playing fields of Ellesmere College, a Woodard school opened in 1884. Canon Nathaniel Woodard (1811-1891) founded eleven eponymous schools, including Lancing, Hurstpierpoint and Ardingly in the south, and Worksop, Denstone and Ellesmere in the north. Amongst the college's alumni is Bill Beaumont, captain of the English Rugby Union team 1979-82. Edward Wilson, author of *The Ellesmere and Llangollen Canal*, was Senior Biology Master at the school for over twenty years.

The towpath hereabouts has been designated as part of the Shropshire Way, though is not particularly well maintained. Val Hill sounds like a fourth-former you might have been so smitten with as to etch her name

Ellesmere Wharf

on your pencil case. But in fact it's a tree-topped glacial mound picturesquely forcing the canal into an extra bend or two on its way to Welsh Frankton. Workmen, mending a fence on the slopes of the hill in the 1890s, uncovered a Bronze Age sword in two halves, obligingly reunited for posterity by the local blacksmith. A public footpath (part of the Shropshire Way) leads from Bridge 63 to Welsh Frankton more directly than the canal. It is a pity that it doesn't cross the summit of Val Hill, because the views from there must be terrific. As it is, even from the canal you can see Grinshill in the middle distance to the south-east and, much further away in reducing chromatic tones, the A. E. Housmanesque outlines of The Wrekin, the Clee Hills, Wenlock Edge; the Caradocs and the Long Mynd.

ELLESMERE MAP 22

Ellesmere is an increasingly rare find: a small, unspoilt country town with no pretensions. Life seems as slowly lived here as the rhythmic lapping of waters on the shores of the meres. Visitors - whether they come by car to feed the ducks, or by boat along the Llangollen Canal - are assimilated without the usual symptomatic rash of tourist paraphernalia. The local economy has traditionally been an agricultural one, though in the past there was an ironworks, an important railway junction, canal workshops and a rennet factory. Worryingly, like resting thespians, some of these buildings are in need of new roles and the local powers that be seem reluctant or clueless how to achieve this. But what the visitor sees today is a late 19th century country town preserved almost in aspic, and all very endearing it is too. There is so much to see and do that only CRT's time limits (72 hours on the arm) curtail an increasing desire to stay put. Early risers get the town and its environs to themselves and can walk into the past with impunity. Go and pay homage to the substantial old railway station before it crumbles beyond redemption. The station master John Hood was sacked in 1892 for standing up to the Cambrian Railways unfair dismissal of a porter. Questions were raised in Parliament and Ellesmere's inhabitants collected enough money for Hood to buy a house which he lived in until he died, never rejoining the railway. If your inclination is for more rural climes, take the path which leaves the towpath half way between Ellesmere Tunnel and Bridge 58. It leads to woodland cared for by the Plantation Wood Ellesmere Charity which was used for allotments during the Second World War. Thence you can find your way to The Mere before the rest of the world has woken up. How satisfying to have it briefly to yourself.

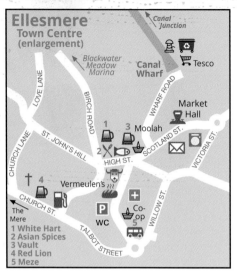

Ellesmere Town Centre (enlargement)

1 White Hart
2 Asian Spices
3 Vault
4 Red Lion
5 Meze

Eating & Drinking

ASIAN SPICES - Birch Road. Tel: 01691 623689. Indian restaurant/take-away from 5pm (ex Mon). SY12 0ET
THE BOAT HOUSE - Mereside. Tel: 01691 623852. Mereside cafe. Open Thur-Mon from 9am-4.30pm for breakfasts, coffees, lunches and teas. SY12 0PA
MEZE - Cross Street. Tel 01691 622660. Authentic Greek/Cypriot restaurant open Wed-Sun from 5pm and Sun 1.30-9.30pm. Take-aways too. SY12 0AW
RED LION - Church Street. Tel: 01691 622632. Thwaites pub en route to Mere. Food served throughout. Accommodation. SY12 0HD
VAULT - Scotland Street. Tel: 01691 239324. Atmospheric cellar bar in the basement of the imposing old Town Hall. Open Wed & Thur from 4pm, 3pm Fri, and from 1pm weekends. SY12 0DE

WHITE HART - Birch Road. Tel: 01691 624653. Half-timbered ale house specialising in for the most part locally sourced beers. SY12 0ET

Shopping

A substantial Tesco supermarket overlooks the canal wharf, absolving shoppers of any real need to patronise the town's traditional retailers. But to venture no further would represent a failure of responsibility and a lost opportunity, for Ellesmere boasts some fine independent shops, the acme of which is Vermeulen's delicatessen on Cross Street (Tel: 01691 622521) by the town square. Their pork pies - often still warm to the touch by mid-morning - are amongst our favourites on the inland waterways, whilst the cold counter contains a mouthwatering array of glazed meats, pates, shellfish and cheeses. A relative newcomer is Moolah (Tel: 01691 623532). Housed in a former bank on Scotland Street, it's billed as a 'local food shop and cafe bar'. The indoor market, housed in a handsome Victorian pile operates on Tuesdays. Thursday is half day. There is a Post Office on Scotland Street and a useful launderette on Victoria Street.

Self-Catering

ABC offer self-catering for up to six people in an apartment at Blackwater Marina - Tel: 0330 333 0590. WINSTON LODGES provide s/c accommodation by Bridge 65. Tel: 01691 622316. SY12 9BA

Connections

BUSES - Arriva service 53 runs to/from Oswestry (ex Sun) and in doing so provides a link with the nearest railhead at Gobowen. Towpath walkers may like to note that it crosses the canal at Bridge 13w, Map 24. Lakeside 449 also runs to/from Oswestry, but via Whittington, crossing the canal at Bridge 5w, Map 23. Lakeside 501 connects Ellesmere with Shrewsbury. TAXIS - Oswestry Cabs. Tel: 01691 661663.

OUT in the middle of the middle of nowhere, Welsh Frankton, or Frankton Junction, was the hub of the Ellesmere canal system. From two junctions in the form of an H, routes radiated to Pontcysyllte, Ellesmere, Weston Lullingfields (the intended main line to Shrewsbury) and Llanymynech. The canal continued onwards from there as the Montgomeryshire Canal through Welshpool to Newtown. This route, amounting to some 35 miles, is now known as the Montgomery Canal. In 1936 a breach occurred where the canal crossed the River Perry by aqueduct (Map 27) and the LMS Railway, who owned the canal, chose not to repair it, stranding the last carrier, George Beck, in the process. Eight years later the canal was legally abandoned. In the ensuing fifty years the Montgomery Canal might well have decayed irredeemably had not its scenic splendour been recognised as the canals underwent a revival for pleasure use. Frankton Locks were restored in 1987 but stood idle for almost ten years, until a further restoration project - involving construction of a new lock named after

the heroic founder of the Waterway Recovery Group - allowed boats to reach Perry Aqueduct. Gradually, navigability has been extended to Gronwen Wharf, beyond Maesbury Marsh, and by 2023 is expected to have reached Crickheath Wharf. Indeed, over half the waterway's thirty-five miles have (more or less) been restored, as described in the text accompanying Maps 27 to 34.

The canalscape at Frankton is typically self-effacing. Pretty enough with its lock flight, but it's not until you begin to poke about a bit that fragments of the past percolate through.
continued overleaf:

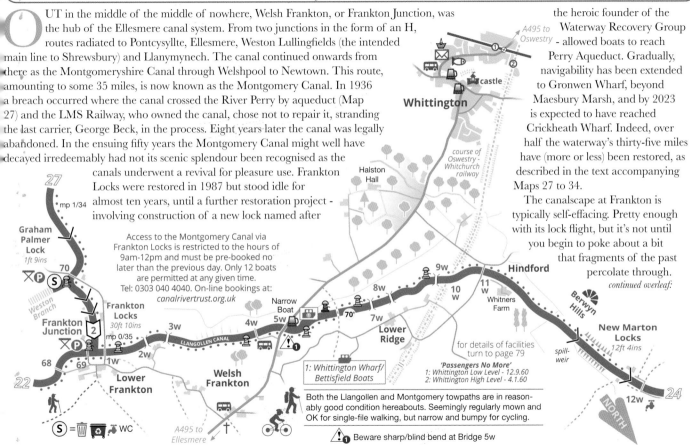

Access to the Montgomery Canal via Frankton Locks is restricted to the hours of 9am-12pm and must be pre-booked no later than the previous day. Only 12 boats are permitted at any given time. Tel: 0303 040 4040. On-line bookings at: *canalrivertrust.org.uk*

1: Whittington Wharf/ Bettisfield Boats

for details of facilities turn to page 79

'Passengers No More'
1: Whittington Low Level - 12.9.60
2: Whittington High Level - 4.1.60

Both the Llangollen and Montgomery towpaths are in reasonably good condition hereabouts. Seemingly regularly mown and OK for single-file walking, but narrow and bumpy for cycling.

⚠1 Beware sharp/blind bend at Bridge 5w

*1ml/5lks on Montgomery Canal - allow 1½ hours

continued from page 77:

No sign of the warehouse and crane which stood where cars now park by Bridge 69; no toll clerk in the check house by the top chamber; no banter from the Canal Tavern at the foot of the staircase, though the curious steps and an iron bar are tangible reminders. A plaque at the tail of the third lock down recalls that L. T. C. Rolt's *Cressy* was converted into a leisure craft at Beech's boat dock in 1929; the dock and workshops lined the lock. *Cressy* had been purchased by an uncle of Rolt's from Peates Mill (see Map 28), having originally been built by the Shropshire Union Canal Carrying Company at Trevor during the First World War. As well as adding extra accommodation, Beech's

Sticking to the Main Line at Frankton Junction

installed a vertical compound steam engine, for hitherto *Cressy* had been horse-drawn. Rolt accompanied his uncle on the refurbished boat's maiden voyage to Barlaston, on the Trent & Mersey south of Stoke-on-Trent, one misty morning in March 1930. With such memories to assimilate, Frankton makes a good spot to moor overnight. It is not only activity on the canal that has vanished: up the lane the former Free Church chapel of 1890 stands skeletally strangled by trees.

Meanwhile, the Llangollen Canal - whose bridge numbers begin again at '1', albeit with the appended suffix 'w' (just in case you thought you'd dozed off and assumed you were back at Hurleston) - traverses a low shelf above the valley of the Perry. The Berwyn and Breidden hills of the Border Marches rise up in the west; benignly blue or intimidatingly black according to weather conditions. At Hindford the Cambrian Railways line crosses the canal again (or at least it did until 1965) and the Vyrnwy Aqueduct passes invisibly beneath the canal, conveying water supplies to Liverpool. Hindford used to be a popular place to moor, though not seemingly enough to save the Jack Mytton pub from closure. At the neighbouring T junction an old signpost points intriguingly to a place called "Iron Mills". Nearby Halston Hall owes much of its architecture to Robert Mylne (of whom more on Map 27) and was the home of John 'Mad Jack' Mytton who was born at Halston with a silver spoon in his mouth in 1797, but died in a debtor's prison thirty seven years later. During a brief life largely devoted to debauchery, he was in the habit of holding up departing guests on the Oswestry road in the guise of a highwayman.

New Marton locks provide the boater with some not unwelcome exercise, though they can be as prone to queues as Grindley Brook when they have a mind to be. Westbound they are the last to be encountered; eastbound it is some twenty miles to the next one: so be inclined to take delays in your stride.

WHITTINGTON   MAP 23

Situated two miles west of the canal on what used to be the A5 London-Holyhead road. The red brick 18th century church is notable for its tracery and Jesse window. 'Sumptuous Victorian Lombardic' according to Piper and Betjeman. They came here (by train) in 1939 to research *Shropshire - A Shell Guide*, though war delayed publication until 1951. Piper had time, between sporadic trains, to sketch Low Level station.

Eating & Drinking

NARROW BOAT - canalside Bridge 5w. Tel: 01691 661051. Purpose-built in 1981 by the owners of the adjacent boatyard. Food served lunchtimes daily, dinner served (from 6pm) Tue-Sat. SY11 4NU *Two other pubs (Olde Boote - Tel: 01691 662250 and White Lion - Tel: 01691 662361) and fish & chips (Tel: 01691 654220) in village centre.*

Shopping

Premier post office stores in village centre.

Things to Do

WHITTINGTON CASTLE - Tel: 01691 662500 Remains of a 13th century castle (pictured here) under the care of the local community. The grounds are always open, but the tea room and shop are from 10am-4pm Wed to Sun. SY11 4DF

Connections

BUSES - Lakeside service 449 operates Mon-Sat to/from Ellesmere and Oswestry (there is a stop beside the Narrowboat Inn at Bridge 5w).

Bridge 19, Wrenbury (Map 18)

Hurleston Top Lock (Map 17)

Beech House, Ellesmere (Map 22)

Whixall Moss (Map 20)

Chirk Bank (Map 24)

Llangollen Horse-boat (Map 26)

Grindley Brook 'Staircase' (Map 19)

SHROPSHIRE'S soft farmlands give way to the rugged mountains of Wales. Well, at least if you're journeying westwards they do. Not that eastbound travellers must brace themselves for an anticlimax. On the contrary, the Llangollen Canal keeps delightful surprises up its sleeve whichever direction you are going in.

St Martin's Moor is low-lying and cross-hatched by drainage dykes. On the horizon to the north stands St Martin's 13th century parish church. Its substantial tower reminded Michael Moulder of the Cotswolds in his 1973 Shell Guide. A far cry from Coventry Cathedral, the village's school was designed by Basil Spence in the 1950s. Thought of as part of the Denbighshire coalfield, Ifton Colliery (1913-68) was the largest in Shropshire, employing thirteen hundred men in its heyday. The mineral line from the pit head to the exchange sidings at Weston Rhyn was steeply graded, and trains officially limited to ten loaded wagons. Imagine the din as one of the mine's internal Hudswell Clarke tank engines, *Richboro* (formerly of a dock

on the Kent coast) or *Unity*, crossed the canal at Rhoswiel on the ferocious ascent to the main line.

Beyond Bridge 13w (where one or two buildings betray their canal heritage) the countryside becomes hilly and wooded. Two extensive country properties have experienced different fates: Henlle Hall is a holiday centre and golf course; Moreton Hall a girls school whose playing fields border the canal. As the canal approaches Chirk it passes the sites of a number of long forgotten basins linked to early coal mines (Preesgwyn, Trehowell, Quinta et al) by primitive tramways. A marshy field betrays scant remains of Gledrid Wharf where the originally horse-drawn Glyn Valley Tramway connected with the canal prior to

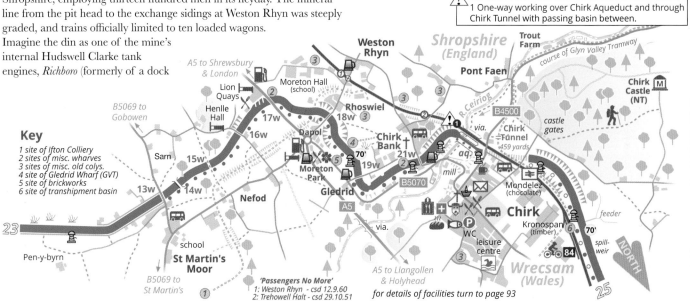

1 One-way working over Chirk Aqueduct and through Chirk Tunnel with passing basin between.

Key

1 site of Ifton Colliery
2 sites of misc. wharves
3 sites of misc. old colys.
4 site of Gledrid Wharf (GVT)
5 site of brickworks
6 site of transhipment basin

'Passengers No More'
1: Weston Rhyn - csd 12.9.60
2: Trehowell Halt - csd 29.10.51

for details of facilities turn to page 93

being converted to steam haulage and redirected to Chirk. At Bridge 19w the canal assumes World Heritage Site status all the way through to Horseshoe Falls (Map 26). A profusely illustrated and well researched handbook, written by Peter Wakelin and published by the Canal & River Trust and Royal Commission on the Ancient & Historical Monuments of Wales, is obtainable from Trevor Basin Visitor Centre.

Chirk Bank was a busy canal centre up until the 1920s. Employed on maintenance duties in the 1950s, previously encountered Jack Roberts was housed in one of the aqueduct cottages, and British Waterways built him a small stable for his boat horse from corrugated iron which still stands. His wife, however, didn't take to Chirk Bank, because the high trees on the offside meant that the house received hardly any sunshine. Nothing has changed in that respect, but apart from one sadly derelict cottage, the others remain occupied and obviously well cared for.

British border crossings don't come much more dramatic than the canal's entry into Chirk. Only the Royal Border Bridge at Berwick can match the excitement of crossing from England to Wales (or vice versa) seventy feet up in the air above the rushing River Ceiriog. Solely the fact that you no longer arrive in Denbighshire subtracts - in our trenchant opinion - from the magic spell. Incidentally, the border follows the original course of the river, for it seems likely that the canal builders altered the Ceiriog's course to avoid the potential for flood damage.

A certain amount of gentlemanly debate centred on exactly how and where the canal would cross the Ceiriog Valley. William Jessop, in a report dated 14th July 1795, wrote: 'It was originally proposed to cross the Chirk (sic) Valley a little above Chirk Bridge, but following an objection by the owner of the land (Richard Myddleton) the line was altered to cross at Pont Faen.' In the event, a course between those two bridges was compromised upon, and Chirk Aqueduct was completed at the end of 1801: 696ft long and 70ft high, consisting of an iron trough carried upon ten arches. In Telford's words: 'there is no earth or puddle made use of; the waterway is formed with a cast iron bottom, and square masonry on the sides; the spandrels of the arches are hollow.' By the way, Chirk Bridge - on what is now known as the B5070, but previously the A5, is Telford's work as well, and according to a plaque on its northern parapet, dates from 1793.

Whatever the Myddletons finally thought of the visual intrusion to their land, the aqueduct was widely accepted as a romantic addition to the landscape, and spanned the Ceiriog valley in splendid isolation for the best part of half a century until a railway arrived on the scene. We used, blithely, to inform Canal Companion users that the watercolourist John Sell Cotman had painted a view of the aqueduct in all its early glory. Indeed, it was believed he had, and it hung in the Victoria & Albert Museum, only for an art historian to declare that the subject was Crambe Beck Bridge near Kirkham in Yorkshire on the road from York to Malton. The past, like a fresh-faced, corduroy-jacketed graduate teacher, marching into class eager to redefine the syllabus, is always rewriting itself. *continued overleaf:*

continued from page 91:

The Shrewsbury & Chester Railway burst onto the scene in 1848, becoming part of the GWR's main line from Paddington to Birkenhead. Designed by Henry Robertson - another of those ubiquitous Scottish engineers who seemed to wander about the world erecting lasting monuments to their endeavours - construction of a rival structure in such close proximity might have been expected to mar the impact of the aqueduct, but in fact the second bridge only served to enhance the setting and drama of the first. From whichever angle you consider their juxtaposition, these two great structures seem to form an homogeneous whole and share such a unity within the landscape that the border would now be inconceivable and significantly less dramatic without them. How pleasant it is to loiter on the aqueduct's railed towpath, gazing up the Ceiriog Valley framed by Robertson's Romanesque arches, whilst spring lambs cavort in the meadows below. We shall encounter another of the indefatigable Scot's railway bridges on the next map, the former home of his siblings at Llangollen, and his chain bridge at Berwyn, but those with an interest in railways and engineering generally, may be interested to learn that he was, in 1854, co-founder of the word famous Manchester locomotive building firm of Beyer Peacock.

At the north end of the aqueduct a broad, and increasingly tree masked pool (where boats frequently jostle (not always courteously) while waiting for the aqueduct or tunnel to clear) leads to Chirk Tunnel, 459 yards long with a cantilevered towpath running through; with typical altruism, Telford considered the hitherto established practice of 'legging' by boatmen to be dangerous and undignified. Pedestrians may find it useful to carry a torch with them through the tunnel - or, of course, these days, a smartphone! The tunnel was constructed on the 'cut and fill' principal. Was it really necessary? Wouldn't a lengthier cutting have provided an equally viable solution? Perhaps the Myddletons

intervened again. Plus ca change: HS2 tunnels beneath parts of the Chilterns for environmental and aesthetic motives.

Beyond the bosky northern portal of Chirk Tunnel the canal penetrates a densely wooded cutting of some magnitude. There are visitor moorings, but television and/or mobile phone reception is patchy. At its far end a winding hole marks the site of a former transhipment wharf between the canal, the collieries at Black Park and Brynkinhalt, and the narrow gauge Glyn Valley Tramway. What a loss this charming line became when competition from lorries and buses precipitated its downfall in 1935. Built to serve mines and quarries at the head of the Ceiriog Valley, it also carried passengers. In *Landscape With Machines*, L. T. C. Rolt describes 'swaying and rattling down a steep gradient through thick woods to the floor of the valley at Pontfaen' on visits to his uncle at Glyn Ceiriog. Perhaps the experience may one day be repeatable, for two separate groups have enthusiastic ambitions of resurrecting the GVT, initially through interpretation, but eventually by re-laying as much of the track as feasible.

The Afon Bradley feeder enters the canal on the offside, a compensating overflow follows. The site of Bottom Wharf, which served Black Park Colliery, is marked by a winding hole. Peter Wakelin's book contains a splendid doublespread of a boat (crewed, apparently, by a pair of waifs) waiting to load at this point circa 1910. No discernible trace remains of the side-bridge which spanned the entrance to the wharf's twin arms; nor, alas, of the GVT narrow gauge rails embedded in the towpath, let alone the tell-tale horse dung of the vessel's out of picture motive power. Back in the present, the railway draws alongside. Look out for Transport for Wales expresses - as pictured on the previous page - linking Cardiff with Holyhead, rare beasts these days with their restaurant cars.

CHIRK

MAP 24

Anxious to push on to Pontcysyllte, many boaters fail to visit Chirk. Their loss, because the village centre is not without a certain intrinsic charm. The parish church of St Mary's boasts a double-aisled interior, lending it the air of a small cathedral. The poet R. S. Thomas was a curate here in the late 1930s. South of the extensive churchyard lie the remains of a motte and bailey castle. At the intersection of Station Avenue and Church Street stands an imposing war memorial of Portland stone carved by sculptor and typographer Eric Gill. Look out for the wrought iron sculpture depicting a boat and train on the bridges on the park gate opposite, and the plaque commemorating Billy Meredith, born here in 1874, the 'wing wizard' who won the Welsh Cup with Chirk FC and went on to play for both Manchester clubs and his country on many occasions. Once almost exclusively a mining community, Chirk is now dominated by the Mondelez (formerly Cadbury) hot chocolate factory and the adjoining vast Kronospan works where timber - brought in by train from Scotland, mid Wales and Devon - is turned into panels for the construction industry. Still on a railway theme, Dapol, the model railway company, have their headquarters (and a shop - Tel: 01691 774455) at Gledrid Industrial Park.

Eating & Drinking

BRIDGE INN - Tel: 01691 773213. Billed as the 'Last pub in England', but nicknamed 'The Trap' this homely pub - just down from Bridge 21w - opens at noon and serves food throughout, (ex Sun eves). LL14 5BU

CAFFI WYLFA - Castle Road. Tel: 01691 770492. Friendly community run cafe open 9.30am-5pm daily (sometimes later in summer). LL14 5B

CASTLE BISTRO - Church Street. Tel: 01691 239133. Excellent eaterie open 10am-9pm daily. LL14 5EZ

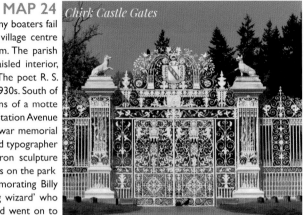

Chirk Castle Gates

CASTLE TANDOORI - Station Avenue. Tel: 01691 772499. Smartly furnished village centre Indian restaurant open from 5pm daily. LL14 5LS

THE HAND HOTEL - Church Street. Tel: 01691 773472. Coaching inn which has long been catering for travellers on Telford's Holyhead road. LL14 5EY

LION QUAYS - canalside Bridge 17w. Tel: 01691 684300. Hotel and conference centre thoughtfully providing moorings for boating patrons. SY11 3EN

LORD MORETON - Tel: 01691 778888. Bar/restaurant, part of the Moreton Park complex best reached from Bridge 19w. LL14 5DG

THE POACHERS - canalside Bridge19w. Tel: 01691 773250. Marston's 'Rotisserie'. LL14 5DG

PLOUGH INN - Station Road, Weston Rhyn. Tel: 01691 772536. Village local about half a mile's walk west from Bridge 18w. SY10 7SX

Self-catering

BELMONT BRIDGE - self-catering by Bridge 16w. Tel 0797 782 0978. SY10 7SX

Shopping

Jamie Ward's butchers offer a wide range of locally sourced produce, and are particularly well known for their home made sausage and dry cured bacon: delicious pork pies and sausage rolls as well. The village also supports Gerrards bakery, Hughes fruit & veg, a pharmacy, and a capacious Spar with a post office and ATM. Dobbies Moreton Park garden centre (accessed via Bridge 19w) offers a wide range of shopping opportunities, including Sainsbury's products. Chirk Trout Farm (Tel: 01691 773101) lies about a mile west of the canal on the B4500. Open Mon-Fri 9am-5pm and Sat 10am to 4pm, they sell their own fish produce together with cheese, eggs, pies and cakes and charming postcards of the GVT.

Things to Do

CHIRK CASTLE - Just over a mile from the north end of the tunnel. Tel: 01691 777701. Probably the best way of accessing the castle for canal users on foot (recommended by Canal Companion correspondent, Richard Carden, of Harleston, Norfolk) is via a public footpath which leaves the road about a hundred yards north of the impressive castle gates. Over seven hundred years of history and habitation to soak up. Open March-October, Wed-Sun, 10am-6pm. National Trust shop, restaurant. Admission charge. LL14 5AF

CHIRK LEISURE & ACTIVITY CENTRE - Chapel Lane. Tel: 01691 778666. Swimming pool etc. LL14 5NF

Connections

BUSES - Tanat Valley service 64 Mon-Fri to/from Llangollen (via Froncysyllte) and Glyn Ceiriog. Arriva services 2/2A to/from Oswestry and Wrexham half-hourly Mon-Sat, hourly Sun.

TRAINS - Transport for Wales services to/from Chester, Wrexham and Holyhead, and Shrewsbury, Cardiff and Birmingham.

TAXIS - B&L. Tel: 01691 776444.

WHITEHOUSES Tunnel ushers the canal into Offa's Dyke country, and the towpath is suddenly swollen by walkers on the long distance footpath of that name. Boater and walker alike are treated to a compelling passage through a mask of woodland on a shelf above the River Dee. Given the right conditions, the delicious aroma of pinewood fills the air. Between the ivy clad boles of the tall trees there are glimpses of the impressive Dee or Cefn Bychan railway viaduct. Consisting of nineteen arches, it stands 148 feet above the river at its highest point, and like the viaduct at Chirk, was designed by Henry Robertson. Old maps show just how many railways, or tramways, either competed with the canal or connected with it. The Great Western's Fron Branch paralleled the canal, initially on the towpath side, before passing beneath the canal via a stone-built aqueduct; traces of the turntables, laboriously employed to manhandle wagons through right-angles may still be discerned.

On the outskirts of Froncysyllte the former Pen-y-Graig limekilns recall what was once a hive of industry alongside the canal. What hectic scenes of activity were once enacted here, though they would have largely quietened down before

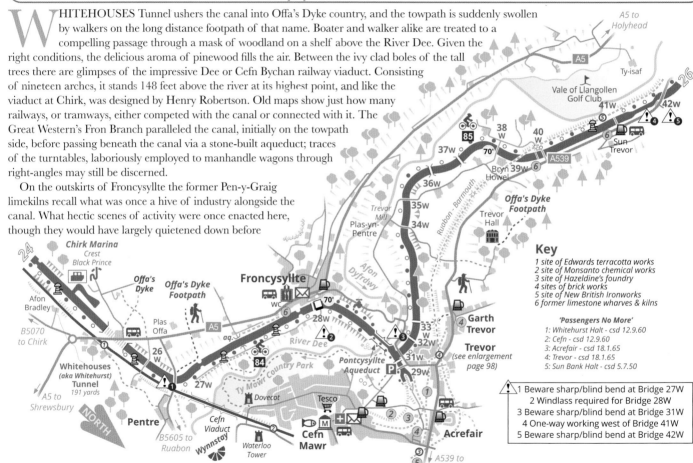

Key

1 site of Edwards terracotta works
2 site of Monsanto chemical works
3 site of Hazeldine's foundry
4 sites of brick works
5 site of New British Ironworks
6 former limestone wharves & kilns

'Passengers No More'
1: Whitehurst Halt - csd 12.9.60
2: Cefn - csd 12.9.60
3: Acrefair - csd 18.1.65
4: Trevor - csd 18.1.65
5: Sun Bank Halt - csd 5.7.50

1 Beware sharp/blind bend at Bridge 27W
2 Windlass required for Bridge 28W
3 Beware sharp/blind bend at Bridge 31W
4 One-way working west of Bridge 41W
5 Beware sharp/blind bend at Bridge 42W

he writer, artist and social historian, Dorothy Hartley, moved into Fron House (overlooking Bridge 28w) in 1933. She must have found the neighbourhood conducive, because she remained here until her death at the age of 92 in 1985. *Food in England* was arguably her best known book, and it is still much revered, but a companion piece of perhaps more appeal to canallers was entitled *Water in England*. Dorothy's devotees - of which there are increasingly, not to say, belatedly many - can make a pilgrimage to her grave, which lies with that of her maternal grandfather, Walter Eddy, amongst the bluebells and primroses of St David's churchyard (right hand side beyond interpretive board). Miss Hartley befriended the Rolts during their three month sojourn aboard *Cressy* at Trevor in 1949, showering them with vegetables from her garden. Lucy Worsley made a documentary about Dorothy for BBC4 in 2013.

Footbridge 28Aw enables those in a rush to cross the canal if the adjoining lift-bridge (plain 28w) has been raised for a boat to pass. Despite its apparent decrepitude, it's a mid-20th century addition. Clearly, in the past, pedestrians were able to exercise more patience. It seems plausible that its neighbour was the mystery bridge encountered by a youthful Jonathan Meades in 1956, as recounted in *An Encylopedia of Myself*; a structure he years later 'half-heartedly searched for and failed to find'. What is more certain, is that this was the Van Gogh-like drawbridge where L. T. C. Rolt witnessed a troupe of Spanish dancers and musicians provide the natives of 'Fron' with an impromptu performance. They were, it transpired, contestants at the Llangollen International Eisteddfod, temporarily residing in the village.

Superlatives are superfluous when it comes to describing Pontcysyllte Aqueduct, approached upon huge earthworks amassed with spoil extracted from the cutting at Chirk. Sacrilege in certain circles, but a bit of judicious tree surgery wouldn't go amiss. Trees planted to stablilise the embankment have a tendency to overpower it visually now. There are paths on either side, linked by a pedestrian tunnel at the aqueduct end of the embankment.

World Heritage Site status ensures that there is no element of surprise concerning the advent of the aqueduct - accolades can be counter-productive - yet it still has the power to take the breath away. Lilian Hayward, writing her walking column for the *Shropshire Chronicle*, and fresh from an encounter with the Rolts, had to be escorted across the structure by a kindly workman, far too scared to look at the bird's eye view of the Dee he was urging her to admire. In *Wild Wales*, written in 1854, George Borrow found the experience of walking across the aqueduct 'awful', though one wonders if he meant to write 'awesome'. His guide, a local weaver who had once been a mountain shepherd, confessed that: "It gives me the pendro, sir, to look down." Borrow, an East Anglian, had gamely insisted on a solely Welsh-speaking companion, and pendro translates to dizziness in English.

It isn't easy for mere Anglo-Saxons to get their teeth around its knotty consonants, but something approximating to 'Pont-ker-sulth-tee' should avoid embarrassment; though some espouse 'tay' for the final syllable. The bare, good old imperial, facts are that it is over 1,000 feet long, 127 feet tall at its deepest point, and consists of an iron trough supported by 18 stone piers. The aqueduct was completed in 1805, the year of Nelson's death at Trafalgar. Four hundred and fifty-eight 'Englishmen' perished at Trafalgar, but only one life was lost in construction of the aqueduct; a misfortune attributed to a moment of carelessness.

Pontcysyllte had been ten years in the making, so it seemed appropriate to celebrate. A flotilla of boats crossed from the southern end. The leader containing bigwigs (no change there then!); the second canal officials; the third a military band playing patriotic airs; the remainder, personages of diminishing importance. The last two boats were earmarked to return with the first two cargoes of coal from the collieries at Plas Kynaston. As the leading vessel began its traverse of the aqueduct, the Shropshire Volunteers fired fifteen rounds from a pair of cannon captured at the Siege of Seringapatam which, as all historians will gleefully tell you, marked the end of the Fourth Anglo-Mysore War

continued overleaf:

The towpath has been surfaced throughout the World Heritage Site, i.e. all the way from Bridge 19w at Gledrid (Map 24) to Horseshoe Falls (Map 26) and is thus in excellent condition for walking and cycling alike.

in 1799. Eight thousand spectators cheered. In other words, about twice as many as Wrexham AFC's seasonal average. While the coal was being loaded, the dignitaries partook of a cold collation and listened to an oration, before returning.

Along with the Menai Suspension Bridge, Pontcysyllte is ranked among Telford's outstanding achievements. But in his final book, *Thomas Telford's Temptation*, the eminent canal historian, Charles Hadfield, felt that posterity had emphasised Telford's contribution at the expense of William Jessop's; the latter being, after all, the Ellesmere Canal Company's Engineer, whereas Telford was merely its General Agent. Didn't we caution you about the past on the previous map? Personally, we'd be loathe to traduce Telford: perish the thought that one day Mr Pearson's life's work might be reattributed to his deadly rival. Whoever you prefer to credit, this remarkable act of civil engineering was contemporaneously dubbed 'the stream in the sky', and fulfils that description in the minds of awestruck spectators to this day. Incidentally, just as Chirk Aqueduct finally materialised in a somewhat different form to that initially conceived, so, early in its conception, it was suggested

that Pontcysyllte be erected at a lower height, reached, at either end by a flight of locks, though Jessop quickly realised that this would create severe water supply difficulties.

Beyond Trevor, the plan was for the canal to have carried on over the neighbouring ridge and then down through Wrexham to the Dee at Chester. Such a course would have required many locks, a very long tunnel or a series of boat lifts. The enormity of this undertaking, coupled with the recession which occurred as an aftermath to the Napoleonic Wars, thwarted the Ellesmere Canal Company's plans to provide a direct canal between the Mersey and the Severn.

In place of the envisaged main line northwards, the canal beyond the aqueduct passed through Bridge 29w and terminated at a twin-armed transhipment wharf from where, first a tramway, then later a railway, connected with quarries and collieries on the higher ground towards Ruabon. A substantial warehouse, with water access, stood at the tip of the easternmost arm, but was demolished in the 1920s. A pity that it could not have still been extant to provide a centrepiece for the redevelopment masterplan announced in 2020, whereby Trevor,

Acrefair and Cefn Mawr will be awoken from their post-industrial trance into a 'world class tourist destination'. Not without a certain amount of trepidation, one waits to see how such lofty ambitions manifest themselves, if indeed they ever do.

Meanwhile, back in the more inherently interesting mists of time, yet another arm - known as the Plas Kynaston Canal - described an arc to the east serving chemical, terracotta and iron works in the vicinity. It was at Plas Kynaston that the ironmaster, William Hazeldine, cast the arches and trough for Pontcysyllte Aqueduct. In the Ellesmere Canal's commercial heyday much traffic was generated in the neighbourhood. Trefynant Fireclay Works was one of the most notable industries. Owned by James Coster Edwards, the business grew to merit being described as the 'largest and most successful manufacturer of terracotta in the world'. On the back of such success, Edwards erected a mansion for himself beside the canal at Bryn Howel (Bridge 38w). The works closed in 1965, but you can still pay homage to the entrance gates - decorated with terracotta, naturally - on Llangollen Road, the A539.

A canal to Llangollen was not in the original scheme of things. Only when it became clear that the main line would never be completed did the company decide to provide a feeder from the River Dee at Llantysilio to the canal at Trevor. The cutting of a canal along the steep slopes of the Vale of Llangollen posed considerable problems and this was the last section of the canal to be completed, over two years after the aqueduct had been opened to traffic. This unforseen waterway is, not without irony therefore, widely recognised as one of the most scintillating lengths of canal in the country.

Moving off the aqueduct onto the feeder, or vice versa, boaters are forced to employ their best turning skills, often to an audience as ready to nit-pick as the judges on *Great British Bake Off*. All but the shortest boats are best advised to do it in at least two turns. A quick sequence of three overbridges ensues, thence the canal/feeder, call it what you will, essays a beguiling hillside course above the precipitous valley of the Dee. By Bridge 34w there are views down to the rooftops of Plas-yn-Pentre and its watermill on the riverbank. On the opposite side, Trevor Hall flaunts its Grade I listed richness. Dating from 1742, it can be hired for ludicrous sums of money. Between bridges 37w and 38w (how tedious this 'W' business becomes) there were wharves on the offside for limestone brought down from the surrounding hills by tramway. Canalside, at Bryn Howel, is a half-timbered gabled boathouse built by James Coster Edwards to keep a pleasure boat in. The delightful image of a teak slipper launch rubbing pristine shoulders with scruffy limestone-carrying narrowboats springs to mind.

Bridge 39w carried the Great Western Railway's Ruabon-Barmouth line over the canal. Opened in 1862, initially as far as Llangollen, passenger services were withdrawn on the frequently flawed recommendations of Dr Beeching in 1965, and goods three years later, yet there was a happy ending, as we shall discover on Map 26. The canal becomes sandwiched between the overgrown trackbed of the former railway and the frenetically busy A539 Wrexham-Llangollen road. There was another limestone wharf at Sun Trevor. Limestone was brought down a 1 in 5 incline on iron-wheeled wagons from quarries on the hillside to the north. Occasionally the chain controlling this Newtonian procedure would snap, with spectacular results. A wooden shute conveyed the limestone onto waiting boats. Some of it went as far as the Black Country for use as a flux in iron smelting. The course of the incline can still be discerned to the left of the Sun Trevor inn, most notably a surviving overbridge.

Unsurprisingly, given its precarious mountainside setting, the section between Trevor and Llangollen has a history of breaches. In the early hours of 7th September 1945 the bank collapsed by Bridge 41w. A torrent of water swept over the adjoining railway line, washing away its ballast and leaving the rails suspended in mid air. As luck - often a crucial participant in such dramas - would have it, the 3.35am mails and parcels train from Chester to Barmouth was bearing down on the scene of the breach, and before any warning could be given, left the rails and plunged down the hillside. The driver, a Mr Jones, was in the words of the official report, 'killed instantly', as his cab was crushed. A poignant image of his empty boots, which remained intact on the footplate, was amongst the

continued overleaf:

continued from page 97:

official photographs taken by the accident investigation team.

Remarkably, the fireman, a Mr Joy, was thrown clear, and, in spite of being half buried, experiencing severe shock, and sustaining a broken wrist, had the presence of mind to walk all the way to Llangollen to report the incident. Scattered firebox embers from the wrecked locomotive (a GWR 'mogul', No. 6315, if you were wondering) set all but the brake van of the seventeen vehicles in the train ablaze. Fire engines attended the scene from as far away as Wrexham, yet the wreckage burned for the best part of five hours. One wonders, in those pre-nationalisation days, if the incident caused any friction between the custodians of the canal, the London Midland & Scottish Railway, and the owners of the washed away line, the Great Western Railway. The Accident Report, however exonerated both parties, whilst hinting that the vibration of modern traffic on the parallel road may have played a part in destabilising the canal bank. Significantly, a month earlier, the area had experienced twenty-four hours of heavy rainfall. Breaches occurred more frequently thereafter and by the mid nineteen-eighties it became apparent to British Waterways that this section would, effectively, have to be rebuilt. Nowadays the canal bed is concrete-lined, under-drained and fitted with a waterproof membrane. Finally, and anecdotally, the best time to travel into Llangollen is during the afternoon, as most boats come out of Llangollen in the morning.

FRONCYSYLLTE   MAP 25

A mountain goat of a village famed for its male voice choir, who have gained a reputation as recording stars in recent years, and whose sixth album features a photograph of Pontcysyllte Aqueduct on its cover. If your legs are up to it, it's worth following the zigzagging lane up to the crest of the ridge for spectacular views across the Dee Valley and up into the Vale of Llangollen; with, perhaps, a lusty rendition of *Men of Harlech* upon reaching the summit.

Eating & Drinking

AQUEDUCT INN - Holyhead Road. Tel: 01691 777118. Free house standing prominently above the canal. Veranda to rear offers panoramic views over the aqueduct's approaches. Open from noon daily, food served throughout until 8pm. LL20 7PY.
FRON PIZZAS & KEBABS - Holyhead Road. Tel: 01691 777111. Fast food outlet open from 4pm daily ex Tuesdays. LL20 7RA.

Shopping

Tiny post office stores on A5.

Connections

BUSES - Tanat Valley service 64 runs aproximately four times Mon-Fri to/from Llangollen and Chirk.

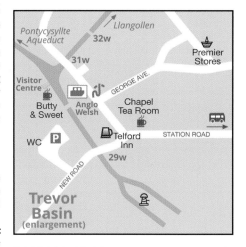

TREVOR/CEFN MAWR   MAP 25

Male voice choirs and villages (Rhosymedre, Gresford et al) that have given their names to well-loved hymns, where else could we be but Wales! The basin is hard by a housing estate, but the canal shrugs off such intrusions and a car park (with overspill) reflects the ever increasing popularity of the aqueduct.

Eating & Drinking

BUTTY & SWEET - Trevor Basin. Floating cafe famed for its bacon sandwiches.
CHAPEL TEA ROOM - Station Road. Tel: 01978 812786. Coffee shop/tea room housed in former chapel. Open 10am-4pm daily. LL20 7TP
TELFORD INN - Tel: 01978 820469. Canalside pub formerly known as Scotch Hall, home to the canal's supervising engineer, Telford being a frequent visitor Canalside adjoining the Anglo Welsh base. LL20 7TT

Shopping

The Premier convenience store (some 200 yards west of the canal basin) is open 7am-10pm daily. Cefn Mawr - pronounced as something vaguely like 'Kevin Mow' (the mow to rhyme with cow) - boasts a large Tesco butcher, pharmacy & PO half a mile east of the canal.

Things to Do

TREVOR BASIN - Tel: 01978 822912. Visitor centre located by north end of aqueduct. Open daily Easter to October 10am-4pm (weekends only in winter).

Connections

BUSES - Arriva service 5 every 30 minutes (Mon-Sat) (40 mins Sun) to/from Llangollen and Wrexham (via Ruabon railhead) from stops on the A539 at the north end of Station Road.

HAVING reached a crescendo at Pontcysyllte, the Llangollen Canal needs little encouragement to provide an encore, and treats you to all the wild majesty that the celebrated Vale of Llangollen can muster. Great buttresses of limestone cliffs tower above conifer plantations, making memories of Hurleston and gentle green Cheshire seem like something that occurred to someone else in another lifetime. When the weather is kind, you find yourself constantly lifting your eyes up into the hills, where sunlight gives the heather-clad ridges the clarity of well-executed marquetry. But Wales wouldn't be Wales if it weren't for the frequent, dripping Celtic mists that come creeping up the valley of the Dee, muffling boat exhausts and dampening the woods, though manifestly not the spirits.

Never exactly wide, the canal/feeder narrows as it approaches Llangollen with 'one way working' along three short sections cut through solid rock. Boaters need to be patient in high season, and a good deal of frustration can be saved simply by sending a member of your party (preferably the most diplomatic) ahead to check if a boat is approaching in the opposite direction. Linear visitor moorings are provided on the approach to Bridge 45w, but you may prefer (as we do) to continue to the basin beyond where pontoons can accommodate over thirty boats. Whichever you decide on, you can stay for up to four hours free; charges thereafter being £6 for up to 24 hours and £12 for up to 48 hours. Tickets - which have to be displayed on your boat in the manner of a car

continued overleaf:

1 Beware narrows west of here.
2 No powered boats beyond this point.

Fron Bache

Llangollen
(see enlargement - page 101)

Geraint Hill

Plas Newydd

Town Centre

Llangollen Pavilion

85

70'

45 w

46 w

47 w

Llangollen Railway

Berwyn

Chain Bridge Hotel

Horseshoe Falls

Llantysilio Hall

Plas Berwyn

A5

River Dee

44w

Geufron

Wern Isaf

A539

Dinbren Hall

48Aw

49 w

P

WC

NORTH

25

43w

Llandyn Hall

Castell Dinas Bran

48w Motor Museum

aq.

Pentrefelin

Valle Crucis Abbey

A542 to Ruthin

River Dee

(S) = 🚽🗑️🗑️ WC

park - are obtainable from the cafe/trip boat booking office just beyond Bridge 45w at Llangollen Wharf. Some may baulk at the notion of paying to moor, but, in the basin at least, each pontoon comes equipped with water and electricity supplies. We have always maintained that other towns should be encouraged to provide

Siambr Wen

similar secure and facility equipped berths for a small charge. Bear in mind, though, that moorings at so popular a destination as this can be at a premium at the height of the season, and the earlier in the day you arrive, the more chance you'll have of finding a space.

Running above the slate roofs and salt-glazed chimney pots of the town, the canal narrows significantly as it squeezes past a handsome crenellated house, whose well-manicured lawns spill down to a low stone boundary wall beside the water's edge. This is Siambr Wen, whose Gothic facade dates from circa 1800. In the mid-19th century it was the home of a Dr Robertson and his three inseparable sisters. Their other brother was no less than Henry Roberston, the railway engineer, whose magnificent viaducts we met at Chirk and Cefn. Dr Robertson died at Siambr Wen in 1883. The three sisters stayed on, two of them died - on consecutive days - from influenza in 1892. The remaining sibling, five years later.

Beyond Bridge 45w stands the aforementioned Llangollen Wharf, where an old warehouse serves as a base for the horse-drawn boats which have been plying the final, narrow, shallow, transparent section up to Berwyn and the Chain Bridge since 1884. Powered boats are prohibited from proceeding beyond the mooring basin, a couple of hundred yards further on, where, in any case, you will need to go to turn, whether you intend to moor or not.

The feeder canal continues for another couple of miles beyond Llangollen to Llantysilio, an enchanting journey by any standards, particularly if you succumb to a voyage aboard one of the horsedrawn excursion boats. Skirting the Pavilion, where the world-famous Eisteddfod, established after the Second World War, is held annually, early in July, the canal passes beneath the main road to Ruthin. Make a mental note of how the railway runs below the canal at this point, and remember to look how high above you it is at Berwyn.

At Pentrefelin (Bridge 48w) a former slate mill - once served by a tramway which crossed the canal via a lift-bridge - now hosts a fascinating display of motoring memorabilia and vehicles, including a nostalgic recreation of a 1950s garage. Eglwyseg Aqueduct follows, parenthesised by a curving causeway. Beyond Ty Craig Bridge (48Aw) the canal is cut into the rock. Soon boat horses reach the limit of their exertions beside the Chain Bridge Hotel. The eponymous suspension bridge, dating from 1817, was re-opened in 2015 after a long period of disuse and provides a delightful means of reaching the Llangollen Railway's Berwyn station perched loftily above the River Dee.

More of a viaduct, really, Kings Bridge (49w) dates from 1906 and was named in honour of Edward VII, its portal ushers you through to the last stretch of the feeder, the gauge house which controls the amount of water fed into the canal, and the massive, crescent-shaped Horseshoe Falls themselves. To do him posthumous justice, it was Jessop who suggested tapping the waters of the Dee to feed the Ellesmere Canal system, but it fell to Telford to design the weir, a feat he accomplished with customary panache, so much so that this purely functional arrangement has been regarded as an arcadian beauty spot ever since.

Don't stop now! Continue the last quarter of a mile to Llantysilio's little church, sign the visitor book, and offer votary thanks for the forty-five mile odyssey from Hurleston, and the ingredients which make the Llangollen one of the great inland waterway experiences in the world.

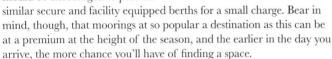

The canal could not have found a more entertaining town to terminate in. Once a year, in early July, this little grey-slated Welsh town takes on a cosmopolitan atmosphere, as singers and dancers in colourful national dress take part in the famous Eisteddfod. In truth, the town is busy with tourists all summer long, as it has been since the 18th century, when early travel writers like Hazlitt and Borrow discovered the wild charm of the Vale of Llangollen. Arguably, Llangollen's heyday coincided with the residence here of the 'Ladies of Llangollen' when such august figures as Wordsworth, Sir Walter Scott and the Duke of Wellington were regular visitors. The canal wharf lies over the river from the bulk of the town, but it's just a short walk over the creaming Dee via the graceful Bishop Trevor Bridge to the centre.

Eating & Drinking

ADYAN'S - Victoria Square. Tel: 01978 860610. Tandoori restaurant open from 6pm daily. LL20 8ET
CHAINBRIDGE HOTEL - canalside Bridge 49w. Tel: 01978 860215. Smartly refurbished hotel in idyllic setting. Bar and restaurant food for non-residents at the 'unnavigable' end of the canal. LL20 8BS
THE CORN MILL - Dee Lane. Tel: 01978 869555. Look no further than this multi-levelled modern restaurant & bar (part of the Brunning & Price group which seldom lets you down) housed within an 18th century mill whose water wheel still turns for the entertainment of diners. Balcony seating for warm days with views across the Dee to the nostalgic shufflings and shuntings of Llangollen's steam trains. Food served from noon daily throughout. LL20 8PN
GALES WINE BAR - Bridge Street. Tel: 01978 860089. Characterful wine bar offering food and they also do accommodation. LL20 8PF

Llangollen (enlargement)

1 The Cornmill
2 Gales
3 Three Eagles
4 Adyan's

SUN TREVOR - adjacent Bridge 41w (Map 25). Tel: 01978 860651. Pleasant roadside pub with good (if somewhat noisy) moorings available away from the crush at Llangollen. Food from noon daily. LL20 8EG
THREE EAGLES - Bridge Street. Tel: 01978 869595. Classy reinvention of former Wynnstay Arms. Food served from noon daily. LL20 8PF

Shopping

Amongst all the gift shops there are many genuinely attractive craft outlets. Plenty of food shops too, notably Llangollen Oggie Shop (offering hugely tasty Welsh Oggies) on Castle Street where you'll also discover Chatwins the bakers who you may have encountered back in Nantwich. Porter's Delicatessen on Market Street is also worth a visit. Watkins & Williams is a long established hardware merchants on Regent Street, as is the Blue Bay launderette.

Rowlands pharmacy can be found on the eastern edge of town on the A539. The Post Office is in Nisa on Berwyn St. Aldi supermarket on the A5.

Things to Do

TOURIST INFORMATION CENTRE - The Chapel, Castle Street. Tel: 01978 860828. LL20 8NU
LLANGOLLEN MUSEUM - Parade Street. Tel: 01978 862862. Local history. LL20 8PW
LLANGOLLEN PAVILION - Abbey Road. Tel 01978 860111. LL20 8SW
LLANGOLLEN RAILWAY - station riverside, below the canal wharf. Tel: 01978 860979. Daily service (April to early October, plus weekends out of season) of steam/heritage diesel hauled trains through delightful Dee Valley scenery to Corwen. Small gift shop and cafe at station overlooking the Dee. LL20 8SN
LLANGOLLEN WHARF - The Wharf. Tel: 01978 860702. Base for motor-boat and horse-drawn trip boats, and also day-boat hire. Gift shop/cafe. LL20 8TA
MOTOR MUSEUM - Pentrefelin Mill. Tel: 0778 030 6220. Engrossing assembly of road vehicles. LL20 8EE
PLAS NEWYDD - Hill Street. Tel: 01978 862834. This delightful black and white timbered house set in charming gardens was the home of the 'Ladies of Llangollen', two daughters of aristocratic Irish families who lived here from 1779 to 1831. LL20 8AW
And all around are hills crying out to be climbed. A particularly fine walk leads from Bridge 45w to the 1000ft summit of Castell Dinas Bran.

Connections

BUSES - services from Parade Street (2nd right across river bridge): 64 approx 5 per day (ex Sun) to/from Chirk via Froncysyllte; 5 every 30 mins (40 mins Sun) to/from Wrexham via Trevor (for Pontcysyllte Aq.) and Ruabon railway station.
TAXIS - Premier Cars. Tel: 01978 861999.

Montgomery Canal

HOWEVER popular the Montgomery Canal may become, as restoration forges ahead, its topographical hinterland will remain remote, ensuring a welcome sense of isolation. After a burst of activity generated by Frankton Locks (Map 23), the junction with the intended main line to Shrewsbury, Graham Palmer Lock and the new aqueduct over the River Perry, the canal soon loses itself in an agricultural landscape, the Berwyn and Breidden hills tantalisingly defining the western horizon.

East of the canal, Woodhouse dates from the 1770s and was designed by Robert Mylne, a Scottish architect and engineer (in the 18th century it was feasible to be both) whose curriculum vitae boasted involvement in a number of canal projects, including the Gloucester & Berkeley Ship Canal where his architectural legacy of elegantly porticoed bridge keeper's cottages may still be appreciated. Mylne (perhaps best known for the original Blackfriars Bridge across the Thames) designed a number of bridges and country houses in Shropshire: q.v. Halston, Map 23.

In his long out of print, but still enjoyably informative *Lapal Towpath*

Guide to the Montgomeryshire Canal, John Horsley Denton brings up the curious detour of the canal essayed circa 1799 through the Woodhouse estate at the instigation of the Rev. John Robert Lloyd, contemporary owner of the estate and a committee member of the Ellesmere Canal Company. Its use, however, was short-lived, for by 1822 the new occupant, William Owen, had the canal returned to its original route.

At Heath Houses the Shrewsbury-Chester railway crosses the canal and a derelict arm extends into the reedy precincts of what was initially a transhipment basin with the railway, but used in later years as a 'Bone Manure Manufactory'. In the mid 19th century a packet boat service operated between Newtown and Heath Houses to connect with the railway. The high-chimnied station house of Rednal & West Felton remains intact and used as a private dwelling complete with a valance-canopied timber goods shed in the grounds. In *Red For Danger*,

continued overleaf:

The towpath is in reasonably good condition between Frankton Junction and Maesbury Marsh: comfortable for walkers, acceptable for cyclists. The latter, however, may find it more comfortable to divert onto the road between bridges 74 and 76.

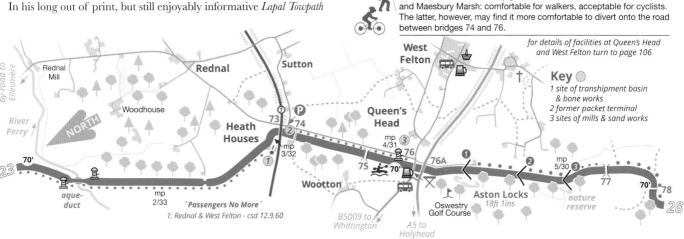

Heath Houses

L. T. C. Rolt described a fatal accident which occurred at Rednal in 1865 when a double-headed excursion from Birkenhead to Shrewsbury was derailed because the driver of the leading locomotive failed to see a warning flag indicating that maintenance was underway on the track which was unable to support the heavy train.

Back on the canal, the quaint brick and timber building (pictured above) abutting Bridge 74 was both a warehouse and a passenger terminal for users of the packet boat. The Wolverhampton Swift Packet Boat Company advertised an astonishing schedule of just over five hours for their boat to cover the 31 miles and 22 locks involved; though, in the event, the service only lasted for a couple of years, and historians can only speculate as to whether this was because it lacked viability or its velocity was doing too much damage to the canal.

The canal parallels a busy by-road which leads to an industrial estate on the site of RAF Rednal, a Second World War aerodrome whose runways are used by go-karters and whose control tower has survived to host paintballing parties. After D-Day the Americans flew wounded servicemen back to Rednal for life-saving treatment in Shropshire's military hospitals.

Skirting woodland, predominantly silver birch, the canal makes its quiet (when there are no boisterous canoeists about) way to Queen's Head, a small roadside community on Telford's road to Holyhead, the A5. In the canal's working days there was a substantial wharf here, together with a flour mill, and a sand pit linked to the canal by a narrow gauge railway which used donkeys as motive power. Travelling with his father aboard the fly-boat *Broxton*, Jack Roberts (*Shropshire Union Fly-boats* - Canal Book Shop 2015) paused briefly in 1904 to unload 'a few bags of sugar, one box of bacon, two boxes of oranges and onions, four boxes of fruit and four boxes of kippers'. From 1996 to 2003 Queen's Head marked a temporary terminus in restoration terms. Aston Locks had been restored for use by boats, but controversy surrounded continuation of the canal through an area designated as being of Special Scientific Interest.

REVELLING in its rural isolation, the Montgomery Canal comes upon Maesbury Marsh, a quintessential country wharf with an inn, stables, boatmen's cottages and dock; the inland waterway equivalent of a country station before the Marples/Beeching massacre. Business used to be brisk at Maesbury Marsh, for this was the nearest wharf to Oswestry (which, surprisingly, no one seems to have ever contemplated building a canal to) and many commodities came and went through here before the railway reached the town. Wharfinger's House, the agent's residence, bears a family likeness to Beech House back at Ellesmere.

Beyond lift-bridge No.81 is the short arm which once led to Peates Mill. Sadly, the mill ceased operating in 2002 - though Lloyd's more modern animal feeds plant continues to be very much in business near Bridge 84; the company also operate mills at Wrexham, Darlington and Langport (Somerset). For their part, Peates once operated a fleet of narrowboats - not least *Cressy* of *Narrow Boat* fame - having purchased eleven craft from the Shropshire Union Company when they ceased trading in 1921. Soon, though, the development of the motor lorry made it unviable to continue carrying by canal. The grain Peates imported by way of Ellesmere Port took three or four days to reach the mill by horse-drawn boat, whereas the company's 13 ton lorry, purchased in 1932, was able to make two round trips to the port in a day. It is hardly surprising, then, that trade had all but evaporated from the canal well before the fateful breach of 1936. But in the next two or three miles you come upon the remains of some of the key industries which made it successful for a time at least. The wharf at Bridge 82 was linked by tramway to a number of collieries up on Sweeney Mountain. Lift-bridge 82A is an entirely new structure, erected in the timber style favoured along the Llangollen Canal.

To comply with Heritage Lottery Fund rules, the canal's navigability has to be extended from Gronwen Wharf to Crickheath Wharf by the end of October 2022, but it would be wise to check with CRT or SUCS for present status to avoid disappointment. Plans are in place to tackle the derelict section towards Pant. Schoolhouse Bridge (No.86) will need to be rebuilt. Welsh Government funding is 'in place' for restoration between Llanymynech and Maerdy Bridge (Map 29).

The canal isn't the only transport mode being slowly brought back to life. In recent times a section of the old Cambrian Railways line has been in use as a preserved railway, though services are currently suspended while the Cambrian Heritage Railways concentrate their efforts on the Oswestry to Weston Wharf section of the route.

continued overleaf:

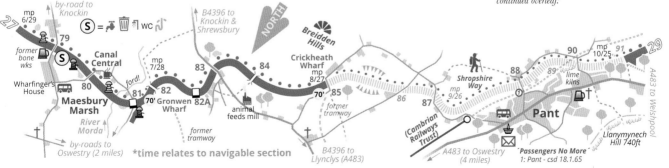

Pant was the scene of more interaction between water and rail. The standard gauge Cambrian Railways squeezed through the gap between the canal and the hillside and a station perched over the waterway by Bridge 88. Narrow gauge mineral lines came swooping down from the hillside quarries - hence the extra arch on the offside of the bridge. By Bridge 90 there is a bank of well preserved limekilns.

QUEEN'S HEAD   MAP 27

Eating & Drinking

QUEEN'S HEAD - canalside Bridge 76. Tel: 01691 610255. Well-appointed pub serving food Wed-Sat 12-9pm and Sun lunchtimes. SY11 4EB

Connections

BUSES - Arriva service 70 operates hourly Mon-Sat to/from Oswestry and Shrewsbury via West Felton.

WEST FELTON   MAP 27

Westernmost of the Ruyton XI Towns, and now spared the A5's elephantine juggernauts, the village boasts a handsome 12th century church whose most recent claim to fame is that a Miss Allegra Mostyn-Owen glided up its aisle in 1987 to be married to a Mr Johnson, Boris of that ilk. But though a bacchanalian reception ensued at Woodhouse (see main text) the marriage was dissolved in 1993, and the subsequent fate of the groom is open to conjecture.

Eating & Drinking

PUNCH BOWL - Holyhead Road. Tel: 01691 611616. Village pub. Lunch served Wed-Sun. SY11 4EH

Shopping

In such remote climes you may be grateful for West Felton Stores Tel: 01691 610863 - SY11 4EA

OSWESTRY   (MAP 27)

Birthplace of Wilfred Owen, Oswestry shares with Berwick upon Tweed the anomaly of having its football team play in a foreign country: in this case The New Saints and the Welsh Premier League. Indeed, it is a town of blurred affinities, as befits its border setting, and amply rewards detours from its adjoining canals.

Eating & Drinking

SEBASTIONS - Willow St. Tel 01691 655444. Michelin listed restaurant. Wed-Sat from 6.30pm. SY11 1AQ

Shopping

Indoor market Wed, Fri & Sat; outdoor market Wed & Sat. Farmers Market last Friday in the month.

Things to Do

VISITOR & EXHIBITION CENTRE - Church Terrace. Tel: 01691 662753. Former 15th century grammar school housing a tourist information centre and coffee shop. Small display devoted to the First World War poet, Wilfred Owen. Open Mon, Wed, Fri & Sat from 10am-4/4.30pm. SY11 2TE

Things to Do

CAMBRIAN HERITAGE RAILWAYS - Oswestry. Tel: 01691 728131. Ambitious plans are on the table to re-open the railway all the way from Gobowen to Llanymynech, though trains currently only operate between Oswestry's grandiose railway station and Weston Wharf, a couple of miles to the south-west. Operations from Llynclys mothballed. SY11 1RE

MAESBURY MARSH   MAP 28

Meresberie in the Domesday Book straddles the River Morda, a tributary of the Vyrnwy and there is evidence of Wat's Dyke a precursor of Offa's. St John's church is one of those sweet little pre-fabricated corrugated iron 'Tin Tabernacles' which travellers on the canals seem to encounter more than most.

Eating & Drinking

CANAL CENTRAL - adjacent Bridge 80. Tel: 0169 652168. Cafe (open Fri-Sun) housed in an eco-friendly Scandinavian style building beside the canal. Self catering, camping, canoeing also available. SY10 8JG
NAVIGATION INN - alongside Bridge 79. Tel: 0169 672958. Comfortable inn nicknamed 'The Navvy' open Thur-Sun. Check internet or telephone ahead for mealtimes. SY10 8JB

Connections

BUSES - Arriva service 576 connects approx four times per day, Mon-Sat with Oswestry and Shrewsbury (via Ruyton XI Towns).
TAXIS - Oswestry Cabs. Tel: 01691 661663.

PANT   MAP 28

A wayside village, more chapel than church, and well sited to take advantage of a fully restored canal in years to come. Buzzards call over the wooded flanks of Llanymynech Hill and there are steep paths up to its nature reserve, a noted habitat of rare butterflies.

Eating & Drinking

CROSS GUNS - Rockwell Lane. Tel: 01691 839631 Main road pub open from noon daily. SY10 9QR

Shopping

Co-op stores with post office at the top of Station Road most easily reached from Bridge 88.

Connections

BUSES - Tanat Valley service T12 provides Pant with a reasonably frequent Mon-Sat link with Oswestry, Welshpool. Tel: 01691 780212.

THE canal skirts the foot of the limestone eminence of Llanymynech Hill. Probably worked for its mineral deposits as long ago as the Iron Age, it now has a golf course on its summit, notable in that fifteen of its holes are in Wales and three in England. [I]an Woosnam started playing on its thymy fairways at the age of nine. [An] Oswestry native, the novelist Barbara Pym, also golfed up there. At the [p]oint where a former railway (known as 'Rock Siding') crossed the canal [Map 28), it becomes navigable again for a short distance and a trip boat [p]lies from Llanymynech Wharf. A high, rook-roosted chimney heralds [the] approach to the hill's eponymous village, and the indents of old wharves eat into the offside bank. The chimney,

erected in 1899 but disused within 15 years, was the flue for a Hoffman kiln used for the continuous burning of limestone. If you have ever travelled on the Settle & Carlisle railway you'll have passed a similar installation north of Settle. There is also one preserved at the Prestongrange Museum in East Lothian.

At Bridge 92 you pass into Wales; Powys since 1974, but formerly, and appropriately, the County of Montgomeryshire. The canal loses its brief navigability at Bridge 93, still intact in its hump-backed innocence, but the by-road to Tanat which crossed it has been directed across the bed of the canal, a cheese-paring act of self-indulgence by the highways authority which will come back to haunt the restorationists when they eventually re-open beyond Llanymynech. A few hundred yards to the west the canal joins a road to cross the trackbed of the old branch railway to Llanfyllin. Carreghofa, a typical GWR halt, lay on the other side of the road, deep in a cutting. When the railway was built a temporary

continued overleaf:

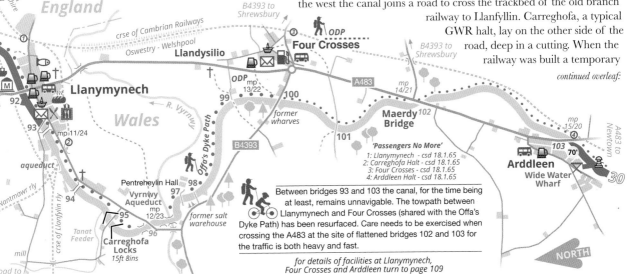

'Passengers No More'
1: Llanymynech - csd 18.1.65
2: Carreghofa Halt - csd 18.1.65
3: Four Crosses - csd 18.1.65
4: Arddleen Halt - csd 18.1.65

Between bridges 93 and 103 the canal, for the time being at least, remains unnavigable. The towpath between Llanymynech and Four Crosses (shared with the Offa's Dyke Path) has been resurfaced. Care needs to be exercised when crossing the A483 at the site of flattened bridges 102 and 103 for the traffic is both heavy and fast.

*for details of facilities at Llanymynech,
Four Crosses and Arddleen turn to page 109*

Carreghofa

aqueduct was constructed pending completion of the permanent one so as not to interrupt canal traffic, and its abandoned arms are still to be seen disappearing into the undergrowth.

Disarmingly picturesque, Carreghofa Locks mark the original junction between the Llanymynech Branch of the Ellesmere Canal and the Eastern Branch of the Montgomeryshire Canal. A feeder comes in from the River Tanat and a wharfinger's office adjoins the upper lock The lockhouse's modest two-storey road frontage masks a much more imposing, bay-windowed rear. It is at Carreghofa that westbound travellers enjoy their first encounter with the Montgomeryshire Canal's unique segmented paddle gear. All the more poignant, then, that notwithstanding a plaque informing them that the site was re-opened by a Baroness and the Chief Executive of the British Waterways Board in 1986, the locks remain effectively moribund.

Bridge 96 was flattened in 1980, another fiasco paying scant regard to the potential of restoration; particularly when, as John Horsley Denton sagely pointed out, its relatively low levels of traffic could have easily been diverted via Four Crosses. An embankment with flood arches leads to Vyrnwy Aqueduct, the canal's major engineering structure. Erected to the design of John Dadford in 1796, it owes more to the Brindley school of aqueduct construction than Dadford's contemporary,

Telford. One of its arches collapsed soon after its opening and, in 1823, George Buck - later to build the magnificent railway viaduct at Stockport - was brought in to strengthen it. Just when he thought he had finished, the walls of the aqueduct bulged and appeared to be collapsing. Buck is said to have smote the ground in despair, but with the help of additional iron tie bars - still prominent (amidst burgeoning vegetation) to this day - the aqueduct has more or less stood its ground ever since. Cogitate upon this colourful past as you lean upon the parapet of the present and watch the waters of the Vyrnwy (which joins the Severn at Melverley, twenty miles upstream of Shrewsbury) glide below. For a better view of the aqueduct, go down the steps from its north end into the meadow below.

A dog-leg bend takes the canal off the aqueduct past a handsomely refurbished salt warehouse built to last from local stone. Bridge 98, which carried the carriage road to Pentreheylin Hall, has some ornate woodwork. Arcing round the attractive hillside of Bryn Mawr, the canal reaches Four Crosses where there were separate wharves and winding holes and basins either side of Clafton Bridge (No.100). Clafton is probably a corruption of the name of a former owner of the wharf, who rejoiced in the euphonious name of Clopton Prhys. Twice in the next three miles the A483 slices across the bed of the canal, presenting a formidable obstacle to full restoration.

LLANYMYNECH MAP 29

oad traffic holds this former quarrying village ostage, bludgeoning the bucolic sensibilities of canal avellers poking their heads up the steps of Bridge 2. Walk down one side of the main street and you re in England, cross the road and you are in Wales. common with all these border communities, the ocals come over as a blurred mixture of Celt and nglo Saxon; presumably the result of all that illicit nter-marrying down the ages. Speaking of progeny, he village's most famous native is Richard Roberts, nventor of the gasometer. Railway enthusiasts may ecognise Llanymynech as the western terminus of he Shropshire & Montgomeryshire Railway, one of Colonel Stephens' impecunious outfits beloved of L.T. C. Rolt, who once propelled a platelayer's trolley from Kinnerley to Llanymynech and back in the same time cheduled for the trains; a statistic which says more bout the generosity of the timetable than Rolt's thletic prowess.

Eating & Drinking
BENGAL SPICES - Tel: 01691 830170. Indian restaurant nd take-away. From 5pm daily. SY22 6ER
BRADFORD ARMS - Tel: 01691 830582. Food and ccommodation. SY22 6EJ
CROSS KEYS - Tel: 01691 831585. Food and ccommodation. SY22 6EA
THE DOLPHIN - Tel: 01691 839672. Food and B&B; eer garden adjacent canal. SY22 6ER
GOLDEN VALLEY - Tel: 01691 830426. Chinese akeaway. SY22 6EZ
LLANYMYNECH FISH & CHIPS - Station Road. Tel: 01691 839692. Fish & Chips. SY22 6EE
There is also a cafe, and a Kebab/pizza takeaway.

Shopping
Small, though well stocked, post office stores. Bakery.

Things to Do
LLANYMYNECH WHARF VISITOR CENTRE - Tel: 01691 831497. Community-run attraction with trip boat, adjoining industrial heritage area, and nature reserve. Open Sunday afternoons Easter to September. Long-term project to build a replica of the packet-boat Duchess Countess. SY22 6EA

Connections
BUSES - Tanat Valley service T12 links Llanymynech to Welshpool (and thence Machynlleth) and Oswestry (some continuing to Wrexham) approximately bi-hourly Mon-Sat.

FOUR CROSSES MAP 29
A plaque at the far end of the whitewashed cottages by Bridge 100 recalls the boxing exploits of Dennis Powell. The long lost railway station appeared in Flanders & Swann's elegiac song Slow Train. Milk lorries occupy the goods yard now, whilst the old rail connected creamery has been turned into apartments.

Eating & Drinking
TY LLEW - Village Centre. Tel: 01691 830295. Food and accommodation. SY22 6RB

Shopping
Costcutter shop & post office at petrol station.

Connections
BUSES - Tanat Valley T12 as per Llanymynech.

ARDDLEEN MAP 29
This roadside village (whose name means 'flax-garden') marks the end of 'navigation' north of Welshpool.

Eating & Drinking
THE HORSESHOE - Tel: 01938 590690. Food and accommodation. SY22 6PU

Connections
BUSES - Tanat Valley T12 as per Llanymynech.

POOL QUAY MAP 30
Severnside settlement of considerable antiquity. Mid-nineteenth century maps depict a barytes grinding mill, corn mill, sawmill, flannel factory, blacksmiths and malt house with drying kilns. Now solely the relentless traffic on the A483 destroys the inherent calm of this lost inland port.

Eating & Drinking
THE POWIS ARMS - Tel: 01938 590255. Former coaching inn with inglenook, real ale, home cooked food and accommodation. Open from 11am. The sign authentically depicts a SUCCCo flyboat in juxtaposition with segmental paddle gear. SY21 9JS
Refreshments are occasionally available at St John's.

Holiday Lets
CROWTHER HALL LOCK COTTAGE - Tel: 01938 590543. Self-catering accommodation. Quarry-tiled floors, wood-burning stove and exposed beams but no phone or television - sounds heavenly! SY21 9JU

GUILSFIELD MAP 30
A substantial village famous for its church and its football team, and how often can you say that! The church is dedicated to St Aelhaiarn, a 7th century Welshman. Pevsner was enthusiastic enough to label it 'one of the richest medieval church interiors in the county'. Guilsfield FC play in the Huws Gray Alliance against such stalwart opponents as Bangor City, Prestatyn Town and Gresford Athletic. Shop and two pubs, buses as per Llanymynech.

Salt Warehouse, Pentre-heylin (Map 29)

Cabin Lock and the Breidden Hills (Map 30)

Luggy Aqueduct (Map 32)

DON'T let the 'dark blue' line of the canal fool you, for whilst officially navigable, to all intents and purposes even a canoe would struggle to negotiate the canal north of Crowther Hall. How has it come to pass that the 'restored' Welshpool section of the canal, stretching from Arddleen (Map 29) to Berriew (Map 32) is, with the honourable exception of the Heulwen Trust trip boats, virtually unused? It remains outside the province of a mere guide book to provide a political answer, but to the casual, if heartfelt observer, the effort put into restoring this part of the Montgomery Canal in the 'eighties and 'nineties appears tantamount to a Sisyphean waste of belief and resources. Singing from the same hymn sheet? The stake-holders don't even appear to be in the same place of worship.

Burgedin Locks were re-opened in the summer of 1998. Above the locks the Guilsfield Arm joins the main canal. An amble along the B4392 offers glimpses of its course and the occasional overbridge remaining intact.

Burgedin Locks drop the canal by sixteen and a half feet to the sump level of the canal, making the Montgomery a peculiarity in a world where most man-made navigations climb up to, and descend from, a central summit. At Wern there is a slipway, winding hole and picnic area; the latter on the site of a former corn mill which derived its power from the sump level's plentiful supply of excess water produced by boats using the locks in either direction. Southwards from Wern the canal rides along an embankment above marshy ground, a remnant of the swamp which surrounded the Severn before it was drained early in the 19th century. On the far side of the river stand the Breidden Hills, seldom out of sight since you left Frankton. Now you can enjoy them in detail: quarry-scarred Breidden Hill itself, the most northerly summit, topped by a monument to Admiral Rodney by way of thanks for using Montgomeryshire timber

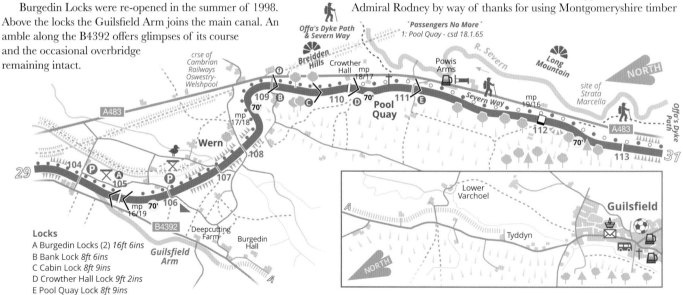

Locks
A Burgedin Locks (2) *16ft 6ins*
B Bank Lock *8ft 6ins*
C Cabin Lock *8ft 9ins*
D Crowther Hall Lock *9ft 2ins*
E Pool Quay Lock *8ft 9ins*

n the building of his navy; and Moel y Golfa to the south with a memorial to Ernest Burton, King of Romanys. In a curious echo of the 18th Century naval memorial, the locality played host to a clandestine radio station built during the Second World War to enable the Admiralty to keep track of its vessels. Dominated by a trio of Eiffel Tower-shaped, seven hundred foot high masts (originally earmarked for erection in Ceylon!), the site continued to be strategically significant throughout the Cold War and into the 21st Century as a means of communicating with Britain's nuclear submarine fleet. The station closed and the masts were demolished in 2003, component of a 'peace dividend' which hasn't quite delivered the profit forecast.

Bank Lock is the first (or last) of four in close proximity which raise (or lower) the canal by some 35 feet. Each chamber has its segmented ground paddles, though these are not in general use. Crowther Hall Lock is the deepest on the canal. The charming lock cottage is available for holiday lets. A bench commemorates a 'land girl' who worked at Crowther Hall farm and lived in the lockside cottage in the late 1940s. Pool Quay's delightful Victorian church, with its elaborate and

distinctively carved timber belfry, overlooks the next pound.

Pool Quay marked the head of navigation on the River Severn. It was, as the name suggests, the port, or quay, for Poole, an earlier name for Welshpool; though previously the settlement, the site of a notable Cistercian monastery, was known as Strata Marcella. The monks brought industry to the banks of the Severn and harnessed the river's power to drive a flour mill, textile works and forge. The Severn could only be navigated this far upstream in winter when there was sufficient depth of water, and with the advent of canal and railway transportation, carrying on the river had ceased by the mid 19th century. The railway, part of the Cambrian system absorbed by the Great Western, closed in 1965, being on the same route from Whitchurch to Welshpool whose scars are encountered at various points along the Llangollen Canal. One of the station masters at Pool Quay was a bee-keeper who won prizes for his honey. Long Mountain assumes the vertical mantle of the Breiddens. Briefly eluding the A483, the canal hides under the wooded, sheep-grazed skirts of Yr Allt - an altogether delightful stretch of waterway.

ROAD schemes seldom benefit canals. You only have to look as far as the Montgomery's flattened bridges to see the truth of this. Yet, paradoxically, the Welshpool by-pass twice came to the rescue of the town's canal: initially in 1969 when it was proposed to route the new road along the bed of the long moribund waterway, the threat of its loss crystallising a latent enthusiasm for the canal; then again in 1992/3 when the by-pass was finally constructed along a different course, allowing the previously flattened Gallows Tree Bank Bridge (117) to be rebuilt with headroom for boats. Final completion of the by-pass and subsequent rebuilding of Whitehouse Bridge (120) in 1998 resulted in the release of those dozen or so miles of navigable waterway. Initially everything looked rosy. A pair of Anglo Welsh hire boats were

outstationed at Welshpool, a day boat was made available for hire and a number of privately owned craft were drawn to the route. But such initiatives proved unsustainable, and a vicious circle of under-use and weed growth has - Heulwen Trust trip boats apart - rendered the canal effectively disused once more, a melancholy state of affairs which does little to promote the benefits of canal restoration to the wider public.

Buttington Wharf (just north of Bridge 115) was an early development under the Montgomery Canal restoration programme, being home to *Heulwen Sunshine*, a specially built trip boat for disabled people which pioneered navigation on this length of canal from 1976. The wharf, popular with local people, has picnic tables and a trio of preserved limekilns; discipline being maintained by a rotundly sculptured wharfinger.

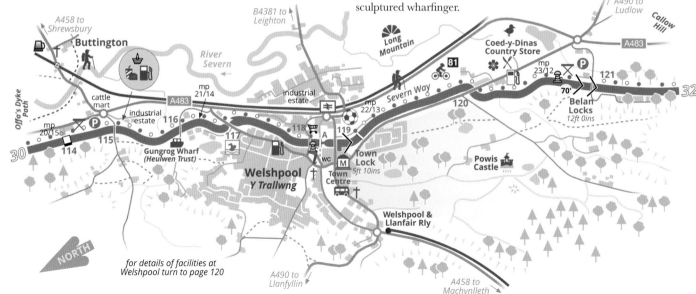

for details of facilities at Welshpool turn to page 120

The Heulwen Trust's trip boats, however are based these days at Gungrog Wharf by Bridge 116. Milepost 21 remembers Jack Roberts, the fly-boat captain whose enchanting book is referenced on a number of pages in this guide.

A Leisure Centre overlooks Bridge 117. Two notable industrial premises lined the canal on its way into Welshpool: on the towpath side a gasworks flourished briefly before being resited when the railway opened; on the offside a large mill, grandiosely known as the Welshpool Company for the Manufacture of Flannel by Steam, stood canalside until the 1930s, latterly being employed as an ordnance works and, briefly, for the manufacture of motorcycles. Some flannel workers terraced cottages remain occupied.

Bungalows with neat gardens and Victorian villas - one with a monkey puzzle tree and a gazebo - herald the approach to the town centre. Empty mooring pontoons emphasise the dearth of boats. Bridge 118A once carried the celebrated Welshpool & Llanfair Light Railway across the canal to its transhipment sidings by the standard gauge Cambrian Railways station, now it carries shoppers to Tesco. Eight miles of the 2ft 6ins gauge line pass through delightful countryside from Welshpool's Raven Square station to the rural terminus of Llanfair Caereinion.

Immediately south of the old railway bridge a small aqueduct, dated 1836, carries the canal over Lledan Brook. The semi-circular weir was part of a scheme whereby water was extracted by a local mill. Welshpool's canalscape is quite delightful, the heart being centred on the old canal yard with its imposing and photogenic warehouse which now serves as a local museum. Interestingly, archive photographs reveal that the overflow from Town Lock provided power for the water wheel of an

Welshpool

adjoining corn mill. Beyond the lock, the canal effects its exit from Welshpool rapidly, the urban environs being exchanged for sports grounds, housing and, before long, the gracious landscape of Powis Castle's parkland. A right angled turn takes the canal under Bridge 120 and along a short new section of the canal, wide and deep compared to the original course which is still in water and well utilised for fishing. The extensive premises bordering the canal on the far side of the A490 belonged to the sawmill and smithy of the Powis Estate. Excess water from the canal was used to power the yard's machinery until the canal became disused and silted up, thereafter the yard's machinery was converted to electric power in the 1940s. The yard's two-storey, stone-built office and blacksmith's shop remains clearly visible from the towpath. Stephen Hughes' *The Archaeology of the Montgomeryshire Canal*, though long out of print, contains fascinating detail of the sawmill, and indeed many of the other buildings and installations associated with the canal.

Hugging the western slopes of the broad Severn valley, the canal affords commanding views of the wooded flanks of Long Mountain to the east. The high spired church is at Leighton, whose towered hall - partly designed by Pugin - is also visible to the south. Belan Locks soon follow, raising the level of the canal by a total of twelve feet. Close by the lock cottage, with its neatly kept garden, is a group of amazingly ornate black and white cottages, occupied in bygone days by agricultural workers. On the horizon the green hills of Mid Wales enticingly beckon the southbound traveller onwards. But pause for a moment, turn and enjoy again the most splendid view of the Breidden Hills. Sometimes, it seems, the landscape - like life itself - is even better when looking back.

BUTTINGTON MAP 31

Roadside village notable for trefoiled cast-iron bridge of 1872 across the Severn, and pretty whitewashed Grade I listed 14th century church of All Saints. Boasting four platforms, Buttington railway station lay a mile to the north-east at the point where the Oswestry and Shrewsbury lines bifurcated.

Eating & Drinking

GREEN DRAGON - half a mile across the Severn and railway on pavemented A458. Tel: 01938 553281. Quaint whitewashed 17th century pub offering camping, glamping and caravanning. Open from noon daily and serving food throughout. SY21 8SS *McDonald's drive-thru adjacent Bridge 115.*

Shopping

Tuffins 24 hour convenience store (well-stocked with local products) and petrol station adjacent Bridge 115.

WELSHPOOL MAP 31

If ever a town deserved to be linked to the canal network, Welshpool is it. One can only look at the empty moorings and weep. Monday is the day to immerse yourself in the town when, as well as the general market, the weekly sheep and cattle market makes its colourful presence felt, even though the cattle market itself has moved away from its previous canalside location to the vicinity of Buttington Wharf. Down from the hills, farming folk congregate in the town to buy and sell, and to assuage the loneliness of their isolated lives in the freemasonry of the auction ring. And all day the town's pubs hum to the sing-song accents of Mid Wales, whilst the steeply climbing High Street, relatively quiet on other days, reverberates to the passage of cattle lorries, Landrovers and battered old cars plastered in the mud and slurry of far-flung farms.

Eating & Drinking

ANDREWS - High Street. Tel: 01938 552635. Award-winning fish & chips. SY21 7JP

BAY TREE - Church Street. Tel: 01938 555456. Quirky vintage tea rooms open from 9am daily (ex Sun). Evening meals served Fri-Sat. SY21 7DL

THE CORN STORE - Church Street. Tel: 01938 554614. Restaurant. SY21 7DL

HOWARD'S RESTAURANT - Coed-y-Dinas. Tel: 01938 555545. Breakfasts, lunches, teas and regular themed evening meals at the garden, home and country centre to the south of the town. SY21 8RP

OLD STATION RESTAURANT - Old Station. Tel: 01938 556622. SY21 7AY

ROYAL OAK HOTEL - Severn Street. Tel: 01938 552217. Imposing hotel offering bar and restaurant food for non-residents. Local Welsh beers such as Monty's and Stonehouse usually on tap. SY21 7DG

THE SMITHFIELD BELL - Mill Lane. Tel: 01938 559472. New-build Marston's pub and restaurant adjacent Bridge 118. SY21 7BL

Shopping

Good facilities for a relatively small town reflect Welshpool's importance as a centre for a wide agricultural hinterland. Tesco, Aldi, Morrisons and Sainsbury's all have supermarkets in the town, but there are plenty of local retailers too, such as Rikki Lloyd's butchers on High Street who've won prizes for their steak and kidney pies. There's a useful launderette adjacent to the imposing Victorian Town Hall on High Street and Brooks bicycle shop (Tel: 01938 553582) on Puzzle Square. There are food markets on Mondays and Saturdays centred on the Town Hall and Broad Street.

Things to Do

TOURIST INFORMATION CENTRE - Vicarage Garden Car Park (adjoining Bridge 118A). Tel: 01938 552043. Heulwen trip-boat bookings. SY21 7DD

POWYSLAND MUSEUM - Canal Wharf. Tel: 01938 553001. Charming displays of local history in the restored canal warehouse. SY21 7AQ

THE OLD STATION - Severn Road. Tel: 01938 556622. Conglomerate of specialist outlets housed in handsome former station building. SY21 7AY

COED-Y-DINAS - Tel: 01938 555545. Attractively laid out garden centre and country store. Impressive food hall. Farmers Market on 1st Friday in the month. Cafe, restaurant. SY21 8RP

POWIS CASTLE, MUSEUM & GARDEN - Tel: 01938 551920. Famous garden, medieval castle and Clive Museum displaying treasures from India including textiles, armour, bronzes, jade, ivory etc. National Trust shop and licensed tea room. SY21 8RF

WELSHPOOL & LLANFAIR RAILWAY - Tel: 01938 810441. Services operate March to October, though not necessarily daily in the quieter months either side of high summer. Departures from Raven Square station at western edge of town. SY21 7LT

Connections

BUSES - Tanat Valley service T12 links Welshpool approximately bi-hourly (Mon-Sat) with Oswestry via Arddleen, Four Crosses, Llanymynech and Pant shadowing the course of the Guilsfield Arm in the process. At Welshpool this connects with Celtic Travel service X75 which runs at similar intervals to Newtown via Berriew, Garthmyl and Abermule. Service T81 runs twice daily (ex Sun) to Montgomery TRAINS - Transport for Wales services to/from Shrewsbury, Newtown and the Cambrian Coast TAXIS - Amber Cars. Tel: 01938 556611.

NOT so much a canal, more a Welsh hymn tune, the Montgomery shadows the Severn's broad flood plain. Your head is turned, and it is difficult to avoid subjectively labelling it the network's prettiest waterway; a status enhanced by the well-surfaced towpath and well-painted locks: both far better kept than many so-called working waterways. Heave a phlegmatic sigh and let the scenery work its balm. Callow Hill, at 1,247 feet, dominates the skyline to the east, part of the wonderful Shropshire hill country in the vicinity of Bishop's Castle.

Flattened Bridge 129, carrying the B4385 road to Berriew, brings to an end the supposedly navigable section from Arddleen. The winding hole is filled with water lilies. Financial constraints meant that construction of the Montgomeryshire Canal stalled in 1797 and for over twenty years Garthmyl, just over 16 miles from Carreghofa, was its terminus. What came to be known as the Western Branch through to Newtown was not completed until 1821. At Garthmyl were concentrated wharves, warehouses, maltings, coal yards, stables and limekilns. In its

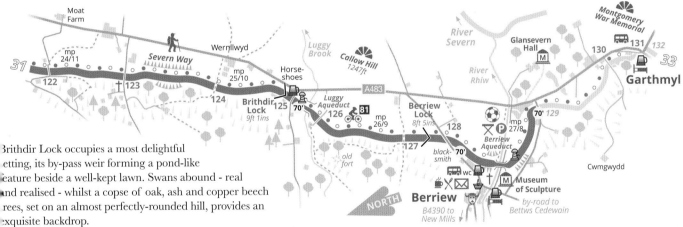

Brithdir Lock occupies a most delightful setting, its by-pass weir forming a pond-like feature beside a well-kept lawn. Swans abound - real and realised - whilst a copse of oak, ash and copper beech trees, set on an almost perfectly-rounded hill, provides an exquisite backdrop.

Beyond Berriew Lock, the canal is carried on an embankment across the Rhiw Valley and on to Berriew Aqueduct. An 1889 rebuild in brick of an earlier stone structure, the four-arched aqueduct (two river and two land arches) takes the waterway over the fast flowing waters of the Rhiw and the minor road into Berriew. The village's football team, who ply their trade in the Mid Wales League, along with nearby Welshpool, have a surprisingly impressive 'stadium' between the canal and the river.

heyday the hamlet must have witnessed scenes of intense activity. It still does, but only from cars and lorries thundering along the A483, the widening of which in 1949 obliterated most of the wharf area, although the old maltings are still in evidence beside an infilled section of canal. Prominent to the south-east, a Doric column of Portland stone commemorates Montgomeryshire's fallen: innocents who failed to return from the First World War to this delectable corner of the globe.

BERRIEW MAP 32

Enchanting village beside the River Rhiw, with clusters of black and white cottages huddling around the church of St Beuno's and a handsome 18th century single span stone bridge downstream of some falls. Privately owned Dolphin Lane leads to properties enchantingly known as 'The Pleasantaries' and 'River Whispers'.

Eating & Drinking

THE HORSESHOES - on A483 by Bridge 125. Tel: 01686 640198. Comfortably refurbished country pub open from noon daily. Self-catering. SY21 8AW
LION HOTEL - village centre. Tel: 01686 640452. Half-timbered inn offering accommodation, restaurant and bar meals. SY21 8PQ
THE TALBOT HOTEL - Tel: 01686 640881. Comfortable small hotel idyllically located beside the River Rhiw. Bar and restaurant food. SY21 8PJ
LYCHGATE COTTAGE - village centre. Tel: 01686 640750. Tea room and deli. Closed Suns. SY21 8PG
UPPER RECTORY - Tel: 01686 640930. Restaurant offering seven course tasting menus Thur-Sat evenings from 7pm, reservations essential. Plus accommodation in one bedroom self-catering cottage, and Shepherd's Hut. SY21 8AN

Shopping

Post office stores open daily 8am-6pm daily (1pm Sun). PO 10am-4pm ex Sun, 1pm Sat. Alan Davies butcher open Tue-Sat, and small gift shop.

Things to Do

ANDREW LOGAN MUSEUM OF SCULPTURE Tel: 01686 640689. A 'glittering, sparkling, fantasy wonderland' founded by the originator of the Alternative Miss World contest. Shop selling jewellery and sculpture. Mostly only open summer weekends. Cafe and shop. SY21 8AH

Berriew Blacksmith

GLANSEVERN HALL - Tel: 01686 640644. Gardens in grounds of Greek Revival house on banks of the Severn. Open Spring-Autumn Tue-Sat and Bank Hol Mons 10.30am-5pm. Tea room. SY21 8AH
WILLIAM O'BRIEN - The Wharf. Tel: 01686 640739. Artist blacksmith. SY21 8AN

Connections

BUSES - Celtic Travel service X75 operates approximately half a dozen times Mon-Sat to Newtown and Welshpool.

GARTHMYL MAP 32

Wayside village on the busy A483 Chester-Llandovery main road. Notable for its four-column Tuscan porch,

Grade II listed Garthmyl Hall is now a wedding venue. The former county town of Montgomery lies a couple of miles to the south-east and is well worth visiting whilst in the area. Buses run from Welshpool.

Eating & Drinking

NAGS HEAD - adjacent bridge 131. Tel: 01686 640600. Well-appointed inn with comfortable accommodation. Food served throughout from noon. SY15 6RS

Accommodation

PENLLWYN LODGES - Brynllwyn Lane. Tel: 01686 640269. Self-catering timber lodges in woodland overlooking the canal. SY15 6RU

Connections

BUSES - Celtic Travel X75 as Berriew.

ABERMULE MAP 33

Expanding village at the confluence of the Mule and Severn. A lovely cast iron bridge spans the Severn adjacent to canal Bridge 147. Large characters carry the inscription: 'THIS SECOND IRON BRIDGE CONSTRUCTED IN THE COUNTY OF MONTGOMERYSHIRE IN THE YEAR 1852'. Less than a mile to the north-west, lie the ruins of 13th century Dolforwyn Castle, cared for by CADW.

Eating & Drinking

THE ABERMULE - village centre. Tel: 01686 639110. Village pub with restaurant open from 4pm Mon-Thur and from noon Fri, Sat & Sun. Caravanning and camping.
SY15 6ND

Shopping

Village stores open daily 7am-7pm. Tel: 01686 630405.

Connections

BUSES - Celtic Travel X75 as Berriew.

CANOEING is encouraged along this otherwise unnavigable stretch of the Montgomery Canal and portaging points are thoughtfully provided either side of fixed or flattened bridges. The towpath, in default of one along the Severn, is the pleasantest and easiest walk along the valley' wrote Brian Waters, the poet and topographical writer in *Severn Stream* published in 1949, and seventy odd years later we're not inclined to quibble with his assertion; indeed, the towpath has become officially adopted as the route of the Severn Way between Pool Quay and Newtown and National Cycle Route 81 between Welshpool and its latter terminus.

Two more flattened bridges (coincidentally in the same year as Brian Waters' book was published) provide a stark reminder of the difficulties facing the return of full navigable status. William Pugh, one of the prime movers in the canal's extension westwards, was born at Pennant. Wealthy, educated, and philanthropic, he built the Flannel Exchange in Newtown and put so much money into the canal and the local economy that he was forced to flee across the Channel to escape his creditors, dying a pauper's exile in 1842. The creditors may have been confounded, but retrospectively we can thank Pugh for this ravishingly beautiful canal.

By Bridge 140 there's a most life-like wooden sculpture of a navvy. At Brynderwen Lock the towpath briefly changes sides to accommodate a former coal wharf. On the death-defying road side of the adjoining corrugated iron clad warehouse an authentic sign still proclaims SHROPSHIRE UNION RAILWAYS & CANAL CO. GENERAL CARRIERS. Grants have been awarded in recent years to sustain the intrinsic biodiversity of the Montgomery Canal, especially in relation to its rare and indigenous floating water plantain *Luronium natans*.

Abermule is remembered for being the site of a railway accident in 1921. Two trains - an Aberystwyth-Manchester express and a Whitchurch-Aberystwyth stopping train - collided head on along a stretch of single track; 17 people were killed and 36 injured. A happier railway memory is of the branchline from Abermule which threaded the gorge of the River Mule to the famous sheep-rearing centre of Kerry. Closed in 1956, in its final days cattle trains struggled up the grass-grown line solely to serve monthly sheep fairs.

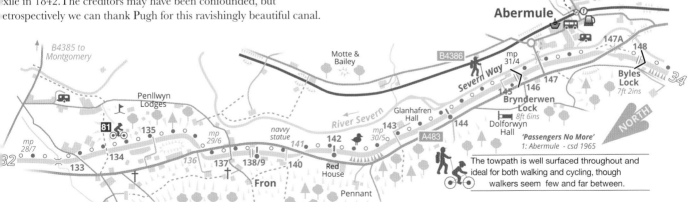

The towpath is well surfaced throughout and ideal for both walking and cycling, though walkers seem few and far between.

SAVOURING its proximity to the Severn, the Western Branch of the Montgomeryshire Canal probes deeper and deeper into the delectable, sheep-rearing heart of mid-Wales, 'The Mont', as it is bluntly but affectionately known to its core supporters, reaches its illogical conclusion on the outskirts of Newtown. Illogical, that is, because even the most zealous revivalist of the canal's fortunes would conclude that restoration of the Montgomery's last couple of miles, together with its once extensive terminal basin, is too far-fetched a proposal to bear close scrutiny.

Newhouse Lock is the last of a restored trio which would suggest to the random passer-by that the canal is more navigable than is the case. Bechan Brook is crossed on a three arched aqueduct before Bridge 152 carries the B4389 road into the hamlet of Aberbechan, the last settlement of any sort before Newtown. Freestone Lock is derelict and gateless, its keeper's house roofless, windowless and strangled by trees, whilst the canal bed beyond is a mass of rushes. Pwll Penarth Nature Reserve is accessible from the towpath.

The Severn broadens and Penarth Weir becomes audible, seeming to mock the moribund canal's inactivity. The weir was constructed by the canal's engineers in 1819 to convey water from the river into the canal. A cast iron sign again reminds us that this was once the property of the Shropshire Union Railways & Canal Company.

Barely discernible, Dolfor Lock stands alongside a large sewage works. The Shropshire Union Canal Society have relaid the hedge here full restoration may be a pipe dream but small contributions like this are still worthwhile. The canal as such vanishes, but its course may be followed along a well defined pathway.

Apart from an abrupt rise in the asphalt path, there is no obvious clue as to the site of Rock Lock, the most westerly on the canal. Quarter of a mile further on, an old pumping house which drew water for the canal up from the River Severn restores your faith that there was indeed a waterway here once. Together with an adjoining cottage and a cast iron overbridge, it looks more like a former railway station. Briefly the course of the canal runs at the rear of terraced houses, but beyond

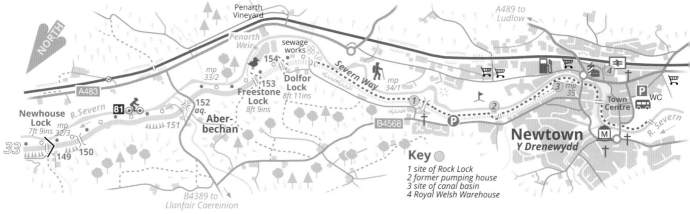

Key
1 site of Rock Lock
2 former pumping house
3 site of canal basin
4 Royal Welsh Warehouse

his point the canal has been built over and it is necessary to follow the riverside Severn Way into the centre of Newtown.

Should this abrupt end appear an anti-climax after the thirty-five mile journey from Welsh Frankton, consider instead the heady days of the nineteenth century when the area was a cornucopia of limekilns, foundries, coal and timber wharves. No less than seven dock arms extended from the main basin, each capable of holding two narrowboats simultaneously. By the twentieth century Newtown's mills were mainly mechanised and, whilst some used water power, others were steam operated and received their coal by canal. The last to do so were the Commercial Mills of Jones, Evans & Co, manufacturers of blankets, shawls and knitted goods. When they closed in 1935, they were still using 20 tons of coal a week. Mined in the collieries at Chirk, it was delivered by Tom Moody in his narrowboat *Endeavour*. Bearing in mind the ever deteriorating state of the Montgomery Canal, the round trip from Chirk probably took around a week to complete and it is doubtful whether he was able to carry any other traffic. When Jones, Evans & Co closed in 1935, Tom Moody stopped work, leaving George Beck as the last surviving boatman on the canal, until the breach of the following year put him out of business too.

NEWTOWN MAP 34

The second town (Llanidloes is the first) that the Severn encounters on its long hike south to the Bristol Channel. Moreover, charm oozes from almost every non-porous brick in this market town whose longevity belies the mundanity of its name. Edward I granted the town a charter in 1279 but it was not until the nineteenth century that Newtown grew significantly with development of the woollen industry at its zenith it acquired the sobriquet 'The Leeds of Wales'. Newtown's most famous son was Robert Owen (1771-1858), the successful capitalist whose socialist ideals inspired the Co-operative movement. His statue stands in Shortbridge Street and his tomb in the grounds of St Mary's ruined riverside church. Prominent on the southern edge of the town by the railway station is the Royal Welsh Warehouse. Erected by Pryce Pryce-Jones, a local draper, it is thought to have been the first mail order business in the world, numbering amongst its customers, Florence Nightingale and Queen Victoria. Pryce-Jones patented the Euklisia Rug, a forerunner of the sleeping bag and is credited with the concept of the parcel post. Another fine feature of this most likeable town is a plethora of impressive nonconformist chapels: Zion Baptist, Welsh and English Calvinistic, Wesleyan et al.

On Severn Street a plaque commemorates local novelist Geraint Goodwin (1903-41) whose life and literary output was cut short by tuberculosis.

Accommodation

YESTERDAYS - Severn Street. Tel: 01686 622644. Superior guest house accommodation for the benefit of tired walkers. Huge Welsh breakfasts. SY16 2AG

Eating & Drinking

JARMAN'S FISH RESTAURANT - High Street. Tel: 01686 625505. Filling fish suppers for hungry walkers. SY16 2NX

PARKERS - Shortbridge Street. Tel: 01686 626095. Comfortable bed & breakfast and cafe from 9am Mon-Sat. SY16 2LW

SPORTSMAN - Severn Street. Tel: 01686 623978. Town centre pub owned by Monty's Brewery from Montgomery. SY16 2BQ

Shopping

Chain stores lurk in the Bear Lanes Precinct and Ladywell Shopping Centre. Pearsonites are more discerning and make for the charming indoor market (Tue, Thur, Fri and Sat) or the launderette on Severn Street should all this walking have resulted in an embarrassing level of dishevelment.

Things to Do

ROBERT OWEN MUSEUM - The Cross, Broad Street. Tel: 01686 625544. Museum (housed in glorious Arts & Crafts 'confection' of a building) telling the remarkable story of the man who inspired the Cooperative movement. Admission free. Open Mon-Fri throughout the year, plus Sats in summer. SY16 2BB

W. H. SMITH MUSEUM - High Street. Tel: 01686 626280. The shop has been restored to its original state when first opened in 1927 and on the first floor is a small museum open shop hours. SY16 2NP

TEXTILE MUSEUM - Commercial Street (north bank of Severn). Tel: 01686 622024. Splendid museum housed in a hand-loom weaving factory dating from the 1830s. Open May to September, Tue, Thur, Fri & Sat, 12-4pm. SY16 2BL

Connections

BUSES - Celtic Travel X75 (Mon-Sat) parallels the Montgomery Canal offering opportunities for one-way walks between Newtown and the likes of Abermule, Garthmyl and Berriew.

TRAINS - Transport for Wales services to/from Welshpool, Shrewsbury and the Mid-Wales coast.

TAXIS - Ross Cabs. Tel 0777 637 5342

Monmouthshire & Brecon Canal

PERCEIVED by many canallers as being too remote and short to be worthy of exploration, what is now known as the Monmouthshire & Brecon Canal was built as two separate waterways, the Monmouthshire Canal and the Brecon & Abergavenny Canal. The former, opened in 1799, ran for eleven miles from the Usk Estuary at Newport to Pontnewynydd, north-west of Pontypool, with an eleven mile branch from Malpas to Crumlin. The latter, opened throughout in 1812, linked Brecon with Pontymoile, junction with the Monmouthshire, a distance of some 33 miles. In 1865 the Brecon & Abergavenny Canal was bought by the Monmouthshire Company. Commercial trade ended in the 1930s and the

Monmouthshire Canal was largely abandoned, but the Brecon & Abergavenny Canal survived, primarily as a water feeder. With financial support from local authorities, the waterway was reopened for navigation between Brecon and Pontymoile in 1970. Subsequent restoration work has seen the limit of navigation pushed south as far as Five Locks, Cwmbran. Further proposals exist to restore the Mon & Brec all the way down to Newport and thus provide a link with the rest of the inland

continued overleaf:

Pontymoile Basin

Pontypool

Tesco

Town Centre

Dry Ski Slope

A472 to Crumlin

WC

51 A

52

Junction Cottage

Griffithstown

50A

St Hilda's

hosp.

50

51

52

53

Cwmbran Tunnel

Sebastopol

Five Locks

60'

Forge Hammer

46

47 48

49

49

492

57'

49

Open Hearth

Pontnewydd

Cwmbran

Afon Llwyd

Knauf Insulation

A4051

Pontypool & New Inn

New Inn

36

A4042 to Abergavenny

cemy

'*Passengers No More*'
1: Upper Pontnewydd - csd 30.4.62
2: Pontnewydd - csd 9.6.58
3: Pontrhydyrun Halt - csd 30.4.62
4: Sebastopol - csd 30.4.62
5: Panteg & Griffithstown - csd 30.4.62
6: Pontypool Blaendare Road - csd 30.4.62
7: Pontypool Clarence Street - csd 15.6.64
8: Pontypool Crane Street - csd 30.4.62

A4042 to Newport

Key
1 site of Panteg Steel Works
2 site of Pontypool Road mpd 86G
3 site of Phoenix Galvanising Works
4 site of Lower Mills Sheet Works

1 Low Headroom

NORTH

Scale: 2½ inches to a mile

continued from page 127:

waterway network (somewhat challengingly) by way of the Usk and Severn estuaries. But for the time being navigability begins, or ends, at Five Locks, where a lowered road bridge and a flight of derelict locks bar any further progress south. In homage to the Great Western Railway's trademark weight limit signs, which still preside over a number of bridges, a lozenge shaped sign records the various agencies involved in the Five Locks restoration scheme, but the fact that it is dated 1983 speaks volumes as to the rate of further progress. Nevertheless, a mooring basin and winding point were provided (in 1997 according to another sign) amidst bland but unthreateningly suburban surroundings.

The first half mile or so of navigable canal is in the care of Torfaen County Borough Council as opposed to the Canal & River Trust. Often pea soup green with algae, the canal water betrays a prevalent hesitancy amongst boaters to venture south of Pontymoile. But an absence of boats is more than compensated for by high numbers of pedestrians - both purposeful and lolling - and cyclists on the metalled towpath.

Cwmbran Tunnel - just 87 yards long with a path over the top - looks rather disconcertingly like a toy, albeit one cradled endearingly in a leafy bower. Such bucolic overtones are shortlived, however, for housing developments have all but gobbled up what was until comparatively recently a pastoral interlude between Cwmbran and Sebastopol. Doubtless the canal will have been a keynote in their marketing strategy. Indeed, mooring pontoons have been put in place, but for who's benefit remains to be seen.

At Bridge 47 TCBC pass the baton of responsibility to CRT and urbanisation sets in. Some may find the post-industrial communities of Pontnewydd, Sebastopol (which gained its name from the Crimean War) and Griffithstown too dour for their holiday-making sensibilities, but this is the real South Wales, a throwback zone of terraced houses, telegraph poles and ice cream van jingles. Griffithstown was eponymously named after Henry, the first stationmaster at Pontypool Road, who founded a building society which enabled railway workers to become owner-occupiers, so that it is, in effect, as much a railway town as Crewe or Swindon. A memorial at St Hilda's church commemorates his altruism.

Surviving Monmouthshire Canal mileposts measure the distance from Newport to the south. Housing smothers the site of Panteg Steel Works, closed in 2004. In its heyday it boasted nine open hearth melting furnaces and sixteen sheet mills. At one time the plant was owned by Baldwins, the midland tinplate manufacturers, who could count a Prime Minister amongst their progeny.

The gaunt, four storey building of plum coloured sandstone and creamy Ebbw Vale brickwork (dated 1900) overlooking Bridge 50 was originally the Pontypool Poor Law Institution workhouse. Designed to cater for a hundred paupers, its occupancy rapidly doubled. Later it became an isolation hospital. Sprouting ivy and buddleia now, it comes as a shock to learn that it is still in use by NHS Wales, stark evidence of chronic underfunding if ever it were needed.

Converted into a cycleway, the trackbed of the Monmouthshire Eastern Valleys railway crosses the canal on high, skewed girders by Bridge 51, a neighbouring masonry arch provoking photogenic juxtaposition. A competent transport artist could do worse than capture a nostalgic encounter between a train and a working boat at this point. Passenger services were withdrawn between Newport and Blaenavon (Low Level) on 30th April 1962. They had been dieselised, to no avail, five years earlier.

Pontymoile Basin marks the former junction of the Monmouthshire and Brecon & Abergavenny canals. Not without irony the busy dual-carriageway A472 running west to Crumlin and Ebbw Vale was built over the course of an abandoned railway, itself built over the course of the Monmouthshire Canal. History can be awfully unkind to transport undertakings. Nowadays Pontymoile Basin is a popular leisure asset for nearby Pontypool. A tea bar and picnic site draw the locals, though it was sad to see the bow-fronted junction house boarded-up on the occasion of our most recent sortie. Here, in the canal's working past, boats were assessed for tolls as they went from one canal to the other. Close by, an aqueduct - the tallest on the Mon & Brec - carries the canal over the Afon Llwyd ('Grey River') where the young turks of the neighbourhood are apt to dive noisily in on hot days.

CWMBRAN MAP 35

A 'new town' established in 1949, and now the sixth largest urban area in Wales. Arguably best known as the location of Burton's biscuit factory, makers of Jammie Dodgers and Wagon Wheels.

Shopping

Local shops at Pontnewydd

Connections

TRAINS - Transport for Wales offer links with the outside world and the possibility of one-way towpath walks to/from Abergavenny.
TAXIS - Gwent Cars. Tel: 01633 866665.

SEBASTOPOL MAP 35

Mid-19th century industrial village which grew up around St Oswald's canalside church, and which gained its name from the Black Sea port of Sebastopol and the contemporary siege which occurred there during the Crimean War.

Eating & Drinking

OPEN HEARTH - Wern Road, Sebastopol (between bridges 48 & 49). Tel: 01495 763752. The lost tradition of steel-making gives this friendly canalside pub (and Good Beer Guide fixture) its curious name, though the buildings origins can be traced back to the 17th century when it was a cowman's cottage. Real ales and a wide-ranging menu make this probably the best port of call in the vicinity. Open from 9am daily and, apart from a quarter of an hour's break before noon, food enterprisingly served throughout. NP4 5DR
PAGES FISH BAR - Greenhill Road, Sebastopol (Bridge 48). Tel: 01495 753185. Open from noon Wed-Sat. Established in 1949, still in the same family, and reputedly one of the best in South Wales. Sister restaurant in 'downtown' Cwmbran. NP4 5BQ

GRIFFITHSTOWN MAP 35

Grid-like streets of terrace houses interspersed with non-conformist chapels. Profoundly Welsh in feel.

Shopping

Co-op convenience store on Windsor Road accessed west of bridges 49 & 50.

PONTYPOOL MAP 35

A much older town than Cwmbran, having grown dramatically during the industrial revolution. Once renowned for its decorative 'japanned' goods. These days the jewel in its somewhat tarnished crown is a large municipal park, complete with leisure centre, ski slope and home to Pontypool RFC, one of the most illustrious rugby clubs in Wales.

Eating & Drinking

Tea bar at Pontymoile Basin open daily (ex Thur) Wed-Sun 9am-2.30pm. Harvester Restaurant (Tel: 01495 751551) KFC and McDonald's at nearby junction of A472/A4042. The Horse & Jockey stands downhill from Bridge 55. (Map 36) Tel: 01495 762723.

Shopping

Petrol station shop 5 mins from Pontymoile Basin. Tesco supermarket and town shops 20 mins away.

Things to Do

TORFAEN MUSEUM - Park Road. Tel: 01495 752036. Splendid museum of local history housed in Georgian stable block. Fine collections on local industry. Open daily (ex Mon & Fri) 10am-4pm. Shop and refreshments. Admission fee (children gratis) NP4 6JH

Connections

TRAINS - Transport for Wales services to/from Cwmbran and Abergavenny etc. from station best reached on foot via Bridge 53.
TAXIS - Dragon Cars. Tel: 01495 781781.

MAMHILAD MAP 36

A hamlet rather than a village. The pretty little red sandstone church of St Illtyd, notable for a yew tree of exceptional girth and antiquity - perhaps two thousand years old. Of equally significant duration was the Reverend Christopher Cook, incumbent for seventy years.

Eating & Drinking

STAR INN - Old Abergavenny Road (Bridge 62). Tel: 01495 785319. Comfortable country pub open from noon daily. Lunch and dinner (from 6pm), lunch only on Sun. NP4 0JF
HORSESHOE INN - Old Abergavenny Road (Bridge 65). Tel: 01873 880542. Another well appointed and welcoming country pub. Lunches (from noon) and evening meals (from 5.30pm) open lunch & evenings Mon-Thur and from noon throughout Fri-Sun. Local ales. NP4 8QZ

PENPERLLENI MAP 36

GOYTRE ARMS - Penperlleni (10 mins walk east of bridges 71/72). Tel: 01873 880376. NP4 0AH. The village also boasts a fish & chips bar.

GOYTRE WHARF MAP 37

Penelope's Cafe (Tel: 01873 880899 - NP7 9EW) provides refreshments, and ABC offer self-catering for up to four in Aqueduct Cottage - Tel: 0330 333 0590. CRT charge for parking.

LLANOVER MAP 37

Comfortably furnished, Hummingbird coffee shop (Tel: 01873 881044) is a pleasant walk down from Bridge 80. They do a nice line in local gifts too. NP7 9HA Stagecoach X3/33 buses run hourly to/from Cardiff (via Cwmbran and Pontypool) and Abergavenny.

FORMING the eastern boundary of the Brecon Beacons National Park - not that the landscape beyond appears any less meritorious - the canal winds picturesquely between frequent overbridges. The pretty little primrose coloured church of St Michael lies just downhill from Bridge 55. Even when it´s locked, as is sadly so often the case, you can admire its unusual double bell-cote.

Through the towpath hedge there are glimpses of Mamhilad Park Estate, a business park located on the site of a vast works erected by British Nylon Spinners in 1948. At its zenith the works employed five thousand people and could boast a ballroom for whatever leisure hours were available to them. The industrial photographer, Maurice Broomfield, visited the plant in 1964 and took an iconic image of a headscarfed woman at work on one of the warp machines. Somewhat emasculated, the remaining buildings host myriad activities, many of them local and regional government based. In 1971 it gained a neighbour in the shape of a pharmaceutical works erected for the

Parke Davis company which was said to have the longest internal corridor in the UK. Subsequently it fell out of use and was used for filming episodes of Dr Who in 2007. Now it has been demolished and the site is to be redeveloped.

Prominent on the neighbouring ridge to the west stands the Folly Tower, erected in the 1770s as a summer house and lookout for deer hunting. During the Second World War it was more or less completely demolished against fears that enemy aircraft might employ it to pinpoint the munitions plant at Glascoed. Not until 1994 was it fully rebuilt.

Throughout its working existence, the canal's main traffic was in coal. Other significant cargoes included iron and timber. Barges were typically of nine foot beam and just over sixty feet in length. They were horse drawn and could carry twenty tons. The last recorded toll - for a boatload of lime - was recorded at Llangynidr (Map 42) in 1933.

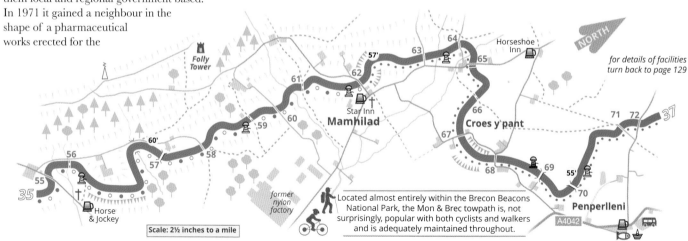

for details of facilities turn back to page 129

Located almost entirely within the Brecon Beacons National Park, the Mon & Brec towpath is, not surprisingly, popular with both cyclists and walkers and is adequately maintained throughout.

Scale: 2½ inches to a mile

TREE-LINED, secretive, and often demarcating the boundaries of traditional hill farms, the canal sustains its idyllic progress between, to the west, the steep flanks of a ridge which separates it from the once heavily industrialised South Wales Valleys and, to the east, a pastoral landscape levelling out past clumps of woodland towards the banks of the Usk. Frequent occupation bridges - most humped, some flat-decked - punctuate the canal's progress along the 367 foot contour line. Thomas Dadford Junior's feat of essaying a twenty-five mile pound in such mountainous surrounds is a remarkable achievement. Occasionally you find yourself wishing, heretically, that there were less trees, because they do tend to mask the views, though, by the time the bridge numbers are in the early eighties, you begin to glimpse the mountains which lie ahead, notably Sugar Loaf to the left and the Ysgyryds (Skirrids), Fach (Small) and Fawr (Great), to the right.

Goytre Wharf has long been a showcase for the Mon & Brec, and continues to fulfil that role, having been acquired by the ABC Leisure Group

from the Canal & River Trust. A microcosm of a typical canal wharf of its era, it attracts a surprising number of visitors by road; though if they are curious to see the canal in its historic setting, or simply desperate for a cup of tea and a slice or two of cake is anyone's guess. Certainly the setting, with its aqueduct and rank of lime kilns, is worth savouring, although visitor moorings - squeezed between angler's perches and a water point - are at a premium.

Between bridges 77 and 78 there is a circular cattle drinking pond fed from the canal. The house on the offside by Bridge 81 features an internal boathouse. Glimpsed below through the trees, Llanover House belonged to one Benjamin Hall, who, as Commissioner of Works, gave his name to London's most famous horological landmark, Big Ben. To cross precipitous water courses, the canal is twice forced into horseshoe curves: challenging engineering feats in their day, whilst demanding of vigilant maintenance even now; but hugely scenic in effect.

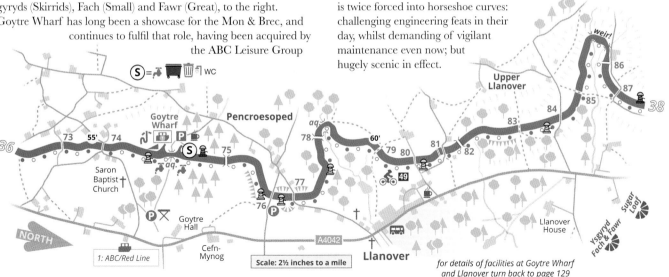

for details of facilities at Goytre Wharf and Llanover turn back to page 129

ALEXANDER CORDELL'S historical saga, *Rape of the Fair Country*, contains sequences featuring the canal in which he writes vividly of lying on the prow of a barge watching the water lilies and bindweed waving as sunlight streams through the trees casting golden patterns on the boat. Cordell's ashes are buried in the extensive municipal cemetery at Llanfoist. Picturesque to a fault, Llanfoist Wharf was once the scene of intense industrial activity. Hill's tramroad linked the ironworks at Blaenavon and forge at Garnddyrys with the canal wharf and the Llanvihangel tramroad on the valley floor below. To explore the route of the tramroad, go down the steps adjacent to Bridge 95A to reach the road and the entrance to the tunnel, which leads uphill beneath the canal to the tramroad incline. The route can be followed up the hillside and on to Blorenge Mountain whose 1,833ft summit can be reached in a couple of hours. North of Llanfoist Wharf the canal passes the imposing Llanfoist House, once the home of Crawshay Bailey, the ironmaster of Nantyglo and MP for Monmouth. A major breach occurred at White House Turn in 1975, when thousands of gallons of water cascaded down onto parts of the village below the canal. Six years were to pass before the breach was repaired and the section reopened.

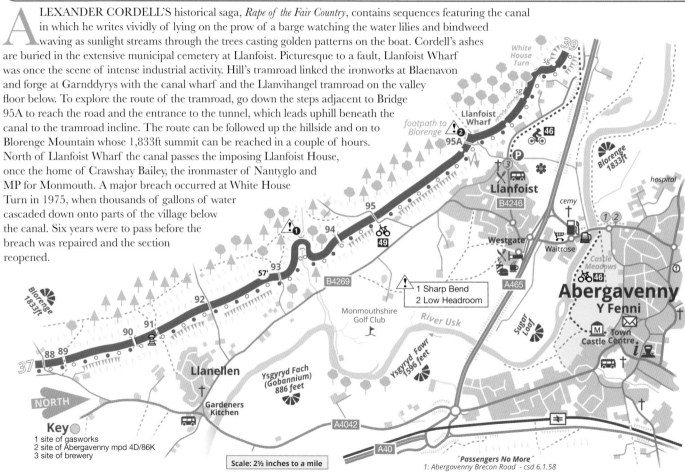

1 Sharp Bend
2 Low Headroom

Monmouthshire Golf Club

River Usk

White House Turn

Llanfoist Wharf

footpath to Blorenge

95A

95

94

93

92

91

90

88 89

57'

37

B4269

B4246

B4246

Blorenge 1833ft

Llanfoist

Westgate

Waitrose

A465

Blorenge 1833ft

hospital

cemy

Castle Meadows

Abergavenny
Y Fenni

Town Castle Centre

Sugar Loaf

Ysgyryd Fawr 1596 feet

Llanellen

Ysgyryd Fach (Gobannium) 886 feet

Gardeners Kitchen

A4042

A40

NORTH

Key
1 site of gasworks
2 site of Abergavenny mpd 4D/86K
3 site of brewery

Scale: 2½ inches to a mile

'Passengers No More'
1: Abergavenny Brecon Road - csd 6.1.58

LLANELLEN

Map 38

Village tucked below the canal on the busy Pontypool to Abergavenny main road. Gardeners Kitchen deli/farm shop/cafe - Tel: 0780 589 8132. NP7 9HT

LLANFOIST

Map 38

The remains of the ironmaster Crawshay Bailey lie in the cemetery of the church of St Faith's (a 3rd Century martyr) which you pass on your steep descent from the canal. Edward's Brewery - noted for 'Jolly Brew' - ceased brewing in 1945.

Eating & Drinking

BREWERS FAYRE - Westgate. Tel: 01873 776294. Chain restaurant open for food throughout from 6.30am weekdays and 7am weekends. NP7 9LH

BRIDGE INN - Merthyr Road. Tel: 01873 854831. Pub overlooking the Usk. Open from noon daily. Food and accommodation. NP7 9LH

SPICE LOUNGE - Merthyr Road. Tel: 01873 855720. Indian rest. & t/a daily (ex M) from 5.30pm. NP7 9LP
There are branches of Costa and McDonald's at Westgate adjoining the Heads of the Valleys A465.

Shopping

Waitrose supermarket - open from 7.30am (10am Sun) about 15 minutes walk from Bridge 95A. Abergavenny Garden Centre is also located in Llanfoist.

Self-Catering

Beacon Park Cottages have a trio of idyllically situated properties (two sleeping two, and one sleeping six) for holiday hire at Llanfoist Wharf - Tel: 01873 858277.

ABERGAVENNY

Map 38

Canallers may legitimately wish that Hamelin of Ballon had sited his 11th century castle on the *west* bank of the Usk and that Abergavenny had subsequently developed much closer to where the canal was eventually dug. Similarly, railway enthusiasts may mourn the closure of the Heads of the Valleys line in 1958, prior to which they could have caught a local train at Govilon and passed triumphantly over the Usk into Abergavenny (Brecon Road) in a cloud of smoke and steam. More mundanely, nowadays you will need to catch a bus or call a taxi, or make the mile long journey under your own steam. But make it one must, for it is well-nigh impossible to resist the siren call of the town hall tower - positively Ruritanian in its lofty eminence - and the town itself is of enormous appeal.

Eating & Drinking

ANGEL HOTEL - Cross Street. Tel: 01873 857121. Old coaching inn offering bar and restaurant food and accommodation. NP7 5EW

BOTANICAL CAFE - Frogmore Street. Tel: 01873 853306. Nicholls department store coffee shop with outdoor courtyard open daily 9am-4.30pm. NP7 5AH

GURKHA CORNER - Nevill Street. Tel: 01873 855800. Nepali cuisine. Sister est. in Brecon. NP7 5AD

KINGS ARMS - Nevill Street. Tel: 01873 855074. Comfortable accommodation and 'gastropub' food. We enjoyed coracle-caught sewin! NP7 5AA

MARKET STREET FISH & CHIPS - Market Street. Tel: 01873 855791. Restaurant/take-away. NP7 5SD

PIZZORANTE - Market Street. Tel: 01873 857777. Italian serving lunch & dinner Tue-Sat. NP7 5SD

WALNUT TREE INN - Llanddewi Skirrid. Tel: 01873 852797. Michelin starred dining at internationally famous restaurant 3 miles NE of A. NP7 8AW

Shopping

Waitrose notwithstanding, it is Abergavenny's independent shops - like Rawlings the butchers on Market Street, Neil Powell butchers and delicatessen on Flannel Street and Chesters Wine Merchants on Cross Street - which really contribute to the pleasure of shopping here. Look out too for Nicholls department store on Frogmore Street, and Broadleaf Books secondhand bookshop on Monk Street. The lively retail market which they're so proud of takes place on Tuesdays in and around the handsome market hall. There are additional retail markets on Fridays and Saturdays, a vibrant Flea Market on Wednesdays, a Craft Market on the second Saturday, and a Farmers Market on the fourth Thursday in the month. By the way, don't miss the former Burton's men's clothes shop (now Mountain Warehouse) which retains its 'Tailor of Taste' slogan and gold-leafed list of towns with branches. Abergavenny's growing reputation as a food centre culminates each September in an increasingly influential event which has been labelled 'the Glastonbury of food festivals'.

Things to Do

TOURIST INFORMATION - Town Hall, Monmouth Road. Tel: 01873 853254. NP7 EH

ABERGAVENNY MUSEUM AND CASTLE - Castle Street. Tel: 01873 854282. Open daily March-October, closed Sundays November-February. Displays trace the history of the town from Roman times. NP7 5EE

ST MARY'S PRIORY - Monk Street. Tel: 01873 858787. Imposing priory church described as 'the Westminster Abbey of South Wales'. Adjoining 13th century tithe barn houses the Abergavenny Tapestry which took sixty ladies four years to stitch. Locally sourced refreshments and souvenir shop. NP7 5ND

Connections

BUSES - Merthyr Tydfil (Cardiff) service X4 calls at Llanfoist, Govilon and Gilwern; Brecon buses (43) stop at Crickhowell; X3/X33 runs to/from Cardiff via Llanover, Pontypool & Cwmbran.

TRAINS - Transport for Wales services to/from Shrewsbury and Cwmbran, Newport and Cardiff.

TAXIS - Station Cars. Tel: 01873 857233.

GOVILON AND GILWERN provide alliterative punctuation to your journey as the canal veers north-westwards out of Abergavenny's orbit, and in doing so introduces a not entirely unwelcome atmosphere of urbanisation: all those arboreal glades can become a tad repetitive when dawdling along at one and a half miles an hour. Govilon Wharf hosts the Canal & River Trust's maintenance yard as well as Govilon Boat Club. The wharf was once an interchange point with tramroad, and later railway, traffic. In *The Forgotten Railways of South Wales* (David & Charles, 1979) James Page considered the Merthyr Tredegar & Abergavenny Railway the most spectacular in South Wales. The trackbed is now a well-surfaced footpath and cycleway worth exploring, perhaps as part of a circular itinerary incorporating the towpath. Adjacent Bridge 97B stands Llanwenarth Baptist Church whose fellowship, dating from 1652, is reputedly the oldest in Wales. With its hipped roof and cream painted

facade, it presents a memorable sight from the canal, backed by the summit of Sugar Loaf. As is common in Wales, the churchyard - entered through a fine wrought iron gateway - contains many handsome tombs and headstones.

Much encumbered, William Bliss alighted at Govilon station to begin his canoeing trip along the Mon & Brec Canal vividly described in *Rapid Rivers*, published in 1935. He wrote of this section of the canal: 'The canal made a bend to cross the little Llanwenarth brook, and between that and Gilwern there were wonderful open views from the canal itself up the Usk Valley. I was glad I had come. It was late May, and everything was green and happy and there was no-one there but me'. There are still wonderful views up the Usk Valley and across to Sugar Loaf and the Black Mountains, and everything is still 'green and happy'. As for there being 'no-one there', well we can't promise that, but by virtue of its isolation, the Mon & Brec is *Bliss*fully quieter than the main canal network. Govilon's parish church nestles snugly beneath the canal's embankment.

Blorenge

Gilwern Hill

46

B4246

Llanwenarth House

7

aq.

B

98

57'

A

99

100

101

102

96

97

Govilon

Sugar Loaf 1955ft

Monmouthshire

3

103

104 lime kilns

aq.

S

60'

105

P

106

107

60'

Llanelly

NORTH

A4077

R. Clydach

River Usk

Powys

Pen Cerrig-calch 2302ft

A465

38

40

60' A

'Passengers No More'
1: Govilon - csd 6.1.58
2: Gilwern Halt - csd 6.1.58

Scale: 2½ inches to a mile

1	Low Headroom
2	Blind Bend
3	Very Low Headroom

S = WC

134

t dates from the middle of the 19th century, before which villagers crossed the Usk by ferry to pay their devotions. The lych-gate commemorates a former village schoolmaster who rejoiced in the unforgettable name of Ivor Tossell. It was at Llanwenarth House, south of Bridge 100, that Mrs Cecil F. Alexander, an Irish poetess, composed the words for the hymn *All Things Bright and Beautiful* in 1848. Certainly she had a plethora of 'purple headed mountain(s)' to inspire her muse.

At Gilwern a right-angled bend takes the canal dramatically across the Clydach Gorge on a ninety foot high embankment. On the south side was the Clydach Iron Company's wharf and a connecting tramroad, branches of which led to further wharves and to the Clydach Basin, now the base of Castle Narrowboats who, probably uniquely in the UK, offer electric powered boats for hire, charged from points along the canal.

Visitor moorings encourage exploration in the neighbourhood of the aqueduct where steps lead down into the bosky gorge.

It was in the neighbourhood of Bridge 106 that a breach occurred in October 2007 which resulted in the canal being closed for over a year. Subsequently, sixteen miles of canal were closed for a geotechnical survey to be carried out and ninety leaks were discovered. A hundred thousand fish had to be relocated. In the end some £15 million was spent on refurbishing the canal, an outlay commensurate with the canal's annual contribution to the local economy. From Bridge 106 a rocky path climbs to the tiny village of Llanelly whose parish church, dedicated to St Elli, contains stained glass windows depicting the coal and iron industries; frustratingly, the church tends only to be open at weekends.

GOVILON Map 39

Interpretive boards usher you entertainingly around a number of Heritage Trails. The War Memorial is notable in that it lists a female civilian, one May Prosser, believed to have been killed in a munitions factory.

Eating & Drinking

TAFARN Y BONT - Church Lane (best approached via the aqueduct steps). Tel: 01873 830720. Open from 5.30pm Mon-Fri and throughout from noon Sat & Sun. Pub with good choice of food. NP7 9RP

Shopping

Convenience store open 7.30am (8am Sun) to 8pm.

Connections

BUSES - Stagecoach X4 operates hourly Mon-Sat between Abergavenny and Cardiff (an interesting journey through 'The Valleys'). Additional links to Abergavenny on Service 3.

GILWERN Map 39

The industry of the Clydach Gorge has withered with age and been replaced by commuter properties handy for the Heads of the Valleys highway. But there remain fascinating nooks and crannies to uncover, whilst this is a useful point for feeding & watering, especially if you're not planning to visit the fleshpots of Y Fenni.

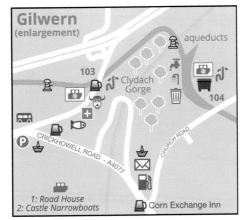

Gilwern (enlargement)

aqueducts

103

Clydach Gorge

104

CRICKHOWELL ROAD - A4077

CHURCH ROAD

1: Road House
2: Castle Narrowboats

Corn Exchange Inn

Eating & Drinking

BEAUFORT ARMS - Main Road. Tel: 01633 846198. Re-opened pub, noted now for food. NP7 0AR
CORN EXCHANGE INN - Crickhowell Road. Tel: 01873 832404. Open from 4pm Mon-Fri and noon Sat & Sun. Food served Sunday lunch only. NP7 0DG
TOWPATH INN - Main Road. Boutique village pub. Street Food pop-ups. Accommodation. NP7 0AR
VILLAGE FISH BAR - Main Road. Tel: 01873 832040. Open Wed-Sat, noon to 8pm. Award-winning fish & chips cooked fresh to order, so you may like to telephone ahead rather than queue. NP7 0AS

Shopping

A good butcher (Bromfields - Tel: 01873 268686), pharmacy, and charming little gift shop (Road House Narrowboats - Tel: 01873 830240 - who also offer B&B) on Main Road leading down from Bridge 103. Two convenience stores, and a post office by petrol station on A4077.

Connections

BUSES - as Govilon.

Ashford Tunnel (Map 42)

139

ECO CYCLE BOAT FROM BEACON PARK BOAT

Talybont-on-Usk (Map 42)

EXCHANGING Monmouthshire for Powys (or, more properly in the Pearson scheme of things, Brecknockshire) the canal glides enchantingly beneath the quarried flank of Llangattock Mountain and above the broad valley of the Usk. You don't get anywhere fast on this shallow canal, yet nor should you want to; this is Stevenson's 'travelling hopefully', not your daily commute. As our headline timings imply, you are unlikely to average even two miles an hour on this canal, half the statutory limit. Plenty of time, then, to mull over the Brecknock & Abergavenny Canal's late 18th century origins, work upon which commenced in 1796, on this very section as it happens. Initially, progress was comparatively swift, and it opened between Gilwern

(Map 39) and Llangynidr (Map 41) within a couple of years. Thomas Dadford Junior was the engineer. Progress, after that initial surge, became more slothful - the Napoleonic Wars were not conducive to investment - and the canal was not completed until 1812. Connecting tramways brought welcome amounts of additional trade. One such, now a public right of way, can be followed from the by-road which crosses Bridge 114, up into the hills to the south-west as far as Craig y Cilau National Nature Reserve. Dramatically located on the site of a former limestone quarry, the reserve is considered one of the most outstanding botanical sites in Wales, a paradise of alpine plants

Craig y Cilau

crse of former tramway

Beacon Park

115

Llangattock Wharf

Llangattock Boat Club

113

114

60'

112

116

Mynydd Llangattock 1735ft

110

111

Llangattock

117

Ffawyddog

120

39

108

109

Heron's Rest Marina

41

industrial estate

Table Mountain 1481ft

P

Old Rectory

Ty Croeso

118

119

Powys

Vine Tree

Horse Shoe

B4558

Dardy

River Usk

A4077

Black Mountains Smokery

Bussiness Park

A40

Castle

Crickhowell

Pen Allt-mawr 2360ft

NORTH

Town Centre

Manor Hotel

Pen Cerrig-calch 2302ft

Scale: 2½ inches to a mile

S = 🗑 🗑 WC

Northbound through Bridge 110 you catch your first glimpse of Table Mountain squatting amiably over the little town of Crickhowell, a community approaching perfection. Try mooring for the night near Bridge 111, then, as daylight fades, watch the lights twinkling in the cottages and farms far across the valley, like a sea of stars in a cloudless sky.

A lofty rank of limekilns dominates the scene at Llangattock Wharf. Published by Crickhowell District Archive Centre, *A History of Llangattock* provides fascinating detail to the working life of the district. A. L. Watkins ran a coal and haulage business from the wharf, and when the former ceased being delivered by barge, it would be collected from Abergavenny railway stations in wagons drawn by a Foden steam traction engine. Another occupant of the wharf was Thomas Edwards, a wheelwright and signwriter. In the 19th century when the limekilns were still in use, it was apparently the habit of tramps to sleep beside them at night for warmth.

Visitor Moorings just south of Bridge 116 provide the easiest access to Crickhowell. By far the nicest way to get there is through St Catwg's churchyard on a path which comes out at Crickhowell Bridge, which from downstream appears to have thirteen arches, whilst from upstream twelve; and this before you've patronised any of the town's drinking establishments.

The buildings clustered above the canal at Bridge 118 are remnants of the Crickhowell Union Workhouse. The largest, once an infamary, is now ironically a luxury Bed & Breakfast establishment. What would the inmates make of such a transformation? Other surviving buildings include the Fever Ward, Master's House, Chapel, Casual Ward and Laundry. The double-doored garage-like building nearest the bridge housed the establishment's hearse, purloined on occasion for the conveyance of pigs to market. Concrete edged, the canal north of Bridge 119 appears to solicit mooring but appearances are deceptive, for the sides are extremely shallow.

LLANGATTOCK — Map 40

Llangattock takes its name from the imposing church of St Catwg, founded in the 6th century and rebuilt in the 12th. Tucked away down a narrow lane, the village stocks and whipping post are in its grounds.

Eating & Drinking

HORSE SHOE INN - Hillside Road. Tel: 01873 268773. Re-opened village pub offering Jamaican pop-up food. NP8 1PA

OLD RECTORY HOTEL - Access from Bridge 116. Tel: 01873 810373. Country house hotel with 9 hole golf course offering food to non-residents. NP8 1PH

TY CROESO - The Dardy. Tel: 01873 740173. Luxury B&B in former workhouse. NP8 1PU

VINE TREE - Llangattock. Tel: 01873 812277. 19th century inn close to the Usk. Restaurant/bar/self-catering. Closed Mon & Tue. Lunches from noon, evening meals from 6pm ex Sun. NP8 1HG

Connections

BUSES - Traws Cymru service 43 connects Llangattock with Crickhowell (and thence Abergavenny), and with Brecon (via Llangattock and Talybont) five times a day, Mon-Sat.

CRICKHOWELL — Map 40

We trust that this peach of a little town - increasingly well-known for its annual Walking Festival at the beginning of March - will rub off on you as favourably as it always does us. The name is the Anglicised form of Crug Hywel, the rampart and the ditch stronghold of Hywel Dda - now known as Table Mountain, which overlooks the town. Eat your heart out Cape Town!

Eating & Drinking

BEAR HOTEL - High Street. Tel: 01873 810408. Immensely comfortable and welcoming 15th century coaching inn; all beams, big fireplaces and flagstones. Bar and restaurant meals plus very tempting accommodation. NP8 1BW

BRITANNIA INN - High Street. Tel: 01873 810553. Wye Valley ales, open from 11am daily. NP8 1BD

COURTROOM CAFE - Market Hall. Tel: 01873 812497. Refreshments in historic setting. NP8 1BD

DRAGON INN - High Street. Tel: 01873 810362. Stylish hotel & restaurant rivalling The Bear. NP8 1BE

LATTE-DA - Beaufort Street. Tel: 01873 810579. Beguiling tea room offering breakfasts, lunches and teas and open daily from 10am to 4pm. Try the American pancakes, replete with bacon and the fluffiest scrambled eggs you'll ever taste. Suntrap of a 'secret' garden to rear, ice creams and first floor craft gallery. NP8 1AD

TREEBEARDS - High Street. Tel: 01873 268668. Craft beer and cordial bar. From noon Wed-Sun. NP8 1BH

VAMOS - The Courtyard, Standard Street. Tel: 0748 828 3800. Cafe open daily (ex Mon) between 9.30am and 5.30pm. NP8 1BP

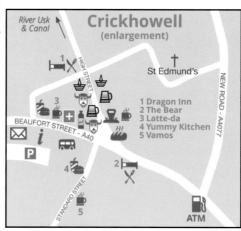

YUMMY KITCHEN - Standard Street. Tel: 0187 811177. Traditional fish & chips, pizzeria and chargr take-away. Open Mon-Sat 10am-9pm. NP8 1BP

Shopping

Supermarket-free Crickhowell is a heavenly place t saunter around and shopping here is the pleasur it ought to be, the emphasis being on characterf individual retail outlets as exemplified by the zer waste wholefood shop Natural Weigh. Maiflou Bakery, Grenfell's Grocery, Cashells and Richarc butchers shops, and Webbs (est. 1936) furnitur hardware and kitchenware store. Nicholls (est. 192 clothes shop also has branches in Abergavenny ar Brecon. Tower Gallery on High Street is home to Us Valley Artists' Co-operative. Enterprising organise of Crickhowell's annual literary festival in Octobe Book-ish on High Street also operate an exceller cafe to the rear. Bacchus (Beaufort St.) stocks good choice of wine together with a thirst-inducir range of bottled Welsh beers. Outdoor clothir and accessories from Crickhowell Adventure. Pos office at the southern end of the town on Beaufor Street. Small market on Thursdays. South of the tow centre, in a business park beside the A40, is the Blac Mountains Smokery, open 9am-5pm weekdays.

Things to Do

CRiC - Beaufort Street. Tel: 01873 811970. Exemplar modern information centre run by gregarious sta upper storey gallery and internet facilities. Open dai (ex Sun) from 10am until 4pm. NP8 1BN

Connections

BUSES - Traws Cymru services X43/43 connec Crickhowell approximately bi-hourly, Mon-Sa with Brecon (via Llangattock and Talybont 43) an Abergavenny.

TAXIS - Crickhowell Taxis. Tel: 01873 811764.

ARE there any limits to the beauty of the Mon & Brec, you catch yourself wondering rhetorically, and, given the visual evidence at your disposal, you are in no position to demur. Why, even those of an industrial archaeological bent, used to salivating their way around the murkier and more arcane corners of the BCN can enjoy a Pavlovian response in the limekilns and tramroads which continue to evoke recollections of this canal's industrial origins.

Amongst other events, Glanusk Park hosts the annual Green Man music festival. The estate was established in 1826 by Sir Joseph Bailey who, like his brother Crawshay (Map 38), had made his fortune in iron production. The original mansion was demolished after being set on fire by the Army, who had requisitioned it during the Second World War, but the imposing Dower House remains. In 1876 the estate's gamekeeper was shot dead whilst trying to apprehend poachers. The stone 'barn' by bridge 125 formerly saw use as a stable for boat horses.

Backed by the conifer forested slopes of Myarth Hill, and the craggy outcrops of Darren and Bryniog, stands Gliffaes. It is an Italianate country house, erected towards the end of the 19th century for a Rev. W. West, a well-travelled clergyman who had managed to mislay three of his family's fortunes in the process. Since the nineteen thirties it has been used as an hotel and is notable for its twin campaniles. When the vicar finally ran out of money the house passed to a man called Sir Shirley Salt, the son - and this will appeal to users of *Pearson's Canal Companion to the Leeds & Liverpool Canal* - of Titus Salt of Saltaire, Bradford. Sir Shirley had married one of the Baileys of Glanusk and had, not surprisingly, become enamoured of the neighbourhood as much as one of its female residents. Gliffaes translates sweetly as 'dewy field' and, by all accounts, the hotel offers considerable luxury to its guests, though unfortunately there is no way to reach it easily from the canal without getting wet.

Approaching Llangynidr (difficult for mere Anglo Saxons to pronounce, but try 'Clan-gun-idder') an aqueduct carries the canal over Nant Cleisfer, and the beauty simply continues ... unabated!

Scale: 2½ inches to a mile

1 Low Headroom

TWENTY-FIVE idyllic miles of northbound lock-free cruising come abruptly to an end at Bridge 132. It makes, however, a pleasant change for boaters to have something to do and non-boaters to have something to watch whilst, like English wickets going down in a Test Match, you don't just get one or two locks, but five in relatively quick succession. Designed - like most locks in South Wales - to accommodate boats of 63ft length and 9ft beam, they are spread over less than a mile and lift the canal up by 48 feet. Local practice is to leave the locks empty with bottom gates open; something of an inconvenience as it means you always have to fill the lock first when locking down, or empty it afterwards when locking up. The apparently random numbers (64-68) date from the Great Western Railway's acquisition of the canal in 1880. Further evidence of GWR ownership includes boundary posts and the lozenge-shaped weight-limit signs familiar to those who know the Stratford-on-Avon Canal.

Between the first and second locks the canal crosses the River Crawnon on a sizeable aqueduct equipped with a plug and conventional windlass to drain this section of the canal. Public moorings are provided nearby, presenting the opportunity to be lulled to sleep by the babbling waters of the Crawnon. Hirers from Country Craft - one of six bases on this isolated canal - can avail themselves of offside moorings handy for a delightful path which runs alongside a feeder into the woods.

Canal & River Trust volunteers are often in attendance to help you through Lock 65; thus 'Llangynidr Welcome Station' invariably lives up to its name. Attended by woodland, the top three locks are overlooked by the almost perfectly rounded summit of Tor y Foel. On the towpath side, in the short pound between locks 67 and 68, a side pond - more like a small lake in appearance - helps to equate water levels. When the canal was being built, a Roman secespita, or sacrificial knife, was discovered at this point. The Visitor Moorings above the top lock are particularly attractive and correspondingly popular.

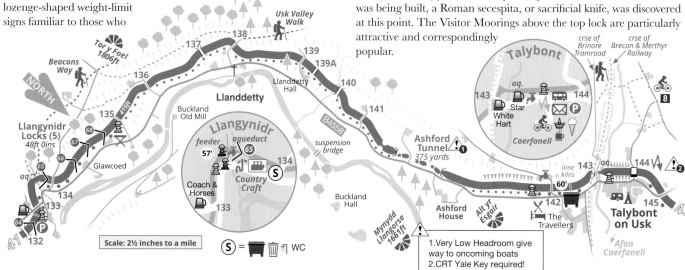

1.Very Low Headroom give way to oncoming boats
2.CRT Yale Key required!

A stroll downhill from Bridge 138 stands the little Tudor church of t Tetti at Llanddetty. Steeped in history, one of its most remarkable ssociations dates back to the Civil War when a Parliamentarian arishioner by the name of Jenkin Jones appropriated the incumbency, sing the church as a farm. He was apparently milking his ewes when e heard of the landing of Charles II at Dover in 1660. Instantly he nounted his horse, rode through the churchyard, discharged a pistol nd cried out: 'Ah, thy old whore of Babylon, thou'll have it all thy own vay now' before riding off and never being seen in the neighbourhood gain. A bullet hole in the priest's door corroborates the story to this lay. Nearby a decrepit suspension bridge spans the Usk. It was probably rected to enable people from Buckland Hall to visit the church. 3uckland was requisitioned by the War Office in 1939 and became a nilitary hospital, receiving many soldiers wounded at Dunkirk. In excess f three hundred servicemen are laid to rest in St Tetti's churchyard. llanddetty Hall can trace its origins back to the 17th century, having een originally built by the aforementioned Jenkin Jones. Down the enturies it has been occupied by many interesting people, not least the romoter of the Brinore Tramroad and a widow who was to become the vife of a certain Benjamin Disraeli.

Ashford Tunnel - so low in the middle that you can get a crick in our neck negotiating it - has no towpath; in bygone days horses went ver the top and boats were poled through. It was built as a 'dig and ll tunnel', whereby a cutting was first made and the tunnel built, then he earth was put back over the tunnel. At the southern portal a plaque ommemorates the fact that, after a period of closure for repair, the unnel was officially reopened on 5th May 1985, the ceremony being erformed by Mr Trevor Luckcuck; his name is depicted in large capital etters. Mr Luckcuck was, as many of you will know, British Waterways' Deputy Chief Executive at the time. None can gainsay the immortality f petty officialdom.

Beyond the tunnel the B4558 runs in close proximity to the canal, the raffic appearing unnervingly rapid. A reedy winding-hole adjacent to 3ridge 142 recalls the existence of a transhipment wharf between the

canal and the Brinore Tramroad which was opened in 1815 to link the canal with a colliery near Rhymney. An interpretive board and replica wagon elucidate. A hefty pipe conveys the Newport water main across the canal. Like someone coughing at a hushed moment in a classical concert, Talybont briefly interrupts the Mon & Brec's default setting soundtrack of plashing water, mewing buzzards and bleating sheep. Just this once you're prepared to forgive the intrusion, though, because you've been dying for an ice cream since Gilwern.

A skeletal girder bridge acts as a sort of lych-gate to the village. This once bore the mountainous Brecon & Merthyr Railway across the canal at the commencement of a severe 1 in 38 gradient known as the 'Seven Mile Bank'. Regrettably the line lost its passenger services in 1962, resulting in the closure of such outlandishly named and unnervingly isolated stations as Torpantau, Pontsticill and Pentir Rhiw. Chunks of it to the south-west of Talybont have been appropriated by the 55 mile Taff Trail which links Brecon with Cardiff. Parts of it have been relaid as the narrow gauge Brecon Mountain Railway.

Just after the awkwardly-sited Bridge 143, an aqueduct carries the canal across the Afon Caerfanell which flows down off the Brecon Beacons through the massive Talybont Reservoir to join the Usk nearby. The canal runs along an embankment parallel with the village's main street. The Visitor Moorings here fill up early. On the offside a cottage bears the inscription 'B&ACCo. 1843.

Lift bridge 144 is electrified and cannot be raised at certain times in the morning and afternoons during school terms lest its use might delay the neighbourhood's darling children from their lessons, or more importantly, their tea. Our intrepid photographer witnessed one baffled crew (obviously using an inferior guide) dither over the bridge's modus operandi for the best part of half an hour. Finally, when the penny dropped that they needed a CRT Yale key to set the structure's machinery in motion, they brought it to the control panel on a key ring shared with their boat's engine key, and as a consequence had to stop the procedure, separate the keys, and start all over again. Either side of the bridge, two lengthening queues of motorists failed to see the funny side.

LLANGYNIDR   Maps 41/42

Set in perhaps the most dramatic section of the Usk Valley, Llangynidr is one of the shiniest jewels in the Mon & Brec crown. The village comprises three distinct parts: Upper Llangynidr, half a mile from Bridge 129; Cwm Crawnon close to the 'Coach & Horses'; and Lower Llangynidr, also known as Coed-yr-ynys, which is down by the Usk. The latter is the most pleasing, an enchanting jumble of cottages by the ancient and extremely narrow bridge over the Usk.

Eating & Drinking

COACH & HORSES - Cwm Crawnon Road (adjacent Bridge 133, Map 42). Tel: 01874 730245. Self-branded 'canal boat pit stop'. NP8 1LS

RED LION HOTEL - Duffryn Road, Upper Llangynidr. Tel: 01874 730223. 15th century coaching inn. Bed & Breakfast. NP8 1NT

Shopping

LLANGYNIDR DELI - Cwm Crawnon Road. (adjunct to Coach & Horses - see above). Tel: 01874 730245. Artisan delicatessen specialising in fresh local produce: bread, cheese, fish, meat, larder goods, alcohol etc. Pre-cooked meals for home/boat cooking. NP8 1LS

WALNUT TREE STORES - Lower Llandgynidr (Bridge 131 is closest on canal). Tel: 01874 730309. Post office stores with cafe bar (Tel: 730358) to rear. NP8 1NA

CYCLE BASKET - Cwm Crawnon Road. Tel: 01874 730368. Bicycle shop. NP8 1LS

Connections

BUSES - Traws Cymru service 43 runs five times a day, Mon-Sat, to/from Abergavenny (via Crickhowell) and Brecon (via Talybont).

TALYBONT-ON-USK   Map 42

This wayside village, where the 'Taff Trail' joins/leaves the canal, is a launch pad for all manner of outdoor

St Meugan's

pursuits. Of rather shorter duration is 'Vaughan Walk', a two and a half mile waymarked trail celebrating the haunts of the 17th century poet, Henry Vaughan, who lies buried in St Bride's churchyard just across the Usk. Another religious building of interest is the Benaiah Chapel which backs onto the canal between bridges 145 and 146 (Map 43); named, apparently, after a commander in King David's army.

Eating & Drinking

CANAL SIDE CAFE - Tel: 01874 676663. Popular cafe adjoining village stores. Open daily 9am-5pm throughout the summer months, shuts 3pm in winter. Take-away food as well. LD3 7YJ

STAR INN - canalside by aqueduct. Tel: 01874 676635. Good Beer Guide entry. B & B. LD3 7YX

THE TRAVELLERS - adjacent Bridge 142 (Map 42). Tel: 01874 676333. Restaurant & rooms. LD3 7YP

WHITE HART - adjacent Bridge 143. Tel: 01874 676227. Traditional pub grub and bunkhouse accommodation. Wide range of Welsh ales. LD3 7JD

Shopping

TALYBONT STORES - Tel: 01874 676663. Friendly and well stocked post office stores open 7am-6pm daily (8am-6pm Sat & Sun). The post office counter operates between 9am and 1.30pm Mon-Sat. LD3 7YJ

Things to Do

BIKES & HIKES - Talybont. Tel: 0790 996 8135. Bik hire based at Talybont Stores. Their fleet of 'specialise pitch' bikes are renewed annually. Helmets and repai kits included in the hire fee. Repairs and servicing als undertaken for private owners. LD3 7YJ

Connections

BUSES - service 43 as Llangynidr.

PENCELLI   Map 43

Shopless village on the B4558. Up an exceedingl narrow and high-hedged lane to the south-west, an beyond the adolescent cries of an outdoor educatio centre, lies Llanfeugan and the isolated church c St Meugan, named after a 7th century Welshma descended from the King of Siluria, who may well hav been a poet, and a man who 'never troubled his hea about religion'. 'Enchanting' we wrote in the visito book, but other bewitching adjectives are equall applicable. The church itself, masked by ancient yew probably dates largely from the 14th century. Cool an dimly lit within, the chancel boasts some particular fine monuments and wall tablets to worthy local One especially caught our eye, commemoratin Arthur Gordon Jones-Williams, who, having surviv the killing fields of Flanders during the First Worl War, mislaid his life in the first attempted non-sto flight from England to Cape Town in 1929.

Eating & Drinking

ROYAL OAK - village centre between bridges 15 and 154; visitor moorings. Tel: 01874 665396. Family run pub backing onto the canal open from noon dail Food served lunchtimes and evenings (from 6pm Mon-Sat and from 12-6pm on Sundays. LD3 7LX

Connections

BUSES - service 43 as Llangynidr.

STURDY beeches clothe a sinuous cutting between bridges 146 and 147. A trio of windlass-operated lift bridges - mostly, in any case, left 'up' for the passage of boats - ensues, supplying visual variety to the prevalent stone arch structures on the rest of the canal if nothing else. Standing on a knoll across the Usk, Scethrog Tower is thought to date from the 14th century and is one of only two tower houses in Breconshire. Canallers from the North of England will acknowledge a family resemblance to their peel or pele towers. At one time it was the home of the jazz stalwart, George Melly, who purchased it so as to be able to indulge in his passion for fly fishing. Before he succumbed to lung cancer at the age of eighty in 2007, he is said to have remarked: 'I would like to die leaving the stage to the sound of applause ringing in my ears, or on the riverbank with two freshly caught trout by my side.' Incidentally, the Usk is renowned in game fishing circles for salmon and brown trout. Indeed, its Welsh name, Afon Wysg, literally translates as abundant in fish.

At Pencelli ('Pencelthly') the canal is said to have incorporated the moat of one of the Marcher Lords' medieval castles. Hints of a motte & bailey fortification are apparent in the unnaturally vertiginous undergrowth, whilst a lofty farmhouse appears to have filched a good deal of the old castle's materials in its construction.

North of Pencelli, some *deus ex machina* appears to have taken a steam iron to all the landscape's extravagantly random creases and left them neatly and more flatly folded; or at least this seems to be the case until you reach Bridge 160, where the upturned ruptures of the Brecon Beacons, dominated by Pen y Fan, remind you that this is Wales and that it is in its DNA to be wild. By bridge 158 stands a former warehouse together with an accompanying boathouse. Cambrian Cruisers' base is the northernmost on the M&B. By Peterstone Court, the canal renews its relationship with the Usk. On the offside there's evidence of an old quarry, and by a weir on the river, a converted mill.

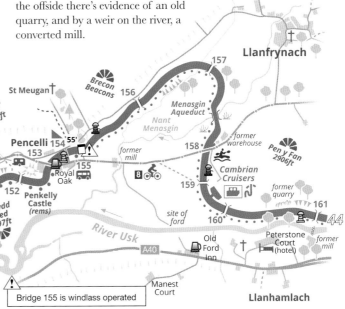

Scale: 2½ inches to a mile

⚠ Bridge 155 is windlass operated

ECHOING E. F. Schumacher's tenet, 'Small is Beautiful', the Monmouthshire & Brecon Canal - all currently navigable thirty-five miles of it - approaches its northern terminus, much as it has journeyed along the Usk Valley, surrounded by astonishingly lovely scenery. Tarrying on Brynich Aqueduct, beguiled by the view through the tree-tops of the Brecon Beacon's highest peak, Pen y Fan, you don't want the experience to end abruptly in Brecon; you want to break out into *Hen Wlad Fy Nhadau*; you want, damn it, to *be* Welsh.

Brynich Aqueduct has familial overtones of Vyrnwy Aqueduct on the Montgomery Canal (Map 29). Its upstream neighbour, Usk Bridge, dates from the 16th century and was the subject of a painting by Turner. The river here is well into its stride on its seventy-eight mile journey from the Black Mountains to the Bristol Channel.

Brynich Lock lifts the canal up by ten feet to its summit level of 425 feet. The trip boat, Dragonfly, makes regular appearances here, carrying appreciative excursionists down onto the

aqueduct, evoking memories of the Sunday School outings which were a feature of the canal in Victorian and Edwardian times. Ripples too, perhaps, of the weekly market boat which took two days to ply the canal from Newport to Brecon (42 miles and 37 locks) up until 1915, retailing domestic commodities to the isolated inhabitants of communities en route. Bridge 164A carries the Brecon by-pass, the A40 being the old London to Fishguard road for the Irish ferry.

National Cycle Route 8 - which traverses the whole of Wales from Cardiff to Anglesey - follows the well-surfaced towpath into Brecon. The army has a strong presence in Brecon, and Dering Lines is a British Army infantry battle school on the off-side of the canal which draws its name from Sir Edward Dering, a Royalist soldier and statesman

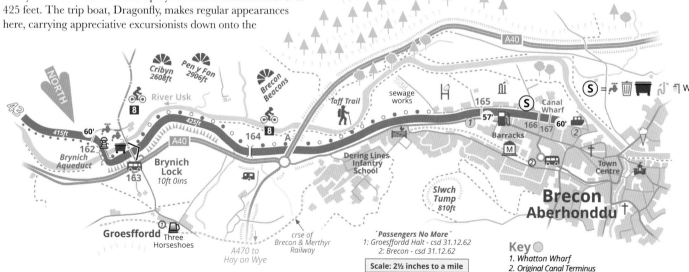

Key ○
1. Whatton Wharf
2. Original Canal Terminus

Scale: 2½ inches to a mile

'Passengers No More'
1: Groesffordd Halt - csd 31.12.62
2: Brecon - csd 31.12.62

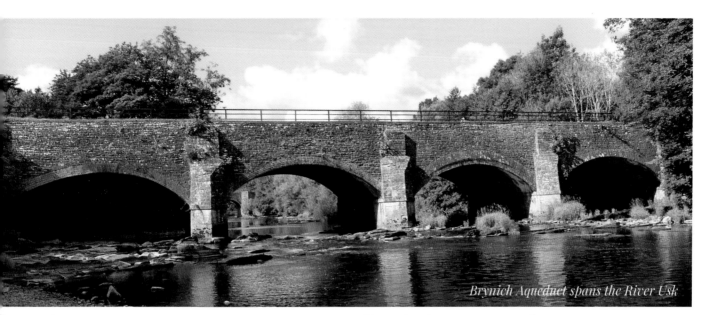

Brynich Aqueduct spans the River Usk

during the Civil War. He raised a foot regiment in 1689. Man's propensity for conflict goes back even further in this landscape, for on the hilltop to the north stands Slwch Tump, an Iron Age hillfort.

The duplicated arch of Bridge 165 recalls the former Hay Railway, a 3ft 6ins gauge, 24 miles long tramroad which opened in 1816. In 1860 it was converted to standard gauge and passenger services from Hereford to Brecon operated over it until 1962, terminating at the town's Free Street station as opposed to Watton Wharf.

Brecon Barracks were built early in the 19th century. Its soldiers fought in the Zulu War at Rorke's Drift, and it houses a Regimental Museum, but that hasn't prevented the Ministry of Defence from announcing that the barracks will close in 2027, though campaigns to reverse that decision are ongoing: armies are never far from their next battle.

Two or three hundred yards short of its original terminal basin, the canal takes its curtain call, appropriately overlooked by Theatr Brycheiniog. The present basin, created in 1997, provides as pleasant an urban mooring as you'll find anywhere on the system. One is reminded, somehow, of Ripon. Day boats are available for hire if you have absentmindedly not brought your own.

Canal Road somewhat ironically follows the original course of the canal to where it dog-legged to the north to terminate. A handsome Victorian mill building marks the spot, now largely covered by a builders merchants yard. Under your feet a pipe feeds the canal from a weir upstream on the Usk.

Don't be in a hurry to turn around. Brecon has much to commend it, whilst the obscurity and brevity of the canal which brought you here are now revealed, not as its weaknesses, but as its strengths.

BRECON

Map 44

Garrison town, administrative centre for the Brecon Beacons National Park, seat of the diocese of Swansea and Brecon and mecca for walkers and climbers, Brecon is a friendly place; certainly no anti-climax at the end of a voyage up the Mon & Brec. The oldest part of town surrounds the castle remains near the confluence of the Usk and Honddu rivers. An attractive 'promenade' by the Usk, reached via Watergate, provides superb views of the Beacons. Every August, New Orleans comes to town with the staging of the internationally-renowned Brecon Jazz Festival.

Eating & Drinking

BRECON TAP - The Bulwark. Tel: 01874 622888. Real ale bar open from 10am Wed-Sat, 12pm Sun-Tue. Bottled beer and artisan produce for sale. LD3 7LB
CASTLE HOTEL - Castle Square. Tel: 01874 624611. Comfortable 'country town' hotel offering bar and restaurant food to non-residents. The restaurant opens out onto a terrace with fine views over the river and distant mountains. LD3 9DB
DEWI'S SECRET GARDEN - St Mary Street. Tel: 01874 620000. Italian restaurant. LD3 7AA
GURKHA CORNER - Glamorgan Street. Tel: 01874 610871. Himalayan & Nepalese cuisine. LD3 7DW
HOP IN - Watton. Tel: 01874 622092. Beer & gin bar open from noon daily (closes 4pm Sun). LD3 7EG
THE HOURS - Cathedral Close. Tel: 0772 637 5274. Delightful cafe/bookshop lately moved from Ship Street. Delicious breakfasts, pastries, soups, sandwiches and cakes jostle for space with a considered stock of new & s/h books. Open Tue-Sat 10am-4pm. LD3 9DP
LLANFAES DAIRY - Bridge Street (far bank of Usk). Tel: 01874 625892. Forty flavours of 'Welsh ice cream made with Italian flair'! LD3 8AH

Brecon
(enlargement)

1 Brecon Tap
2 Castle Hotel
3 Gurkha Corner
4 Llanfaes Dairy
5 The Hours
6 Dewi's Secret Garden
7 Hop In

THREE HORSESHOES - Groesffordd (half a mile's walk north of Brynich Lock). Tel: 01874 665672. Brecon's best eating establishment is neither in Brecon nor on the canal, yet this refurbished village pub is well worth a ten minute walk up from Brynich Lock, though do take care of the road traffic which zips by with unnerving velocity. The bar features a good range of local ales and functions convivially as 'a local'. The restaurant offers panoramic views of Pen y Fan and serves food to match. LD3 7SN

Shopping

Aldi supermarket adjacent canal basin, Morrisons supermarket nearer town centre, Co-op with Post Office on Lion Street. The indoor market dates from 1840 and is open on Tuesdays and Fridays with the addition of Farmers' Markets on the second Saturday of each month. Brecon Books on Lion Yard is a good outlet for secondhand books. Beacon's Laundry on St Mary's Street will refresh your best boating attire.

Things to Do

TOURIST INFORMATION CENTRE - Lion Yard. Tel 01874 620860. LD3 7BA
BIPED CYCLES - Ship Street. Tel: 01874 622296. Bike sales, service and hire. LD3 9AF
Y GAER - Glamorgan Street. Tel: 01874 623346. Open from 9.30am Mon-Fri and 10am Sat & Sun. Revitalised cultural hub housed in Grecian shire hall and assize court. Cafe and shop. LD3 7DW
BRECON BOATHOUSE - The Promenade. Tel: 0187- 622995. Rowing boats for hire on the Usk. LD3 9AY
BRECON CATHEDRAL - Tel: 01874 625222. Former Benedictine priory refurbished by George Gilbert Scott in 1872. Tithe barn heritage centre and restaurant. LD3 9DP
DRAGONFLY CRUISES - Canal Wharf. Tel: 0783 16 5222. Public boat trips from Brecon out to Brynich Aqueduct and back. Also: picnic boat hire. LD3 7EW
REGIMENTAL MUSEUM - The Barracks. Tel: 0187- 613310. Open weekdays 10am-5pm, plus Saturday Apr-Sep and Sundays in August. Features the exploits of the South Wales Borderers at Rorke's Drift in the Zulu War of 1879 when 140 soldiers stood firm against four thousand Zulu warriors. LD3 7PY
THEATR BRYCHEINIOG - Canal Wharf. Tel: 0187- 611622. Performing arts venue. Cafe. LD3 7EW

Connections

BUSES - services X43/43 run Mon-Sat to/from Abergavenny via Crickhowell, the former sticking to the A40, the latter serving canalside villages. Service 3 links Brecon with Hereford via the famous bookselling town of Hay. T4 runs to/from Cardiff via Merthyr Tydfil and Pontypridd.
TAXIS - Brecon Taxis Tel: 01874 623444.

This Guide

Pearson's Canal Companions are a long established, independently produced series of guide books devoted to the inland waterways and designed to appeal equally to boaters, walkers, cyclists and other, less readily pigeon-holed members of society. Considerable pride is taken to make these guides as up to date, accurate, entertaining and inspirational as possible. A good guide book should fulfil three functions: make you want to go; interpret the lie of the land when you're there; and provide a lasting souvenir of your journeys. It is to be hoped that this guide ticks all three boxes, and possibly more besides.

The Maps

There are forty-eight numbered maps whose layout is shown by the Route Planner inside the front cover. Maps 1 to 16 cover the 'main line' of the Shropshire Union Canal between Autherley Junction (Wolverhampton) and Ellesmere Port; Maps 11A-D cover the 'feeder route' between Anderton and Barbridge; Maps 17 to 26 cover the Llangollen Canal from Hurleston Junction (Nantwich) to Horseshoe Falls (Llangollen); Maps 27 to 34 cover the Montgomery Canal from Frankton to Newtown (users should note that this canal is only partially navigable at present); Maps 35 to 44 cover the Monmouthshire & Brecon Canal from Pontnewydd (Cwmbran) to Brecon.

The maps - measured imperially like the waterways they depict, and not being slavishly north-facing - are easily read in either direction. Most users will thus find most itineraries progressing smoothly and logically from left to right or vice versa. Figures quoted at the top of each map refer to distance per map, locks per map and average cruising time.

INFORMATION

Shebdon Wharf

An alternative indication of timings from centre to centre can be found on the Route Planner. Obviously, cruising times vary with the nature of your boat and the number of crew at your disposal, so quoted times should be taken only as an estimate. Neither do times quoted take into account any delays which might occur at lock flights in high season. Walking and cycling times will depend very much on individual fitness and stamina.

The Text

Each map is accompanied by a route commentary placing the waterway in its historic, social and topographical context. As close to each map as is feasible, gazetteer-like entries are given for places passed through, listing, where appropriate, facilities of significance to users of this guide. Every effort is made to ensure these details are as up to date as possible, but - especially where pubs/restaurants are concerned - we suggest you telephone ahead if relying upon an entry to provide you with a meal at any given time.

Walking

The simplest way to explore the inland waterways is on foot along towpaths originally provided so that horses could 'tow' boats. Walking costs little more than the price of shoe leather and you are free to concentrate on the passing scene; something that boaters, with the responsibilities of navigation thrust upon them, are not always at liberty to do. The maps set out to give some idea of the quality of the towpath on any given section of canal. More of an art than a science to be sure, but at least it reflects our personal experiences, and whilst it does vary from area to area, none of it should prove problematical for anyone inured to the vicissitudes of country walking.

We recommend the use of public transport to facilitate 'one-way' itineraries but stress the advisability of checking up to date details on the telephone numbers quoted, or on the websites of National Rail Enquiries or Traveline for trains and buses respectively.

As reliable as we trust this guide will be, the additional use of an up to date Ordnance Survey Landranger or Explorer sheet is recommended as they are able to present your chosen route in a broader context. Should you be considering walking the full length of these paths over several consecutive days, internet accommodation booking websites can usually be relied upon to offer suitable suggestions.

Cycling

Bicycling along towpaths is an increasingly popular pastime, though one not always equally popular with other waterway users such as boaters, anglers and pedestrians. It is important to remember that you are sharing the towpath with other people out for their own form of enjoyment, and to treat them with the respect and politeness they deserve. A bell is a useful form of diplomacy; failing that, a stentorian cough.

Boating

Boating on inland waterways is an established, though relatively small, facet of the UK tourist industry. It is also, increasingly, a chosen lifestyle. There are approximately 38,000 privately owned boats registered on the inland waterways, but in addition to these, numerous firms offer boats for hire. These range from small operators with half a dozen boats to sizeable fleets run by companies with several bases.

Most hire craft have all the creature comforts you are likely to expect. In the excitement of planning a boating holiday you may give scant thought to the contents of your hire boat, but at the end of a hard day's boating such matters take on more significance, and a well equipped, comfortable boat, large enough to accommodate your crew with something to spare, can make the difference between a good holiday and one which will be shudderingly remembered for the wrong reasons.

Traditionally, hire boats are booked out by the week or fortnight, though many firms now offer more flexible short breaks or extended weeks. All reputable

Bridge 45

hire firms give newcomers tuition in boat handling and lock working, and first-timers soon find themselves adapting to the pace of things 'on the cut'.

Navigational Advice

Newcomers, hiring a boat on the inland waterways for the first time, have every right to expect sympathetic and thorough tuition from the company providing their boat. Boat-owners are, by definition, likely to be already adept at navigating. The following, however,

may prove useful points of reference.

Locks are part of the charm of inland waterway cruising, but they can be potentially dangerous environments for children, pets and careless adults. Use of them should be methodical and unhurried, whilst special care should be exercised in rain, frost and snow when slippery hazards abound.

The majority of locks included in this guide are of the narrow variety. However, on the Shropshire Union Canal north of Nantwich they are widebeam and capable of accommodating two narrowboats side by side. There are 'staircase' locks at Bunbury, Chester Northgate, Grindley Brook and Frankton where adjacent chambers share common gates. When working uphill the upper chamber must be full so that the water in it can be released to fill the lower chamber. Going downhill, the lower chamber must be empty to enable the water from the upper chamber to flow into it. Finally, it behoves us all to be on our best behaviour at locks. Remember to exercise a little 'give and take'. The use of foul mouths or fists to decide precedence at locks is one canal tradition not worthy of preservation.

Lift Bridges are a feature of the Llangollen, Montgomery and Monmouthshire & Brecon canals. Great care should be taken to ensure that the bridge platform remains firmly upright as your boat passes through. Most lift bridges are manually operated, employing a windlass, though a couple on the little-used Welshpool section of the Montgomery Canal still rely on the time-honoured method of pulling down on a chain. The lift bridges at Wrenbury (Llangollen Canal) and Talybont (Mon & Brec) are electrically operated using a Canal & River Trust Yale key.

Mooring on the canals featured in this guide is er usual practice - ie on the towpath side, away rom sharp bends, bridge-holes and narrows. An pen, yellow-tinted bollard symbol represents visitor mooring sites; either as designated specifically by the Canal & River Trust and the Shropshire Union Canal ociety or, in some cases, as suggested by our personal xperience.

Turning points on the canals are known as 'winding oles'; pronounced as the thing which blows because the old days the wind was expected to do much f the work rather than the boatman. It is advisable o go in bow first. Winding holes capable of taking full length boat of around seventy foot length are marked where appropriate on the maps. Winding oles capable of turning shorter craft are marked with he approximate length. It is of course possible to turn oats at junctions and at most boatyards, though in he case of the latter it is considered polite to seek ermission before doing so.

Boating facilities are provided at regular intervals long the inland waterways, and range from a simple vater tap or refuse disposal skip, to the provision f sewage disposal, showers and laundry. Such vital eatures are also obtainable at boatyards and marinas long with repairs and servicing. An alphabetical list of oatyards appears overleaf on pages 158 & 159.

Closures (or 'stoppages' in canal parlance) raditionally occur on the inland waterways between November and April, during which time most of the eavy maintenance work is undertaken. Occasionally, owever, an emergency stoppage, or perhaps water estrictions, may be imposed at short notice.

Private Navigations which connect with Canal & River Trust canals covered in this guide are the Manchester Ship Canal at Ellesmere Port (Map 16) and the River Dee at Chester (Map 15). Hire boaters will not be permitted to enter either of these waterways; private pleasure craft may use the MSC only if they comply with a number of strict conditions, such as Third Party insurance and a Certificate of Seaworthiness. A downloadable pdf is available from the ship canal's owners www.peelports.com. Or telephone the MSC Maritime Centre on 0151 949 6000. The Dee below Chester is a tidal, fast flowing river not recommended for use by canal craft. The Upper Dee, however, flows charmingly through the Cheshire countryside and may (or may not!) be reached by prior arrangement with CRT (Tel: 0303 040 4040) via the Dee Branch. To boat the Dee one must additionally contact Chester City Council, The Forum, Chester CH1 2HS. Tel: 0300 123 8123.

Useful Contacts

Canal & River Trust
First Floor North, Station House, 500 Elder Gate Milton Keynes MK9 1BB Tel: 0303 040 4040
www.canalrivertrust.org.uk

Public Transport
National Rail Enquiries - Tel: 0345 748 4950.
Traveline (bus services) - Tel: 0871 200 2233.
Traveline Cymru (Wales) - Tel: 0800 464 0000.

Societies
The Inland Waterways Association was founded in 1946 to campaign for the retention of the canal system. Membership details, together with details of the IWA's regional branches, may be obtained from:

Inland Waterways Association, Island House, Moor Road, Chesham HP5 1WA. Tel: 01494 783453.

The Shropshire Union Canal Society take a keen interest in the canals of the old Shropshire Union system: www.shropshireunion.org.uk

The Monmouthshire, Brecon & Abergavenny Canals Trust are campaigning for restoration of further lengths of their canal: www.mbact.org.uk

Amendments
Updates to current editions can be found on our website: www.jmpearson.co.uk. Feel free to email us if you spot anything worth notifying others about.

Acknowledgements
After forty years and ten earlier editions, we should be acknowledging everyone who has ever contributed, but sadly insufficient space is available, their valued input, however, has not been forgotten. Current correspondents and contributors are, alphabetically, as follows: David Andrew, Richard Carden, Nigel Collier, Pip Elms, Liz Hawkes, David Hymers, David & Karen Nancarrow, Chris & Terry Rigden, Jenny Tyte, and 'Chop' Wales.

Special thanks, as ever, to our esteemed printers, the Short Run Press of Exeter; to Karen Tanguy for her eagle-eyed editing skills; to Meg Gregory for her splendid cover art; and to Jackie Pearson for patiently accompanying the chief compiler on numerous research trips. Let it not be forgotten that the original Monmouthshire & Brecon research was undertaken by Keith Goss over twenty years ago. And finally, 'high fives' to the amazing Beez That Buzz for revolutionising our maps and dragging our antediluvian softwear, kicking and screaming, into the 21st century.

Hire Bases

ABC BOAT HIRE - Ellesmere, Llangollen Canal, Map 22. Tel: 0330 333 0590.
www.abcboathire.com SY12 9DD

ABC BOAT HIRE - Goytre Wharf, Monmouthshire & Brecon Canal, Map 37. Tel: 0330 333 0590.
www.abcboathire.com NP7 9EW

ABC BOAT HIRE - Whitchurch, Llangollen Canal, Map 19. Tel: 0330 333 0590.
www.abcboathire.com SY13 3AA

ABC BOAT HIRE - Wrenbury, Llangollen Canal, Map 18. Tel: 0330 333 0590.
www.abcboathire.com CW5 8HG

ANDERSEN BOATS - Middlewich, Trent & Mersey Canal, Map 11B. Tel: 01606 833668.
www.andersenboats.com CW10 9BQ

ANGLO WELSH - Bunbury, Shropshire Union Canal, Map 12. Tel: 0117 304 1122.
www.anglowelsh.co.uk CW6 9QB

ANGLO WELSH - Trevor, Llangollen Canal, Map 25. Tel: 0117 304 1122.
www.anglowelsh.co.uk LL20 7TX

ANGLO WELSH - Whixall, Llangollen Canal, Map 21. Tel: 0117 304 1122.
www.anglowelsh.co.uk SY13 2QS

BEACON PARK BOATS - Llangattock, Monmouthshire & Brecon Canal, Map 40. Tel: 01873 858277.
www.beaconparkboats.com NP8 1EQ

BETTISFIELD BOATS - Whittington Wharf, Llangollen Canal, Map 23. Tel: 01691 662424.
www.bettisfieldboats.com SY11 4NU

BLACK PRINCE NARROWBOATS - Chirk, Llangollen Canal, Map 25. Tel: 01527 575115.
www.black-prince.com LL14 5AD

BOATING DIRECTORY

CAMBRIAN CRUISERS - Pencelli, Monmouthshire & Brecon Canal, Map 43. Tel: 01874 665315.
www.cambriancruisers.co.uk LD3 7LJ

CASTLE NARROWBOATS - Gilwern, Monmouthshire & Brecon Canal, Map 39. Tel: 01873 830001. www.castlenarrowboats.co.uk NP7 0EP

CHESHIRE CAT - Overwater Marina, Shropshire Union Canal, Map 9. Tel: 0786 779 0195.
www.cheshirecatnarrowboats.co.uk CW5 8AY

COUNTRY CRAFT - Llangynidr, Monmouthshire & Brecon Canal, Map 42. Tel: 01874 730850.
www.country-craft.co.uk NP8 1ND

COUNTRYWIDE CRUISERS - Brewood, Shropshire Union Canal, Map 2. Tel: 01902 850166.
www.countrywide-cruisers.com ST19 9BG

CREST NARROWBOATS - Chirk, Llangollen Canal, Map 25. Tel: 01691 774558.
www.crestnarrowboats.co.uk LL14 5AD

FLOATING HOLIDAYS - Middlewich, Trent & Mersey Canal, Map 11B. Tel: 0790 158 8364.
www.floating-holidays.co.uk CW10 9BD

CHAS HARDERN - Beeston, Shropshire Union Canal, Map 12. Tel: 01829 732595.
www.chashardern.co.uk CW6 9NH

MARINE CRUISES - Swanley Bridge, Llangollen Canal, Map 17. Tel: 01244 373911.
www.marinecruises.co.uk CW5 8NR

NAPTON NARROWBOATS - Autherley Junction, Shropshire Union Canal, Map 1. Tel: 01926 813644. www.napton-marina.co.uk WV9 5HW

NORBURY WHARF - Norbury Junction, Shropshire Union Canal, Map 5. Tel: 01785 284292.
www.norburyhire.co.uk ST20 0PN

PEA GREEN BOATS - Whixall Marina, Llangollen Canal, Map 21. Tel: 0738 892 4636.
www.peagreenboats.co.uk SY13 2QS

ROAD HOUSE HIRE - Gilwern, Monmouthshire & Brecon Canal, Map 39. Tel: 01873 830240.
www.narrowboats-wales.co.uk NP7 0AS

VENETIAN - Venetian Marina, Middlewich Arm, Map 11D Tel: 01270 528122
www.venetianhireboats.co.uk CW5 6DD

WHITTINGTON WHARF - Welsh Frankton, Llangollen Canal, Map 23. Tel: 01691 662424.
www.whittington-wharf.com SY11 4NU

Day Boat Hire

BLACKWATER MEADOW MARINA (ABC) - Ellesmere, Llangollen Canal, Map 22.
Tel: 01691 624391. SY12 9DD

DRAGONFLY DAY BOATS - Brecon, Mon & Brec Canal, Map 44. Tel: 0771 225 3432. LD3 7EW

GOYTRE WHARF MARINA (ABC) - Llanover, Monmouthshire & Brecon Canal, Map 41.
Tel: 01873 880516. NP7 9EW

MIDWAY BOATS - Barbridge, Shropshire Union Canal, Map 11. Tel: 01270 528482. CW5 6BE

NANTWICH MARINA (ABC) - Nantwich, Shropshire Union Canal, Map 11. Tel: 01270 625122. CW5 8LB

NORBURY WHARF - Norbury Junction, Shropshire Union, Map 5.
Tel: 01785 284292. ST20 0PN

WHITCHURCH MARINA (ABC) - Whitchurch, Llangollen Canal, Map 19.
Tel: 01948 662012. SY13 3AA

Boatyards

ANGLO WELSH - Bunbury, Shropshire Union Canal, Map 12. Tel: 01829 260957. CW6 9QB

ANGLO WELSH - Trevor, Llangollen Canal, Map 25. Tel: 01978 821749. LL20 7TX

AQUEDUCT MARINA - Church Minshull, Middlewich Branch, Map 11C.
Tel: 01270 525040. CW5 6DX

BARBRIDGE MARINE - Barbridge, Shropshire Union Canal, Maps 11/11D. Tel: 01270 528682. CW5 6BE

BLACKWATER MEADOW MARINA (ABC) - Ellesmere, Llangollen Canal, Map 22.
Tel: 01691 624391. SY12 9DD

CAMBRIAN CRUISERS - Pencelli, Mon & Brecon Canal, Map 43. Tel: 01874 665315. LD3 7LJ

CASTLE NARROWBOATS - Gilwern, Monmouthshire & Brecon Canal, Map 39.
Tel: 01873 830001. NP7 0EP

CHIRK MARINA - Chirk, Llangollen Canal, Map 25. Tel: 01691 774558. LL14 5AD

COUNTRY CRAFT - Llangynidr, Monmouthshire & Brecon Canal, Map 42. Tel: 01874 730850. NP8 1ND

COUNTRYWIDE CRUISERS - Brewood, Shropshire Union Canal, Map 2.
Tel: 01902 850166. ST19 9BG

GOYTRE WHARF MARINA (ABC) - Llanover, Monmouthshire & Brecon Canal, Map 37.
Tel: 01873 880516. NP7 9EW

CHAS HARDERN - Beeston, Shropshire Union Canal, Map 12. Tel: 01829 732595. CW6 9NH

HERON'S REST MARINA - Llangattock, Monmouthshire & Brecon Canal, Map 40.
Tel: 01873 810223. NP8 1HS

KING'S LOCK CHANDLERY - Middlewich, Trent & Mersey Canal, Map 11B.
Tel: 01606 737564. CW10 0JJ

NANTWICH MARINA (ABC) - Nantwich, Shropshire Union Canal, Map 11. Tel: 01270 625122. CW5 8LB

NAPTON NARROWBOATS (AUTHERLEY) - Autherley Junction, Shropshire Union Canal, Map 1.
Tel: 01902 789942. WV9 5HW

NORBURY WHARF - Norbury Junction, Shropshire Union Canal, Map 5.
Tel: 01785 284292. ST20 0PN

OXLEY MARINE - Autherley, Staffs & Worcs Canal, Map 1. Tel: 01902 789522. WV10 6TZ

OVERWATER MARINA - Audlem, Shropshire Union Canal, Map 9. Tel: 01270 812677. CW5 8AY

ROAD HOUSE NARROWBOATS - Gilwern, Monmouthshire & Brecon Canal, Map 39.
Tel: 01873 830240. NP7 0AS

SWANLEY BRIDGE MARINA - Swanley, Llangollen Canal, Map 17.
Tel: 01270 524571. CW5 8NR

TALBOT WHARF - Market Drayton, Shropshire Union Canal, Map 8. Tel: 01630 652641. TF9 1HN

TAYLOR'S BOATYARD - Chester, Shropshire Union Canal, Map 15. Tel: 01244 379922. CH1 4FB

TATTENHALL MARINA - Tattenhall, Shropshire Union Canal, Map 13. Tel: 01829 771742. CH3 9NE

VENETIAN MARINA - Cholmondeston, Shropshire Union Canal Middlewich Branch, Map 11D.
Tel: 01270 52878. CW5 6DD

WHITCHURCH MARINA (ABC) - Whitchurch, Llangollen Canal, Map 19.
Tel: 01948 662012. SY13 3AA

WHIXALL MARINA - Whixall, Llangollen Canal, Map 21.
Tel: 01948 880420. SY13 2QS

WRENBURY MILL MARINA (ABC) - Wrenbury, Llangollen Canal, Map 18.
Tel: 01270 780544. CW5 8HG

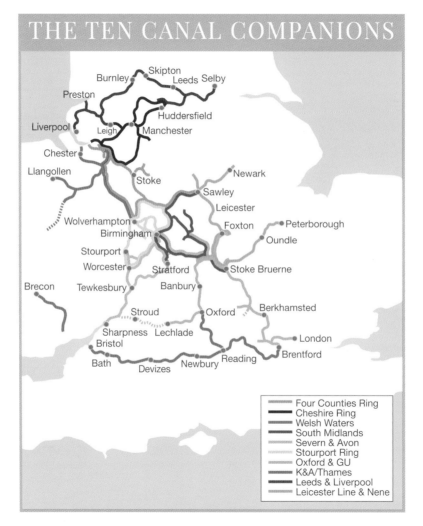

THE TEN CANAL COMPANIONS

Skipton
Burnley
Leeds Selby
Preston
Huddersfield
Liverpool
Leigh
Manchester
Chester
Llangollen
Stoke
Newark
Sawley
Leicester
Wolverhampton
Foxton
Peterborough
Birmingham
Oundle
Stourport
Worcester
Stratford
Stoke Bruerne
Brecon
Tewkesbury
Banbury
Stroud
Oxford
Berkhamsted
Sharpness
Lechlade
London
Bristol
Brentford
Bath
Devizes
Newbury
Reading

Four Counties Ring
Cheshire Ring
Welsh Waters
South Midlands
Severn & Avon
Stourport Ring
Oxford & GU
K&A/Thames
Leeds & Liverpool
Leicester Line & Nene